The Better Elementary School

The Better Elementary School

Hand-Tailored Education for All Kids

Joel Macht

ROWMAN & LITTLEFIELD
Lanham • Boulder • New York • London

Published by Rowman & Littlefield
An imprint of The Rowman & Littlefield Publishing Group, Inc.
4501 Forbes Boulevard, Suite 200, Lanham, Maryland 20706
www.rowman.com

86-90 Paul Street, London EC2A 4NE, United Kingdom

Copyright © 2022 by Joel Macht

All rights reserved. No part of this book may be reproduced in any form or by any electronic or mechanical means, including information storage and retrieval systems, without written permission from the publisher, except by a reviewer who may quote passages in a review.

British Library Cataloguing in Publication Information Available

Library of Congress Cataloging-in-Publication Data

Names: Macht, Joel, 1938- author.
   Title: The better elementary school : hand-tailored education for all kids / Joel Macht.
   Description: Lanham : Rowman & Littlefield, [2022] | Includes bibliographical references and index. | Summary: "This book provides a pupil-centered, teacher-friendly approach where each youngster from his or her own starting point can advance up a school's curriculum ladder as far and as fast as the pupil's skills allow"-- Provided by publisher.
   Identifiers: LCCN 2022001696 (print) | LCCN 2022001697 (ebook) | ISBN 9781475866452 (cloth) | ISBN 9781475866469 (paperback) | ISBN 9781475866476 (epub)
   Subjects: LCSH: Student-centered learning. | Elementary school environment. | Motivation in education. | Educational tests and measurements.
   Classification: LCC LB1027.23 .M22 2022 (print) | LCC LB1027.23 (ebook) | DDC 371.39/4--dc23/eng/20220310
LC record available at https://lccn.loc.gov/2022001696
LC ebook record available at https://lccn.loc.gov/2022001697

*For Professors John I. Goodlad, Robert H. Anderson, and James Lewis Jr.
Their vision, determination, and commitment
to the success of all schoolchildren*

Contents

Opening Thoughts	ix
Chapter 1: Schools and Basic Issues	1
Chapter 2: The Underserved	17
Chapter 3: Celebrating the Individual Child	37
Chapter 4: Age, Grade Level, and Peers	47
Chapter 5: The Consequences of Lumping	59
DIAGNOSTICS, STRATEGIES, AND FORMATS	65
Chapter 6: Tailoring Instruction: Getting Started	67
Chapter 7: Authentic Performance-Based Assessment	81
Chapter 8: Error Analysis	99
Chapter 9: Formative Assessment	107
Chapter 10: Tailored Education for All Schoolkids	125
Chapter 11: Format: Graded	153
Chapter 12: Format: Ungraded	183
Closing Thoughts	211
Bibliography	215
Index	217
About the Author	227

Opening Thoughts

Schools rightfully earn high marks when all their enrolled youngsters succeed; when all their pupils are more capable today than they were yesterday; when because of their teachers' lessons, all youngsters are better prepared for tomorrow's educational challenges. Such would make for a grand accomplishment, an ideal goal for every U.S. school to attain. Impressive as that achievement would be, it's not a current possibility in today's traditional U.S. elementary schools.

In today's schools, not all our school children will advance equally with their reading, writing, and mathematics. While many youngsters will easily progress, some won't advance at all. Skill-wise, able pupils from all backgrounds will leave the school day with little more knowledge than when they first arrived. They are, in essence, moving backward, slipping further away from the skills they'll need. This failure to acquire better skills rests less on the youngsters' shoulders and more on the manner in which they are taught in their classrooms. Know, please, that today's classroom teachers, even the very best, are beset by circumstances that impact their tutorial efforts. These unfavorable conditions have been inescapably approaching our schools for decades. Those complications have arrived; they present challenges to quality teachers unlike anything ever before.

We are experiencing within our schools today what was predicted more than 50 years ago, what then was described as "the nation's greatest educational problem, namely, accommodating successfully in schools a diverse student population exceeding anything we have known so far."[1] Such vast diversity presents to an awaiting classroom teacher "children [who] enter the first grade with a range of from three to four years in their readiness to profit from a 'graded minimum essentials' concept of schooling."[2] In that view, the designated "first-grade teacher" isn't a first-grade educator, but an educator with kids whose skills require kindergarten (if not preschool) or second-or third-or fourth-grade materials and exercises. As the years progress, this range of academic readiness will broaden, certain to tax further the teacher's efforts—to such a degree that even the best public school teachers will find it impossible to ensure that all pupils will end their school day enjoying satisfaction from earned academic accomplishment.

Whereas once it was common for teachers to instruct all youngsters as if they possessed similar abilities, today it's become necessary in theory at least to instruct many or most of the youngsters as individuals, what few teachers are prepared to do. That suggests either the teachers must change, or the educational system adopted by virtually all of American schools must be modified. If neither occurs, the successful school where all youngsters advance will be a goal left to a future generation, leaving behind a large contingent of struggling youngsters and many dissatisfied teachers.

THE BOOK'S OBJECTIVES

In view of the marked differences in culture, financial means, familial support, and academic readiness that currently characterize our schoolchildren, the book has as its aim two objectives. First, the book strives to provide teachers easily acquired sets of diagnostics and strategies necessary to ensure that each child, the high-achievers, the low-achievers, and all others in between, will improve their varied skills within the school day's *first hour*. That emphasized assertion is not hyperbole, rather a testable claim that's to be taken literally.

Second, the book presses for the modification of the nineteenth-century format that governs today's American schools, a format that is neither child—nor teacher—friendly. More than ever, it's beyond reason to expect one teacher with 25–30 (or more) diverse kids using one lesson plan to successfully reach all current schoolchildren. We're talking twenty-first-century schoolchildren, not children who went to school 200-plus years ago, their similarities comparable to a horse pulling an open-air buggy and an all-electric American Tesla.

The book acknowledges that while some people—once aware of the large number of failing U.S. schoolkids—will be quick to accuse the classroom teacher of gross negligence, the more accurate explanation for the academic struggles many children experience point in a different direction.

An alternative to today's ancient school model formulated in the nineteenth century is provided; if enacted, it will benefit all schoolkids and their teachers, bringing closer to fruition the goal of advancing educationally all our schoolchildren—an outcome easily embraced by all who care about America's future.

NOTES

1. Goodlad, J. I., & Anderson, R. H. (1987). *The nongraded elementary school.* New York: Teachers College Press.
2. Goodlad & Anderson (1987).

Chapter 1

Schools and Basic Issues

Educating all our schoolchildren must remain our top priority. Much is at stake, as our future and that of others will be in their hands. Nelson Mandela declared in June 1995

> [Children are] the rock on which our future will be built, our greatest asset as a nation. They will be the leaders of our country, the creators of our national wealth who care for and protect our people. . . . They are our greatest treasure.[1]

Considering the challenges today's American schools face, current secretary of education, Miguel Cardona, remarked, "It's always important we continue to think about how to evolve schooling so the kids get the most out of it."[2]

Such evolving takes effort, a challenge we as a country have accepted throughout the recent decades with only varying degrees of commitment and wisdom. Admirable at first glance, the data tell us what we know all too well: we've succeeded with a portion of our school population but failed to achieve the same ends with a large number of other youngsters who attend our public schools. Such a stubborn, disappointing picture depicting ill-fated youngsters of all stripes has been painted often, in eye-opening detail at a previous point in time.

A NATION AT RISK

In the early 1980s, American President Ronald Reagan struggled with analyst Paul Copperman's grave commentary when he declared

> Each generation of Americans has outstripped its parents in education, in literacy, and in economic attainment. For the first time in the history of our country, the educational skills of one generation will not surpass, will not equal, will not even approach, those of their parents.[3]

To counter what he saw as an unacceptable state of affairs, President Reagan formed his National Commission on Excellence in Education, which released their report, A Nation at Risk. The committee's landmark report affirmed,

> All, regardless of race or class or economic status, are entitled to a fair chance and to the tools for developing their individual powers of mind and spirit to the utmost. This promise means that all children by virtue of their own efforts, competently guided, can hope to attain the mature and informed judgement needed to secure gainful employment, and to manage their own lives, thereby serving not only their own interests but also the progress of society itself.[4]

The committee's declaration represented the president's version of the American drive toward bettering one's life and intellect. "By virtue of their own efforts" was at the core. It summoned the image of an industrious, determined schoolchild who manages to rise above all adversities by tugging his own metaphoric bootstraps. (The secondary phrase, "competently guided," seemed a last-minute add-on—the committee conceding, however reluctantly, the young pupil wasn't expected to carry alone the full burden of his schooling.)

By all accounts, the commission members presumed each American schoolchild would acquire by personal experience or by familial influence a passionate dedication toward self-improvement. The committee's report was commendable and far-reaching. It was also unconditionally naïve.

The Children's Real World

By the mid-to late nineteenth century, those of us who provided direct services to difficult schoolkids, their parents, and their teachers, who had observed firsthand the educational goings on in and beyond the American classroom, knew the commission's precepts though praiseworthy were nevertheless out of touch. In a just, equitable world with all citizens (including professionals) dedicated to the well-being of children, the commission's fundamental planks might have actualized. The reality then and now wasn't—and isn't—so sunny. Due to several factors within schools and classrooms, many children have known mostly failure from their first weeks of school. With home unable *or* disinclined to compensate for school's shortcomings, with teachers treating every child as if equally ready to proceed with the same materials, many children failed to acquire the tools the commission touted as important.

In fairness, the committee members who penned the report likely held scant knowledge of what truly transpires (at the operational level) inside a classroom; inside a classroom packed with diverse kids guided by a single teacher often inadequately prepared for the task. The commissioners would have served America's schoolchildren better prior to issuing their landmark testimony had they visited multiple classrooms across the country to observe firsthand what transpired. If they had done so, one (or more) among them might have possessed the brazen temerity to question who (in a right mind) thought one teacher with 25 vastly different youngsters (with vastly different educational needs) could do anything but fail to effectively educate them all.

Commenting on our inability to meet the Nation at Risk's challenges, James Harvey, executive director of the National Superintendents Roundtable, and David Berliner, educational psychologist, ever the optimists, reminded us,

> The United States has taken a lot of people who looked like losers in Act I of their lives and turned them into winners by Act III. In this great drama, schools aren't just part of the scenery. They're the essential story line. We still have time to make sure the American school story has a happy ending.[5]

Maybe.

FREEDOM AND EDUCATION

Just prior to the twentieth century, George Washington Carver, judged the most prominent Black scientist of his time, raised the bar to new heights when he said, "Education is the key to unlock the golden door of freedom."[6] The same sentiment was avowed much earlier by someone with equal voice though by decree and society's injustice not equal status. A Monticello "personal servant" and housekeeper to Thomas Jefferson, Israel Gillette Jefferson (c. 1800–after 1873), said this about what little of schooling he was afforded. "I consider what education I have as a legitimate fruit of freedom."[7] Mr. I. G., Jefferson's discerning reflection prophesied the future, what he and his brethren knew all too well: education and one's personal freedom were indelibly interwoven. (The gentleman would later purchase his personal freedom after Jefferson's death, at which time he took the surname *Jefferson*.)

Freedom Today

Let's consider the above. Take a moment to contemplate the first quarter of this current twenty-first century. Consider all of America's children, native born and those who have immigrated. View them across the entire social and financial spectrum from the richest to the poorest, from the most privileged to the most marginalized and deprived. Consider the word *freedom* as professor Carver and I. G., Jefferson intended, what freedom entails, what freedom affords. Writing in the year 2001, Linda Darling-Hammond, Stanford University professor emeritus, viewed our ever-changing school population and the manner in which our schools instructed them. Dr. Darling-Hammond intensified the fire under the kettle when she affirmed, "More than ever before in our nation's history, education is not only the ticket to economic success, but also to basic survival."[8]

Conclusion

The educated have access to freedoms the uneducated do not have. The task before us then is clear: provide quality education to all our schoolkids. We know enough to bring that about. A half-century ago, professor of urban studies Ronald R. Edmonds (1935–1983) issued the following provocation:

> We can whenever and wherever we choose successfully teach all children whose schooling is of interest to us. We already know more than we need in order to do this. Whether we do it must finally depend on how we feel about the fact that we haven't so far.[9]

PRESSING BASICS: FUNDING

Where a child goes to school matters. Where a schoolchild lives matters. "Student success comes down to zip code."[10] If a youngster "grow[s] up in a rich neighborhood with a large property tax base, [the youngster will] get well-funded public schools. Grow up in a poor neighborhood, the opposite is true."[11] Some of the following might surprise you.

Expenditures

Author John Merrow stated, "We spend about as much on education as we do national defense, roughly $690 billion [a year]."[12] During George W. Bush's administration, "The federal government [invested] more money in elementary and secondary education than at any other time in American history."[13] President Obama added more to the pot.[14] Beyond traditional expenditures in the multi-billions, the Obama administration spent an additional 7 billion dollars expressly to fix "ailing schools."[15] With unsatisfactory results, it must be said.[16]

While "zip codes should not determine education choices,"[17] they do.

> In every state, inequity between wealthier and poorer districts continues to exist. That's often because education is paid for with the amount of money

available to a district, which doesn't necessarily equal the amount of money required to adequately teach all the students. "Our system does not distribute opportunity equitably [or fairly]."[18]

School districts with high concentrations of Latinx and Black students are much more likely to be underfunded than majority white districts, and face much wider funding gaps, an average deficit of more than $5,000 per student. As the COVID-19 pandemic constrains state and local budgets, policymakers once again face pressure to make cuts that could widen existing gaps. [The Century Foundation] study demonstrates that, even before the pandemic, cuts to public education have a significant cost and, unfortunately, Black, Latinx, and low-income students have paid the highest price.[19]

Jean-Claude Brizard, former superintendent of Rochester City Schools in New York, stated, "We saw schools of similar size, similar demographics, but one school got 50 percent more [money] per pupil."[20] Tony Sanders, superintendent of the Illinois School District, argued, "Kids who need more support to overcome barriers to academic achievement are routinely shortchanged. We [our district] are inequitable. And we are working on that."[21]

Regarding Hartford, Connecticut:

[Connecticut] is one of the wealthiest states in the union. But thousands of children here attend schools that are among the worst in the country. While students in higher-income towns such as Greenwich and Darien have easy access to guidance counselors, school psychologists, personal laptops, and up-to-date textbooks, those in high-poverty areas like Bridgeport and New Britain don't. Such districts tend to have more students in need of extra help, and yet they have fewer guidance counselors, tutors, and psychologists, lower-paid teachers, more dilapidated facilities and bigger class sizes than wealthier districts, according to an ongoing lawsuit. Greenwich spends $6,000 more per pupil per year than Bridgeport does, according to the State Department of Education. In Bridgeport, where class sizes hover near the contractual maximum of 29—with one teacher, students use 15-to 20-year-old textbooks; in New London, high-school teachers must duct tape windows shut to keep out the wind and snow and station trash cans in the hallways to collect rain. Where Greenwich's elementary school library budget is $12,500 per year (not including staffing), East Hartford's is zero.[22]

Our "playing field" has been decidedly lopsided for eons. Parents on the scale's favorable side rarely say anything, quietly pleased with the benefits they and their kids receive. Those parents on the scale's unfavorable side aren't heard. Diego Uriburu, of the Black and Brown Coalition for Educational Equity and Excellence of Montgomery County, stated,

We as Black and Brown folks have always felt it was hard for us to prove our points [about financial inequalities] because we could only speak about our experience and anecdotes, but then suddenly there was the data that was clearly saying what we have been experiencing.[23]

Writing in the *Washington Post,* conservative contributing columnist Gary Abernathy wrote, "It is a tenet of conservatism that a level playing field is all we should guarantee. But that's meaningless if one team starts with an unsurmountable lead before play even begins."[24]

Gaps

An achievement gap is seen as a persistent disparity in academic achievement between minority and disadvantaged students and their more fortunate white counterparts. An opportunity gap differs.

Opportunities

For each of us, opportunities are the doors often closed by prejudice rather than a lack of talent. Raj Chetty, Harvard economist, posted his concerns as they related to minority youngsters (and women) who are often lost within our educational system:

> Kids who have high math test scores in third grade are much more likely to become inventors but only if they're from high-income families. It's largely about opportunity. Black kids [and Hispanics] who are scoring at the top of their class in third grade have essentially very low chances of going on to become scientists and inventors, even though they're doing just as well at that point. . . . [We quantified] how many of these lost Einsteins are there—kids who have the talent to go on to do great things and become inventors who could benefit all of us, but [who] are not coming through the pipeline because of a lack of opportunity in the U.S. [W]e estimated that we would have four times as many inventors in America as we currently do if low-income kids, kids from underrepresented racial and ethnic backgrounds and women were as likely to become inventors as high-income white men with the same early childhood test scores. [W]e're losing a huge amount of talent.[25]

Teacher Mike Yates said it this way:

> Black and Hispanic children are just as bright and academically capable as white students. Racial identity does not influence whether someone wants to learn. There isn't some innate difference in the academic prowess of students based on their race or socioeconomic background. But there are structural inequalities certain groups of students, namely black students, Hispanic students,

and students from low-income backgrounds, face. In other words, there is no achievement gap. There is, however, an opportunity gap [where not all students are provided the same open doors].[26]

Andy Porter, professor emeritus at the University of Pennsylvania, supported Mr. Yate's position:

> The most relevant studies provide no evidence of the genetic superiority of either race but strong evidence for substantial environmental contributions to the . . . gap between blacks and whites. In my view, it is not innate ability but rather the opportunity to learn—an artifact of environment—that underlies the achievement gap.[27]

Reporting for NPR, Anya Kamenetz suggested, "It's not that poor [minority and otherwise diverse] children aren't ready for school; it's that schools and teachers are not ready for these children."[28] If we're honest, we'll admit we haven't been ready for these youngsters for decades. If we wish to reverse that embarrassing reality, we must accept that *our* readiness will require changes within our educational system, what calls for a significant commitment. Author John Merrow expressed doubt: "In order to begin to change, schools [and their administrators] must admit their problems, be willing to change, and use teaching methods that have proven results, things many [in the educational community] just aren't willing to do."[29]

Guaranteeing Opportunity

All American kids are owed the *opportunity* to be successful in school—"a fair chance," President Reagan's committee stated. That's as controversial as saying we're all guaranteed free air to breath. Or so one might think. Author, editor, and activist Kimberly J. Robinson, professor of law and education at the University of Virginia, shared,

> Somewhere in inner-city Detroit, a seventh grader, whose school is closed due to the ongoing pandemic, stares blankly at her science worksheets. Reading at the third-grade level, she does not understand the assignment and without a home internet connection, she cannot reach her teacher for help. . . . That student—like all American children—deserves a full and quality education. . . .
>
> Fortunately, a Detroit schoolchild like her went to court and argued she not only "deserves" an education that enables her to attain literacy, she has a "right" to one. A federal appeals court agreed. . . . Failing to provide the education children need to attain literacy could no longer just be against commonsense, it could be against the law. . . .

The implications for our society and democracy could not be more profound. [For] millions of under-resourced students, like the plaintiffs in Detroit, the decision could prove life-changing, particularly because literacy as a guiding principle is supported by thoughtful leaders on the left and the right.[30]

Critique

Even if everyone within the educational community heard Ms. Robinson's compelling message and read the accompanying legal brief, essential components within the classroom that could lift all children academically might still go missing. Consider the aforementioned seventh grader who failed to possess the necessary skills to complete her science assignment. Do you wonder how such a situation might have come about? Why wasn't the girl prepared? What went missing? What did the youngster's teacher fail to do? Were the teacher's options limited by the educational system's inflexibility? The answer provides insights into what needs to be done, what we will explore in detail.

SCHOOLS FACE A DIFFICULT PREDICAMENT

While funding inconsistencies and opportunity limitations profoundly affect many kids and their schools, such disparities *do not* qualify as the foremost obstacle to pupil achievement in today's schools. Academic achievement problems generated by a more confounding issue than monetary inequality persist even at affluent, *fully funded* schools (i.e., schools flush with cash). (Please see Jay Mathews below.)

Dealing effectively with this formidable situation will require a major shift in school's instructional method, the bones of which this book will present. Maintaining our current approach, we make a quality teacher's job impossible, the resulting consequences significant: the less prepared children slip backward while the advanced youngsters often fail to move forward. The late Seymour Sarason, emeritus professor at Yale University, wrote this piece in 1990. It's equally relevant today, three decades later:

> I cannot refrain from noting one respect in which our schools and society are unique, a point that is as obvious as it is grievously ignored or simply not taken seriously. We are all familiar with studies that demonstrate that, in terms of student achievement, the United States is significantly poorer than many other countries, such as Japan and Korea. . . .
>
> It is both inexplicable and discouraging that discussions of these findings have virtually ignored the fact that the United States is unique in the world in the racial-ethnic-cultural composition of its population, a heterogeneity that in the

past and present has no precedent. Indeed, in light of this fantastic heterogeneity one might seek to explain *not why schools are as bad as they are but rather why they are as good as they are*. (Emphases are mine.) "It may be true that no country in human history has ever had anything resembling our immigration experience. I do not, however, offer these conclusions as an excuse, let alone a justification, for our education ills, or as an argument for inaction. They are conclusion that indicate again how difficult it is to take the obvious seriously."[31]

DECADES IN THE MAKING

In retrospect, what may have appeared to happen overnight didn't. It was decades in the making having its beginning when the U.S. school population more closely took on the characteristics of the expanding, ever-changing U.S. diverse general population. The metamorphosis was caught in a 1980s screenshot when John Goodlad and Robert Anderson raised the caution flag, revealing starkly the "nation's greatest educational problem," "namely, accommodating successfully in schools a diverse student population exceeding anything we have known so far."[32] Administrators in the school system saw what was happening; they'd have been blind not to have seen it. But observing and dealing with it were not one and the same. Exploding right before their eyes, classrooms filled with diverse kids, everything about them differing: their academic strengths and weaknesses, their native intelligence, their life and school histories, their interests, their demeanor, their special personal challenges.

The educational system ignored what was patently obvious. It chose to maintain what had been its course of action since the mid-1800s: treat the kids as if they were all the same, as if they were all ready to learn the same, all ready to benefit from an educator's single lesson, all ready to ride the bike at the same speed. "Teach to the middle; opt for a one-size-fits-all." No one-room-schoolhouse approach for these leaders. Don't listen to the teachers' expressed concerns. Make them teach fast, squeezing everything into the hour even if it can't fit; make them teach behind the classroom doors; make the instructional process furtive. Maybe no one will notice. Maybe no one will care. Maybe no one will voice any objections.

A Daunting Presence

Michael J. Petrilli, president of the Thomas B. Fordham Institute, remarked, "The greatest challenge facing America's schools today isn't the budget crisis, or standardized testing, or 'teacher quality.' It's the enormous variation in the academic level of students coming into any given classroom."[33] Mr. Petrilli described this astonishing reality:

> By the 4th grade, public schoolchildren who score among the top 10 percent of students on the National Assessment of Educational Progress (NAEP) are reading at least six grade levels above those in the bottom 10 percent. For a teacher with both types of students in her classroom, that means trying to challenge [4th grade] kids ready for middle-school work while at the same time helping others to decode [basic letter/sound relationships]. . . . So, if you're a teacher, how the heck do you deal with that?[34]

A fair *and* serious question.

An anonymous Maine teacher offered this answer to Mr. Petrilli's piercing question:

> The problem with our schools is not that they are not what they used to be, but that *they are* what they used to be. In terms of time, our schools are unchanged despite a transformation in the world around them.

The conundrum's answer is found in the teacher's final 12 words. Change will require . . . change.

SUCCESS FOR ALL SCHOOLKIDS

Everything we need to ensure that virtually all of our schoolkids will advance academically is within our reach. Such school success, however, will not welcome itself through the school's front door. It will require that the educational system completely revamp the manner in which it assigns and delivers curriculum to all its enrolled children. Specifically, the curriculum will need to fit the child, every child—a necessary prerequisite.

Accommodating each and every schoolchild may sound overwhelming. It can be done; frankly, it must be done. Continuing with our current approach used to instruct all our kids will only maintain the status quo and the dismal effects it produces: "Education is integral to [a child's] intellectual, emotional, and physical development, [yet] every year, millions of children fall through the cracks of a broken system and lose hope for a fulfilling, prosperous life."[35]

The mechanics necessary to bring about significant change include most of what good teachers do every day. With administrative and colleague support (which is essential), with time made available to teachers to enable them to exercise their talents (which is essential), groundbreaking educators can get us and our schoolkids where we and they need to be.

Atypical Kids

As a prelude to examining the body of the present book, I wish to share an event with considerable promise—if we take heed, what a group of parents did on behalf of their youngsters. No timid folks, these moms and dads.

From the start, the pupils are not typical youngsters, not common to typical homes or typical families. But these kids are *not* our issue. Instead they could be *any* kids in *any* school with *any* type of academic advantage or disadvantage. It's their parents and to some extentd the formerly entrenched school district I'd urge you to think about. Without the parents, this relatively average school district might have been satisfied to continue its dulling instructional approach *without* monitoring what effect its methods had on these stellar youngsters.

The Math-Talented Kids

The kids were high-achieving youngsters whose assigned curriculum did not fit their extraordinary talents—that is, the youngsters' advanced skills and their teachers' curriculum were thoroughly *mismatched*. Just as easily, these kids might have been impoverished low-achieving, crestfallen minority youngsters with limited skills in reading, writing, and arithmetic, their entering skills, curriculum, and lessons equivalently mismatched. One scenario is as thoroughly unacceptable as the other.

The Story

In the *Washington Post,* dated July 5, 2019, columnist Jay Mathews asked, "Why are so many 8th-graders taking AP [advanced placement] calculus at this school district?" Mr. Mathews wrote,

> Two years ago, I encountered an accelerated math class at a public school in Pasadena, Calif., that I found hard to believe. Six eighth graders—four boys and two girls—were taking Advanced Placement Calculus BC, a course so difficult fewer than 5 percent of high school seniors ever try it. For decades, the public schools in Pasadena had no better than a mediocre academic reputation. To see such acceleration is startling, and so is this: The program—called the Math Academy—was designed by parents, who are usually told to butt out of school curriculum decisions. The math-savvy parents who originated the Pasadena program [said] that if a district wants to keep families from abandoning its schools, administrators [would need to] offer math courses for the best students that competing charters, private schools and wealthier districts don't have.[36]

"We've heard from a lot of parents that [without the Math Academy], they would have left the district for private school," said Jason Roberts, a software developer. "One new enrollee," Mr. Roberts reported, "transferred *in from* a private school." Jay Mathews wrote,

> Parents of [similar] children in the rest of the country know aggressive acceleration complicates school scheduling and takes administrators out of their comfort zones. But they still wonder why their kids can't get what so many kids in Pasadena are getting.[37]

Points to Keep in Mind

The young teens in the above news story were poorly matched with their regular classroom curriculum, curriculum that was determined by *their age* not their entering/readiness skills. The dissatisfied parents initiated the program and the teachers (with the superintendent on board—a no-brainer) carried it out. What did these sharp, incentivized Pasadena kids really get, thanks to their parents? They were assigned an energetic curriculum commensurate with their individual academic strengths, what all schools/teachers can do whether the topic is advance calculus, remedial reading, emerging story writing, or just mastering the English alphabet, the latter no small feat in itself.

WHAT'S TO COME

Teachers are challenged in today's schools to reach all school youngsters, those who abilities reside at the upper ends of the skill ladder, those kids situated nearer to the lower rungs, and those who find themselves in between. In a classroom filled with 25–30 kids, the teacher's task is to consider each pupil within the group and program for that pupil to assure he or she consistently moves up the school-skill ladder. In the best of all educational worlds, every youngster should have the opportunity to advance as far and as fast as his or her skills allow.[38] Currently, we are not residing in the best of all possible educational worlds. We haven't been altogether successful in advancing to any degree the school-skills of many of our schoolkids. That represents a serious *system* problem.

In the coming chapters, we will consider the underserved. Technically, our mathematically precocious youngsters qualified initially as *underserved*. Had their parents not interceded, they would have been left to drift aimlessly with their restricted, poorly matched curriculum. You will also be asked to rethink the concept of *peers*, a term thoroughly misused, producing unwanted outcomes. We will celebrate each youngster as someone unique from all others.

And we will examine strategies that will help teachers assure that at the end of every school day, each youngster will know more than he or she knew the previous day—and thus be better prepared for what's to be learned tomorrow.

We will look briefly at "anchors" that hold back educational progress for many youngsters, and we will look at modifying the classroom format used to instruct our diverse pupils, eyeing one that embraces the essential point made by education professor Carol Ann Tomlinson: "Teachers are obliged to ensure that each learner . . . moves forward consistently from his or her starting point."[39] The key words are *starting point*. Knowing that measurement, the quality teacher *will* enrich a child's educational life.

On that positive upside, we leave this chapter with advice from education professor James Kauffman, a timely reminder of what teaching is all about. Keeping Dr. Kauffman's perspective in mind will help us expand each child's educational skills—what schools must be all about.

> Our job as educators . . . is to try to figure out what differences are most important for teaching. As far as I can figure out to date, the differences we need to be most concerned about—maybe the only ones—are (a) what the student knows about whatever we're trying to teach and (b) what that student needs to learn next about whatever we're trying to teach. Then we need to find out how to teach that next thing most effectively and efficiently. And I think this is true regardless of any other differences that we may know exist, many, most, or all of which may be irrelevant to the task of teaching.[40]

NOTES

1. Mandela, N. (1995, June). *Nelson Mandela quotes about children.* https://www.nelsonmandelachildrensfund.com/news/nelson-mandela-quotes-about-children

2. St. George, D., Strauss, V., Meckler, L., Helm, J., & Natanson, H. (2021, March 15). How the pandemic is reshaping education. *Washington Post.* https://www.washingtonpost.com/education/2021/03/15/pandemic-school-year-changes

3. National Commission on Excellence in Education. (1983). *A nation at risk.* https://edreform.com/wp-content/uploads/2013/02/A_Nation_At_Risk_1983.pdf

4. National Commission on Excellence in Education (1983), emphasis added.

5. Strauss, V. (2018). "A Nation at Risk" demanded education reform 35 years ago. Here's how it's been bungled ever since. *Washington Post.* https://www.washingtonpost.com/news/answer-sheet/wp/2018/04/26/the-landmark-a-nation-at-risk-called-for-education-reform-35-years-ago-heres-how-it-was-bungled

6. George Washington Carver Quotes. (n.d.). BrainyQuote.com. Retrieved February 17, 2022, from https://www.brainyquote.com/quotes/george_washington_carver_157103

7. Kerrison, C. (2018). *Jefferson's daughters.* New York: Ballantine Books.

8. Hammond-Darling, L. (2001). Inequality in teaching and schooling: How opportunity Is rationed to students of color in America. In Adrienne Y. Stith, Clyde H. Evans, & Brian D. Smedle (Eds.), *The right thing to do, the smart thing to do: Enhancing diversity in the health professions*. National Academies Press. https://www.ncbi.nlm.nih.gov/books/NBK223640/

9. Edmonds. R. (1979). Some schools work and more can. *Social Policy, 9*, 28–32.

10. Elgart, M. A (2017). Student success comes down to zip code. *Huffington Post*. https://www.huffpost.com/entry/too-often-student-success_b_10132886

11. Raikes, J., & Darling-Hammond, L. (2019). *Why our education funding systems are derailing the American dream*. https://learningpolicyinstitute.org/blog/why-our-education-funding-systems-are-derailing-american-dream

12. Merrow, J. (2017). *Addicted to reform: A 12-step program to rescue public education*. The New Press.

13. On the Issues. (n.d.). *George W. Bush on education*. Retrieved January 24, 2022, from https://www.ontheissues.org/celeb/George_W__Bush_Education.htm

14. U.S. Department of Education. (2016). *President Obama's 2017 budget seeks to expand educational opportunity for all students*. https://www.ed.gov/news/press-releases/president-obamas-2017-budget-seeks-expand-educational-opportunity-all-students

15. Layton, L., & Brown, E. (2015, November 11). Feds spent $7 billion to fix failing schools, with mixed results. *Washington Post*. https://www.washingtonpost.com/local/education/feds-spent-7-billion-to-fix-failing-schools-with-mixed-results/2015/11/11/b984f9aa-8885-11e5-be39-0034bb576eee_story.html?utm_term=.06acd67e5432&tid=a_inl_manual

16. Smarick, A. (2017). *The $7 billion school improvement grant program: Greatest failure in the history of the US Department of Education?* https://www.aei.org/education/greatest-failure-in-history-us-department-of-education

17. Flanders, W., & Roth, C. (2017). *Zip code should not determine education choices*. https://rightwisconsin.com/2017/07/14/zip-code-should-not-determine-education-choices

18. Semuels, A. (2016, August). Good school, rich school; bad school, poor school: The inequality at the heart of America's education system. *The Atlantic*. https://www.theatlantic.com/business/archive/2016/08/property-taxes-and-unequal-schools/497333

19. The Century Foundation. (2020, July 22). *TCF study finds U.S. schools underfunded by nearly $150 billion annually*. https://tcf.org/content/about-tcf/tcf-study-finds-u-s-schools-underfunded-nearly-150-billion-annually

20. Mathewson, T. G. (2020, October). *New data: Even within the same district some wealthy schools get millions more than poor ones*. https://hechingerreport.org/new-data-even-within-the-same-district-some-wealthy-schools-get-millions-more-than-poor-ones

21. Mathewson (2020).

22. Semuels (2016).

23. Mathewson (2020).

24. Abernathy, G. (2021, April 22). Opinion: Why I support reparations—and all conservatives should. *Washington Post.* https://www.washingtonpost.com/opinions/2021/04/22/why-i-support-reparations-all-conservatives-should

25. Chetty, R. (2020, November 19). Why 3rd grade matters [podcast]. *New York Times.* https://www.nytimes.com/2020/11/19/opinion/sway-kara-swisher-raj-chetty.html?referringSource=articleShare

26. Yates, M. (2018). *Opinion: Let's stop calling it an "achievement gap" when it's really an opportunity gap.* https://www.weareteachers.com/stop-calling-it-an-achievement-gap/

27. Porter, A. (2009). *Brighten up.* https://www.apa.org/monitor/2009/09/intellect

28. Kamenetz, A. (2018, June 1). Let's stop talking about the "30 million word gap." *NPR.* https://www.npr.org/sections/ed/2018/06/01/615188051/lets-stop-talking-about-the-30-million-word-gap

29. Merrow, J. (2010). *Below C level: How American education encourages mediocrity—and what we can do about it.* CreateSpace.

30. Robinson, K. J. (2020). *A constitutional right to education fulfills our democratic promise.* https://www.realcleareducation.com/articles/2020/05/08/a_constitutional_right_to_education_fulfills_our_democratic_promise_110417.html. The term *equity* has been removed. Where it once meant "evenhandedness," "parity," "fair play," and "impartiality," it has been made into a divisive political lightning rod, with political sides arguing over what it represents. In the sentence within which it occurred, we're talking about the legal right to "proper resources," what the school child did not receive. That's not political. That's obligatory decency and at the very least good educational practice. Please see https://www.bloomberg.com/news/articles/2021-02-15/what-presidents-mean-when-they-talk-about-equity

31. In Fried, R. L. (Ed.). (2003). *The skeptical visionary.* Temple University Press, emphasis added.

32. Goodlad, J. I., & Anderson, R. H. (1987). *The nongraded elementary school.* New York: Teachers College Press.

33. Petrilli, M. J. (2011). *All together now?* https://www.educationnext.org/all-together-now

34. Petrilli (2011).

35. GLS5272 [username]. (2019, February 7). *Education—a broken system.* https://sites.psu.edu/glscivicblog/2019/02/07/education-a-broken-system/

36. Mathews, J. (2019, July 5). Why are so many 8th-graders taking AP Calculus at this school district? *Washington Post.* https://www.washingtonpost.com/local/education/why-are-so-many-8th-graders-taking-ap-calculus-at-this-ordinary-school-district/2019/07/05/a78d2220-9d4b-11e9-b27f-ed2942f73d70_story.html

37. Mathews (2019).

38. Goodlad & Anderson. (1987)., p. 27.

39. Tomlinson, C. A. (2015, January 28). Differentiation does, in fact, work. *Education Week.* http://www.edweek.org/ew/articles/2015/01/28/differentiation-does-in-fact-work.html

40. Personal communication, December 1, 2014.

Chapter 2

The Underserved

PRELUDE

Diane Ravitch was a former assistant secretary of education. The author of *The Great School Wars*, Ms. Ravitch has been a strong advocate for the underserved, particularly minorities. Once characterized as "one of the conservative school-reform movement's most visible faces,"[1] Ms. Ravitch has had a change of heart and mind. So said Sol Stein, a contributing editor of *City Journal* and a senior fellow at the Manhattan Institute. Stein said Ms. Ravitch confessed,

> I don't care if my two grandsons—one now entering second grade, the other not yet 1—have higher or lower scores than children their age in California, Finland, [or] Japan. I don't think their parents care either. Let's all read *Walden*, read poetry, listen to good music, visit a museum, look at the stars, and think more about what matters most in life.[2]

In reply, Mr. Stein responded,

> Too bad poor minority parents can't afford Ravitch's newly discovered educational romanticism. Their kids often enter school far behind Ravitch's middle-class grandchildren, and if they aren't taught lots of content knowledge in the early grades, they're doomed to fall further behind. They will never be able to read *Walden* or understand poetry.[3]

THE UNDERSERVED

Three decades ago, Jonathan Kozol wrote his impassioned book *Savage Inequalities*.[4] The volume laid bare America's educational system's contemptuous approach to its most vulnerable and underprivileged schoolchildren. Responses to its content were swift and unrelenting. Alex Haley wrote in review, "This book digs so deeply into the tragedy of the American system of public education that it wrenches the reader's psyche."[5] Robert Wilson of *USA Today* wrote, "I was unprepared for the horror and shame I felt. Savage Inequalities is a savage indictment."[6] Equally offended by the system's treatment of the schoolkids, an ever-hopeful Thomas J. Cottle of the *Chicago Tribute* wondered, "Whether a sequel to *Savage Inequalities*—written, say, twenty-five years from now [1992] will document a country that decided [finally] to embrace and educate all its children."[7]

If Mr. Kozol addressed a twenty-first-century symposium evaluating *today's* state of our education three decades after writing his scathing exposé, he'd inform his audience, "No, we still do not embrace all our school kids, and 'no' we still do not educate all the school children equally." He'd go further, challenging the country's pledge to assure a good education for all its kids. "The flag in every [American] classroom is the same. The words of the pledge are very clear: [The children] pledge allegiance to 'one nation indivisible.'" But,

> the nation is hardly "indivisible" where education is concerned. It is at least two nations, quite methodically divided and skillfully maintained, with a fair amount of liberty for some, no liberty that justifies the word for many others, and justice, in the sense of playing on a nearly even field, only for kids whose parents can afford to purchase it.[8]

Professor Jack Schneider affirmed, "[Today's educational system] works to deliver a high-quality education to those [students] we collectively embrace. And it works in a different way for those [students] we have collectively refused. When a school fails, it is because we have failed."[9] Mr. Kozol would have agreed.

Others, too:

- Diane Ravitch, *The Death and Life of the Great American School System: How Testing and Choice Are Undermining Education.*[10]
- Charles M. Payne, *So Much Change, So Little Reform: The Persistence of Failure in Urban Schools.*[11]
- Thomas Sowell, *Inside American Education: The Decline, the Deception, the Dogmas.*[12]
- Neil Postman, *The End of Education: Redefining the Value of School.*[13]
- John Merrow, *Addicted to Reform.*[14]
- Natalie Wexler, *The Knowledge Gap.*[15]
- Pérsida and William Himmele, *Why Are We Still Doing That?*[16]

In different words, authors and researchers called for basic changes in the manner in which we educate our kids. In place of teaching to a classroom's middle, curriculum, lessons, and homework need to be personalized, individualized, tailored to each youngster's readiness. Instruction needs to be differentiated, suited to all kids. The current educational system must refashion itself to accommodate those prerequisites. (See chapter 12, please.)

At the government-funded charter school, touted as a model of "progress," less than 15% of students were proficient in math. The man who runs a boys-only charter school in Baltimore pointed out that reading scores are terrible, too. "Nine out of ten black boys in Baltimore City are not reading at grade level." He added, "The real numbers are probably even worse."[17]

According to Melanie Asmar,

> At the current pace of progress, it will take the . . . school district 13 years to reach its goal that 80 percent of all [non-minority, white] third graders will be reading and writing at grade-level. It will take black and Latino students up to three decades to reach that benchmark.[18]

Eric Hanushek, senior fellow at the Hoover Institution at Stanford University, estimated that if the achievement gaps continue close to today's incremental rate, it will be roughly two and a half *centuries* before the black-white math gap closes and over one and a half centuries until the reading gap closes.[19]

According to Andreas Schleicher, director of education and skills at the Organization for Economic Cooperation and Development, "about a fifth of American 15-year-olds [including White youngsters] scored so low on the PISA [reading] test that it appeared they had not mastered reading skills expected of a 10-year-old."[20]

Peggy Carr, associate commissioner of the National Center for Education Statistics, stated, "Over the past decade, there has been no progress in either mathematics or reading performance, and the lowest performing students are doing worse."[21]

> The [Baltimore] Sun reported that Baltimore school students scored near the bottom in reading and math compared to children in other cities and large urban areas on an important national assessment. . . . In fourth and eighth grade reading, only 13 percent of city students are considered proficient. In fourth grade math, only 14 percent were proficient, and in eighth grade math only 11 percent were proficient, putting Baltimore ahead of only Detroit and Cleveland.[22]

Special education teacher Sharon Thoner said,

In one of my classes, there was a young man who approached me after school. He, at seventh grade level, begged me to teach him the alphabet. I could not fathom that anyone who had reached seventh grade did not know the alphabet, but he did not. Being a new teacher, not familiar with any protocols within the school system, I met with his parent, and he was referred for Special Education. I lost track of him and did not know if he [was] doing well. I did get a letter from him after he graduated high school; it was written by his girlfriend because he still could not write. She also struggled with writing.[23]

FEDERAL MONEY IMPRUDENTLY SPENT

"As the Obama administration came to a close, it quietly released a study reporting that the massive School Improvement Grant investment—(a seven-billion-dollar expenditure), had no significant impacts on math or reading test scores."[24] The Fordham Institute's Chester Finn conceded, "With so many children crammed into rundown classrooms that lack textbooks, well-trained teachers, and other critical resources, with no sweeping remedies to such problems coming from the states," and without "any common set of ends for education, nor any common metric for judging whether we are getting there," the Obama administration and Arne Duncan tried "earnestly" to make the best of a bad setup.[25]

"WORST ELEMENTARY SCHOOLS"

Below, find a sample of schools drawn from a 2017 compilation labeled "Worst Elementary Schools."[26] The list was compiled by Dr. Andrew Shiller, who assembled an information database parents can use when considering schools for their youngsters. The glaring numerical inefficiencies speak for themselves.

The Numbers' Meaning

The percentages reported below are *combined* math and reading pupil proficiencies. At a selected school (names found on the website), you'll see for example results of kids who demonstrated 19% proficiency in reading and 9% proficiency in math. (Those two numbers added and divided by two.) *Combined*, the pupils were said to be 14% proficient in reading and math, which is truly dreadful. (That depiction holds even acknowledging that the standardized test used was a decidedly poor choice. See chapter 6.)

The "worst" schools were chosen without attention to their names or their city locations. They are American schools, mostly public schools with a sprinkling of charters. Percent proficiencies were derived from "No Child Left Behind" standardized test scores. The following will be displayed below: "Third grade (at this school), 14% [55%]." The *first* number represents the pupils' grade level: "third grade." The *second* number, 14%, represents the pupils' combined reading and math proficiencies expressed in percentages for that school's entire grade level. The *third* bracketed number represents the state average for the combined score, [55%].

Large differences between a school's percentage and the state's percentage mean some youngsters are getting educationally healthy at the expense of some youngsters remaining educationally sick.

- Third-grade pupils at this school were 12% proficient in reading and math. *The state average* for third-grade math and reading was 70%.
- Seventh-grade pupils at this school were 19% proficient in reading and math (state average: 64% proficient).
- Sixth grade at this school, 27% proficient (state average: 53% proficient).
- Third grade at this school, 10% (state average: 48%).
- Third grade at this school, 9% (state average: 70%).
- Third grade at this school, 5% (state average: 48%).
- Third grade at this school, 14% (state average: 50%).
- Third grade at this school, 10% (state average: 48%).
- Sixth grade at this school, 30% (state average: 77%).
- Third grade at this school, 13% (state average: 70%).
- Third grade at this school, 15% (state average: 48%).
- Third grade at this school, 8% (state average: 70%).
- Third grade at this school, 12% (state average: 50%).
- Sixth grade at this school, 17% (state average: 48%).
- Third grade at this school, 10% (state average: 48%).
- Third grade at this school, 78% (state average: 48%).
- Third grade at this school, 9% (state average: 70%).
- Third grade at this school, 29% (state average: 70%).
- Third grade at this school, 10% proficiency combined math and reading standardized scores (the state combined percentage was 50%).[27]

Only one school's third grade performed better than the state average. The rest were below the state's numbers, in some instances well below. We're talking kids. Period. Their color, culture, circumstances not relevant. (Don't be lulled into believing the numbers are exclusive to a "minority" population. You'd be wrong.) We're talking about quality teachers being given a chance to exercise their talents; we're talking about *all* kids being given a chance to advance their educational achievements. We're talking about our current educational system not being up to either task.

PANDEMIC EFFECTS: OUR EDUCATIONAL SYSTEM DISPLAYS ITS IGNORANT SIDE

The *Washington Post*'s Valerie Strauss wrote,

> More American K–12 students than ever got F's in the first semester of the 2020–2021 [pandemic] school year. Millions of kids are living through the most disruptive school year of their lives because of the coronavirus pandemic. They are forced to learn at home online or wear masks in classrooms without the benefit of their usual social, sports and artistic outlets.

Ms. Strauss asked rhetorically, "Is it fair to give kids regular A-F grades when nothing has been regular about the way they are living and learning since March [2020], and won't be for some time?"[28]

Justin Parmenter, a seventh-grade English language arts teacher, said,

> When a student's ability to access instruction depends on what kind of Internet signal they have, it's a huge equity issue. Add to that the fact that these conditions make it very difficult for us to provide the kind of individualized instruction that our students need (and in some cases, legally require) and so many other reasons. This is just not the time for it.[29]

Lizzy Francis, an associate editor at *Fatherly*, wrote,

> It feels surprising that teachers and administrators who set policy would choose to punish students with punitive grades right now, especially as many schools, and selfless teachers are struggling to make ends meet themselves. Perhaps the problem is that children have been unjustly thrust into increasingly inequitable learning situations that already existed—and at disparate rates—and that instead of punitive punishment measures to help kids "get with the program," it is the schools who should get with the program themselves. Kids are struggling. More punishment [assigning failing grades] will not suddenly lift them out of the weeds to success. There is no amount of bootstrapping that can deal with a pandemic.[30]

Karen Hawley Miles, chief executive of Education Resource Strategies, argued,

> Schools [need to] rethink the school day, increase social and emotional supports for pandemic-traumatized children, and figure out a way to send the

highest-quality, highest-paid teachers to serve the neediest students. It will be an uphill climb. . . . Schools weren't serving these students to begin with.[31]

Celia Evans, a mathematics professor at Montgomery College, stated,

The pandemic has made urgent the unanswered problems of education in general. The way we think of education and teaching is not robust, it has come apart during the pandemic and attempts to try to transpose the old approaches to the new reality have been largely unsuccessful. . . . A change in philosophy is needed.[32]

In Crisis?

Is the U.S. system of public education as a whole in crisis? William Galston, professor and director of the Institute for Philosophy and Public Policy, believes the answer is "no":

It would be more accurate to say that we have two systems of public education, not one. The first is based principally, though not entirely, in the suburbs of this country and [in] some of the wealthier urban districts. That public-school system could be better and should be better.

The second system of public education, which is based principally in poorer urban and rural areas, is indeed in crisis. Too many of the students in those schools are dropping out well before high school graduation. Too many are receiving high school diplomas that do not certify academic confidence in basic subjects. Too many are being left unprepared for the world of work. Too many are being left unprepared to go on to higher education and advanced technical training. Those schools are indeed in crisis and they require emergency treatment.[33]

Rudy Crew, executive director of the University of Washington's new Institute for K–12 Leadership and former chancellor of New York Public Schools, stated,

Certainly ["crisis"] would be applicable in some places. The real issue is the tremendous variation between and among schools. In every city across this country, there's huge variation in the outcomes for kids. There are some that are doing extraordinarily well, and then you have some in the same system who are chronic occupiers of that lower rung of achievement. We've got some kids in the middle, and then you've got an enormous number of kids on the bottom end.[34]

THE INFLUENCE OF PARENTS' MISPERCEPTIONS

Unbeknown to many affluent parents, financially well-off youngsters are also prone to drift while in school. Unwittingly, parents contribute to their capable youngsters' lack of effort and school performance that's well below their capability. The parents' potentially mistaken attitude prompted NPR's Anya Kamenetz to report that "9 out of 10 parents think their kids are on grade level. They're probably wrong."[35]

Ms. Kamenetz continued,

> In public radio's mythical Lake Wobegon, "all the women are strong, all the men are good-looking, and all the children are above average." The first two conditions are merely unlikely. The third one is a mathematical absurdity. However, a new survey suggests that almost all parents believe it to be true.
>
> In a recent survey of public-school parents, 90 percent stated that their children were performing on or above grade level in both math and reading. Parents held fast to this sunny belief no matter their own income, education level, race or ethnicity. The standardized National Report Card (a poor choice to use) suggested a very different reality. Only about half of white students are on grade level in math and reading by fourth grade; the percentages lower for African Americans and Hispanics school youngsters.[36]

Bibb Hubbard, founder of the organization Learning Heroes, commissioned a nationwide survey of kids in grades K–8.[37] Ms. Hubbard called the results "shocking." She said, "We've got to find good, productive ways to educate and inform parents."[38]

(Have you wondered what "grade level" represents? University of Michigan emeritus professor John M. Lawler answered tersely, "In the United States it means precisely nothing. It refers to an imaginary set of skills that should have been (but never are) mastered by students who successfully complete the Nth grade in elementary school."[39])

OFFERED EXPLANATIONS FOR YOUNGSTERS' UNDERACHIEVEMENT

A Cautionary Tone

We turn our attention to several prominent factors often thought to be responsible for kids' poor school performance: poverty, parental indifference, educational disabilities, and teachers. As you'll see, there's more to consider than what each category portends.

A youngster's academic underachievement can easily trigger parental dismay and worry. Struggling to understand a child's lackluster school performance, those concerned search, speculate, and listen to others who've experienced similar problems with their youngsters, all reasonable approaches, with this important thought considered.

Beyond vision and/or hearing issues that are *verifiable* and often correctable by medical intervention, rather than accept entirely what might be a mistaken or imprecise answer offered as an explanation for a child's school-related difficulty, *no answer* is better than an *incorrect* answer. Incorrect answers waste valuable time. Worse, they can be "false positives," an answer thought to be true when it's not. "Faulty brain wiring" as the reason a child does poorly in school sounds impressive and medically authentic, but it provides no practical path toward helping the child improve his or her academic deficits. A skilled teacher who assumes that responsibility always takes precedence. That teacher will focus on what the child is doing in the classroom; that's his or her province. With that in mind, let's look at a few "false positives."

Poverty

Joe Williams wrote, "Poverty does not cause academic failure, [rather] it is a factor that profoundly influences the character of schools and student performance. Poverty affects a child acutely, the persistent lack of sleep, food and feeling safe." Pedro Noguera continued,

> This does not mean that poor children cannot learn or that until we eliminate poverty and related social issues, we will not be able to educate all children in this country. Schools across the country . . . have shown that it is possible for poor children to achieve at high levels when we respond to their needs and create conditions that are conducive to learning.[40]

The Many Downsides of Poverty

Nothing good comes from being extremely poor, nothing good from going to bed hungry, dirty, frightened, and with no assurances that tomorrow will be better than today. Such drastic conditions can reduce school learning to an irrelevancy. As if the youngsters don't suffer enough, we often add an indifferent, if not defeating, school experience. Kati Haycock, president and CEO of the Education Trust, stated,

> We take the very children who enter school with less and give them [even] less in school. We spend [even] less on their education. We expect [even] less of

them. [Sometimes], we assign them our least effective and least experienced teachers.[41]

Ms. Haycock chastises schools, declaring, "Low-income children need our most expert teachers. Unless our schools are held accountable for the achievement of all groups of children, too many schools will continue to sweep poor outcomes under the rug."[42]

Conclusion

Poverty did not force Connecticut to send to New Britain and Bridgeport schools the least-ready teachers. We can blame disappointing achievement outcomes on a child's poverty when the youngster's poor achievement results more from our educational system's poverty. A quality teacher may not be able to lift a child out of poverty, but that individual can give the youngster the educational legs for him to extricate himself. Poverty in itself is *not* an acceptable explanation for a child's poor school performance. It hides a different failing.

Uninvolved Parents

Dr. Matthew Lynch wrote,

> Of all the things out of the control of teachers, the lack of parental involvement is perhaps the most frustrating. Time spent in the classroom is simply not enough for teachers to instruct every student, to teach them what they need to know. There must, inevitably, be some interaction outside school hours. Of course, students at a socio-economic disadvantage often struggle in school, particularly if parents lack higher levels of education. But students from middle-and upper-class families aren't off the hook, either. The demands of careers and an over-dependence on schools put higher-class kids at risk too when it comes to the lack of parental involvement in academics.[43]

Overwhelmingly, research supports the following conclusions: Academic achievement increases when parents are involved in their children's education; parental involvement leads to better classroom behavior; training helps parents of disadvantaged children get involved; reading together at home greatly improves reading skills; and parental involvement lifts teacher morale.[44] Psychologist J. Richard Gentry wrote in *Psychology Today*,

> Parents who back their children make a difference in school success by helping develop an appropriate mindset, motivation, and self-discipline at school.

Disengaged parents promote school failures and are helping create a generation of children who are less well-educated than they are.[45]

A Step Too Far

Suggesting in the same breath, however, that the parents are the *cause* of their child's low achievement is too easy an assertion. That belief ignores too much, namely the educational system's adverse influence over both teachers and their pupils. Under the right conditions, a strong teacher can enhance a child's achievement despite a paucity of support at home.

Conclusion

Uninvolved parents in themselves are *not* an acceptable explanation for a child's poor school performance. That lets something else off the hook.

Educational Disabilities

In the 1970s and 1980s until today, a child thought to be brighter than most whose classwork was less than expected would often find himself labeled "learning disabled (LD)."

> The designation appeared to be an almost ideal solution. It implied no stigma on either the child or his parents, carried no racial overtones, and suggested an ailment that was the metaphorical corollary of an electronic malfunction—faulty wiring in the cortex or central nervous system.[46]

The determination "LD" derived from the "IQ-Achievement discrepancy model," the belief that an intelligent, capable child who doesn't achieve accordingly must be disabled. That conclusion holds as much truth as a sieve holds water. This *discrepancy* model was irreparably flawed from its very beginning.[47] The problem has always centered around the measure of "capacity" or "innate intelligence." We have no instrument that provides us an answer to that question.

> David Wechsler, author of the most widely used test of intelligence [the WISC] administered to children as part of the discrepancy model, voiced the opinion that IQ test results are environmentally influenced and, at best, reflect a momentary level of intellectual functioning.[48]

"If [reading] the right cereal box can enhance a youngster's IQ score,"[49] we know clearly that an IQ test is a measure of prior learning of skills and knowledge, and "not a measure of some underlying native ability."[50]

Despite that, the model is still the default measure used by some schools.[51] Why? The offered justification is a professional embarrassment. "It's an established practice; schools have been using it for many years; and, it demands little or no time from classroom teachers."[52] And little thought as well. In 1978, professor Thomas Charles Lovitt told his special education colleagues,

> If we continue trying to define learning disabilities by using ill-defined concepts, we will forever be frustrated for it is an elusive concept. We are being bamboozled. It is though someone started a great hoax by inventing the term then tempting others to define it. And lo and behold tasks forces and other have taken the bait.[53]

Fortunately, smarter minds have prevailed. Professionals at kidneeds.com wrote,

> The label "learning disabilities" does not assist in teaching [the labeled children]. Parents and teachers need to concentrate on the individual child. They need to observe how well the child performs, to assess strengths and weaknesses, and develop ways to help each child learn.[54]

We're advised that "Samuel Kirk's personally coined term 'learning disability' no longer says anything meaningful. It is time we get past the attempt at a consensus definition and onto the children who need assistance."[55]

Dyslexia

Dr. Shaywitz, a physician and dyslexia expert, recognized the importance of proper instruction delivered by the proper instructor when a child experiences reading difficulties. She suggested a "year-long reading program that consisted of a very good set of reading strategies,"[56] delivered by a very good reading teacher was the best strategy. With that advice, it's right to speculate that many children may have suffered their problems with literacy difficulties having experienced a *poor set* of reading strategies delivered by an inadequately prepared educator.

Conclusion

Educational disabilities are *not* acceptable explanations for a child's poor school performance. Regardless of the label we attach to a child, we still need a quality teacher to take immediate responsibility, what we needed *before* we wasted time tracking down an elusive (convenient and controversial) construct. Schools' insistence on ambiguous "proof" is an undisguised attempt to save money at the kids' expense. Given the importance of reading, that absurd cost-saving ploy directed by our educational system should painfully rile every parent's spleen. And FYI:

> Children who don't read proficiently by third grade are four times more likely to drop out of school than those who read well, according to a recent study by the Annie E. Casey Foundation. Third grade has become a flashpoint in primary education because it's the stage when children are no longer learning to read but are reading to learn. If children haven't mastered reading by third grade, they will find it hard to handle increasingly complex lessons in science, social studies and even math.[57]

Ineffective Teachers

Professor Matthew Lynch wrote,

> Once upon a time, enthusiasts designed a formal education system to meet the economic demands of the industrial revolution. Fast forward to today and, with the current global economic climate, it seems apparent that the now established education system is unable to meet the needs of our hyper-connected society, a society that is in a constant state of evolution. [Today] there is a lack of teacher education innovation. It stands to reason that if students are changing, teachers must change too. More specifically, it is time to modify teacher [college] education to reflect the demands of the modern K–12 classrooms.[58]

Peter Greene stated,

> Kids cannot succeed without teachers. Teachers help students learn to read and write and figure and draw and make music and play games and know history and understand science and become smarter, wiser, more capable, more confident, and better educated.[59]

Research in Tennessee revealed that students who were placed with highly effective teachers for three years in a row significantly outperformed comparable students on a mathematics assessment (96th versus 44th percentile). Data from Dallas reveals that a student who has an outstanding teacher for just one year will remain ahead of her classmates (*not* peers, please) for at least the next few years. (See "Peers" in chapter 4.) A study of third-grade teachers in an urban Virginia school district found that students of teachers ranked in the top quartile of effectiveness score approximately 30 to 40 scale-score points higher than expected on the Virginia Standards of Learning Assessment in English and mathematics.

And this, too, unfortunately: Virginia students with teachers in the bottom quartile scored about 24 to 32 points lower than expected on state tests. If a student has an ineffective teacher, the negative effect on her achievement may not be fully remediated for up to three years.[60]

Dart Throwing

Since a school child spends most of every school day with teachers, parents and others in the general public look first to educators when assigning blame for school failures and youngsters' curriculum struggles. Admittedly, some teachers should be discharged from the field, those who are not a credit to the profession. In today's public school, identifying and removing those who weigh down the system can be a major challenge. Former President Barack Obama said,

> If we're honest with ourselves we'll admit that in too many places, we have no way—at least no good way of distinguishing good teachers from bad ones. We have 300,000 teachers in California. The top 10 percent are 30,000 of the best that are out there. The bottom 10 percent are 30,000 of the worst out there. The problem is, we have no way to tell which is which.[61]

Consider this incredible eye-opening admission. After all the countless years we've been teaching kids, after all the weighty books written by studious men and women dissecting and reassembling the art and science of teaching, education as field has yet to figure out what represents an effective classroom teacher.

Current literature on this topic clearly demonstrates that there is no consensus on exactly what traits and characteristics truly define an effective teacher. Given this lack of agreement, the question directed at college instructors asks, "How do we prepare teacher candidates to be effective in the classroom when researchers, policymakers, and administrators can't agree on the traits that encompass what the system has come to deem an 'effective' teacher?"[62] Imagine a student graduating from a college teacher-prep program, lacking a definitional rudder, placed in a classroom of small people knowing little about them other than their age. The fledgling (or newly experienced) educator is left to do what an undersized sailboat does when battered by heavy seas and erratic winds. That is hardly the fault of the ship's captain or the overwhelmed classroom's teacher.

Hold the Darts

We assign teachers youngsters who bring with them their name and age but rarely anything about their different readiness skills, their special talents, their curriculum weaknesses. Before anyone slings darts, hand quality teachers a fistful. The good ones know the location of the bullseye.

- Many classrooms exceed 30 diverse students. Teachers understand they will not get to know each student on a personal level.[63] Yet our educational system insists that the classroom teacher instruct the entire class of diverse kids as if they are all ready for the same material. That's like mixing a hundred different colors in a paint can, the brilliance of vermillion gone, the shock of lemon no longer enjoyed, the calm of blue hijacked.
- To deal with the challenge, educators teach to the middle of the class, a practice that overlooks students with higher and lower readiness skills. Teachers are not provided time to program for "extremes," though some at the extremes are often no more than a small step away from a misjudged center. Struggling students fall further behind; advanced kids sit and wait . . . and wait. The teacher's ability to make achievement better for all kids is restricted by the educational system's imposed limitations.[64] There's your bullseye.

The Effective Teacher: A Definition

At the very least, an *effective* teacher is one who helps *each* pupil in a classroom know more today than what *each* knew yesterday. As a result of the teacher's talents, the child can do more, know more, solve more, analyze more. It means each child will read better, write better, and solve math problems better. Each will think better, problem-solve better, communicate better. Each will feel better, smile more, and look forward to school. It's not overly complicated. That's the good news.

In today's rigid educational system, however, where teachers have very limited flexibility, none of those grand outcomes are likely.[65] That's not such good news. But before we assail teachers for pupils' insufficient academic achievement, here's a look at what this teacher faced, what might give the discontented among the general population a sense of what a day is like within today's system where kids *aren't* priority.

The following is a Facebook post that went viral, written by Wendy Bradshaw, a doctoral-level teacher who resigned from what she loved to do—teach kids:

The children don't only cry. Some misbehave so that they will be the "bad kid" not the "stupid kid," or because their little bodies just can't sit quietly anymore, or because they don't know the social rules of school and there is no time to teach them. I can say with confidence that it is not the children who are disordered. The disorder is in the system which requires them to attempt curriculum and demonstrate behaviors far beyond [their readiness skills]. The disorder is in the system which bars teachers from differentiating instruction meaningfully, which threatens disciplinary action if [teachers] decide their students need a five-minute break from a difficult concept, or [decide] to extend a lesson which is exceptionally engaging. The disorder is in a system which has decided that students and teachers must be regimented to the minute and punished if they deviate. The disorder is in the system which values the scores on wildly inappropriate [standardized] assessments more than teaching students in a meaningful and research-based manner.[66]

NOTES

1. Stein, S. (2013). The closing of Diane Ravitch's mind. *City Journal.* https://www.city-journal.org/html/closing-diane-ravitch's-mind-13600.html
2. Stein (2013).
3. Stein (2013).
4. Kozol, J. (1992). *Savage inequalities: Children in America's schools.* HarperCollins.
5. Kozol (1992).
6. Kozol (1992).
7. Kozol (1992).
8. Kozol (1991), p. 212.
9. Strauss, V. (2018). How are American schools really doing? *Washington Post.* https://www.washingtonpost.com/education/2018/10/15/how-are-americas-public-schools-really-doing
10. Basic Books, 2016.
11. Harvard Education Press, 2013.
12. Free Press, 1993.
13. Alfred A. Knopf, 1995.
14. The New Press, 2017.
15. Avery, 2019.
16. ASCD, 2021.
17. Newman, A. (2017). *33% of Baltimore schools have NO students proficient in math.* https://freedomproject.com/the-newman-report/427-33-of-baltimore-schools-have-no-students-proficient-in-math; Papst, C. (2017). 13 Baltimore City High Schools, zero students proficient in math. *Fox Baltimore.* https://foxbaltimore.com/news/project-baltimore/13-baltimore-city-high-schools-zero-students-proficient-in-math
18. Asmar, M. (2018, June 1). Far from reaching its ambitious goals, the Denver district plans to ask for community input. *Chalkbeat Colorado.* https://denverite.

com/2018/06/01/far-reaching-ambitious-goals-denver-district-plans-ask-community-input

19. Smith. B. (2016, May 4). Why is there a huge academic-achievement gap between White students and their peers of color? *Parent Herald.* https://www.parentherald.com/articles/41239/20160504/why-is-there-a-huge-academic-achievement-gap-between-white-students-and-their-peers-of-color.htm

20. Goldstein, D. (2019). "It just isn't working": PISA test scores cast doubt on U.S. education efforts. https://www.nytimes.com/2019/12/03/us/us-students-international-test-scores.html

21. Camera, L. (2019, October 30). Across the board, scores drop in math and reading for U.S. students. *U.S. News.* https://www.usnews.com/news/education-news/articles/2019-10-30/across-the-board-scores-drop-in-math-and-reading-for-us-students

22. Bowie, L. (2018). Baltimore students score near bottom in reading, math on key national assessment. *Baltimore Sun.* https://www.baltimoresun.com/education/bs-md-nations-report-card-20180409-story.html

23. Personal communication.

24. Kahlenberg, M. (2017, January). Can vouchers save failing schools? *The Atlantic.* https://www.theatlantic.com/education/archive/2017/01/can-vouchers-save-failing-schools/515061

25. Darby, S. (2009). Arne Duncan's seductions—and why schools need them. *New Republic.* https://newrepublic.com/article/68758/arne-duncans-seductions-and-why-schools-need-them

26. Schiller, A. (2017). *Top 100 worst public schools (school year 2016–2017).* https://www.neighborhoodscout.com/blog/top-100-worst-schools

27. Schiller (2017).

28. Strauss, V. (2020, December 6). More students than ever got F's in first term of 2020–21 school year—but are A–F grades fair in a pandemic? *Washington Post.* https://www.washingtonpost.com/education/2020/12/06/more-students-than-ever-got-fs-first-term-2020-21-school-year-are-a-f-grades-fair-pandemic

29. Strauss (2020).

30. Francis, L. (2020). *Kids are getting flunked at record rates—WTF, schools?* https://www.fatherly.com/news/teachers-failing-students-record-rates-covid-remote

31. Meckler, L., & Natanson, H. (2020). "A lost generation": Surge of research reveals students sliding backward, most vulnerable worst affected. *Washington Post.* https://www.washingtonpost.com/education/students-falling-behind/2020/12/06/88d7157a-3665-11eb-8d38-6aea1adb3839_story.html

32. In Strauss (2020), comment section.

33. W. Galston, quoted in *Is there a crisis?* (n.d.). Retrieved January 24, 2022, from https://www.pbs.org/wgbh/pages/frontline/shows/vouchers/howbad/crisis.html

34. Quoted in *Is there a crisis?*

35. Kamenetz, A. (2016, April 21). 9 out of 10 parents think their kids are on grade level. They're probably wrong. *NPR.* https://www.npr.org/sections/ed/2016/04/21/474850688/9-out-of-10-parents-think-their-kids-are-on-grade-level-theyre-probably-wrong

36. Kamenetz (2016).

37. *Who can be a learning hero? Every parent*. (n.d.). Retrieved January 24, 2022, from https://bealearninghero.org

38. Ms. Hubbard—who graduated cum laude from Dickinson College—served as senior vice president and managing director of Widmeyer Communication's New York office; directed Innovation America, a National Governors Association policy initiative; and led government relations at Scholastic, the world's largest publisher and distributor of children's books. She also served in the Clinton administration at the U.S. Department of Labor and at the White House in the Office of Cabinet Affairs.

39. Lawler, J. (2015). *What exactly does "reading at grade level" mean?* https://english.stackexchange.com/questions/274226/what-exactly-does-reading-at-grade-level-mean

40. Williams, J., & Noguera, P. (2010, Winter). *Poor schools or poor kids?* http://educationnext.org/poor-schools-or-poor-kids

41. Taylor, K. (2017). *Poverty's long-lasting effects on students' education and success*. https://www.insightintodiversity.com/povertys-long-lasting-effects-on-students-education-and-success

42. Taylor (2017).

43. Lynch, M. (2015). 10 reasons the U.S. education system is failing. *Education Week*. https://www.edweek.org/leadership/osinion-10-reasons-the-u-s-education-system-is-failing/2015/08

44. Chen, G. (2020). *Parental involvement is key to student success*. https://www.publicschoolreview.com/blog/parental-involvement-is-key-to-student-success

45. Gentry, J. R. (2011). A lack of parent engagement helps create failing schools. *Psychology Today* [Blog]. https://www.psychologytoday.com/us/blog/raising-readers-writers-and-spellers/201107/lack-parent-engagement-helps-create-failing-schools

46. Schrag, P., & Divoky, D. (1975). *The myth of the hyperactive child & other means of child control*. Pantheon Books, pp. 48–50.

47. Sussan, T. A., Greenwald, S. J., & Wesler, J. M. (2015, March 25). *How does the school decide if my child has a specific learning disability?* http://www.special-ed-law.com/blog/item/64-how-does-the-schooldecide-if-my-child-has-a-specific-learning-disability; Schrag & Divoky (1974).

48. Cited in Baldwin, R. S., & Vaughn, S. (1988). Why Siegel's arguments are irrelevant to the definitions of learning disabilities. *Journal of Learning Disabilities, 22*, 513.

49. Begley, S. (1996, May 6). The IQ puzzle. *Newsweek*, p. 70.

50. Albee, G. W. (1980). Open letter to D.O. Hebb. *American Psychologist, 35*, 386–387.

51. *The discrepancy model: What you need to know*. (n.d.). Retrieved January 24, 2022, from https://www.understood.org/articles/en/the-discrepancy-model-what-you-need-to-know

52. *The discrepancy model* (n.d.).

53. Lovitt, T. C. (1978). *Reactions to planned research.* Paper presented at Institute for Research on Learning Disabilities' Roundtable Conference on Learning Disabilities. Minneapolis, MN. p. 3.

54. *Learning disabilities.* (n.d.). Retrieved January 24, 2022, from http://www.kidneeds.com/diagnostic_categories/learning.htm

55. Attributed to Learning Disability Association of America, author unknown.

56. Shaywitz, S., & Shaywitz, J. (2020). *Overcoming dyslexia.* New York: Alfred A. Knopf.

57. Layton, L. (2013, March 10). Can't read? Can't move on to 4th grade. *Washington Post.* https://edreform.com/2013/03/cant-read-cant-move-on-to-4th-grade

58. Lynch (2015).

59. Greene, P. (2014, December 31). Peter Greene. *Huffington Post.* http://curmudgucation.blogspot.com/2014/12/the-biggest-ed-win-of-2014.html

60. Stronge, J. E., & Hindman, J. L. (2003) *Hiring the best teachers.* http://www.esc4.net/Assets/hiring-the-best-teachers.pdf

61. The White House, Office of the Press Secretary. (2009, July 24). *Remarks by the president on education.* https://obamawhitehouse.archives.gov/realitycheck/the-press-office/remarks-president-department-education

62. Greathouse, P., Eisenbach, B., & Kaywell, J. (2019). Preparing teacher candidates to be "effective" in the classroom: Lessons learned from national teachers of the year. *The Clearing House: A Journal of Educational Strategies, Issues and Ideas, 92*(1), 39–47.

63. Meador, D. (2019). *7 factors that make teaching so challenging.* https://www.thoughtco.com/factors-that-make-teaching-challenging-and-hard-4035989

64. Meador (2019).

65. Meador (2019).

66. Einenkel, W. (2015, November 5). Teacher's Facebook resignation post goes viral because she is 100% right. *Daily Kos.* https://www.dailykos.com/stories/2015/11/05/1445148/-Teacher-s-Facebook-resignation-post-goes-viral-because-she-is-100-right#

Chapter 3

Celebrating the Individual Child

UCLA professor emeritus W. James Popham stated,

> I wish I believed that all children were born with identical intellectual abilities, but I don't. Some kids were luckier at gene-pool time. Some children, from birth, will find it easier to mess around with mathematics than will others. Some kids, from birth, will have an easier time with verbal matters than will others. If children came into the world having inherited identical intellectual abilities, teachers' educational problems would be far more simple.
>
> I wish I could tell you that all kids have learned the same lessons outside of school, but I can't. Children from advantaged families and stimulus-rich environments will be exposed to more beneficial experiences and will have an easier time with school than children from disadvantaged families and stimulus-poor environments.[1]

Over and over, the message reminds us what makes teaching so demanding—when done right. *Right* means teachers (and their administrators) agree that schoolkids' readiness to learn what their teacher currently teaches differs appreciably, that believing all third-graders are equally ready for a teacher's third-grade lesson is equivalent to purchasing for those youngsters the same size shoes without first looking at their feet. By chance, some will fit. Most will not.

RETHINKING DIFFERENCES

Many teachers and parents preoccupy themselves trying to understand why a child differs from other children. Better to understand all children *are* biologically programmed and environmentally shaped to be different, the latter by accident or by design. Children can no more be peas in a pod than they can be equally quiet, orderly, responsible, studious, playful, and makers of good choices. Everything about them ensures they will be different, effectively reducing the concept of school-aged "peers" to arithmetically manipulated nonsense.

THE AMAZING, ENIGMATIC, *UNIQUE* YOUNGSTER

Introduction

The Curriculum Development Institute wrote,

> The aim of education is to enable each student to attain all-round development according to his/her own attributes. Each student is a unique individual, different in cognitive and affective development, social maturity, ability, motivation, aspiration, learning styles, needs, interests and potential. Apart from this, there are other factors underlying student differences. These include innate differences in intelligence, differences in social and economic background, variations in past learning experiences, and variations in the level of congruence between the learner and the curriculum. . . . [Holding to] the conviction that all students can learn, schools [should] adopt different modes of assessment to find out the strengths and weaknesses of students *before* deciding on the appropriate curriculum and teaching strategies for them.[2]

Drs. Arina Bokas and Rod Rock agreed:

> Too often, formal education begins with a preconception that biology determines the intellectual characteristics with which children are born, that they are fixed and unfold independent of experience. Research in neuroscience, however, shows that children's experiences shape their biology as much as biology shapes their experiences. Conclusion: [Schoolkids] are not equally smart in all settings. Thus, it is time for a mindset change in our educational systems to a growth mindset. In a growth-mindset system, [we] focus on strengths, aptitudes, and individual differences in children. We notice each child's natural proclivities and strengths, and we use this knowledge to help individual children learn math, science, social studies, art, music, and communication skills in ways that work best for each one of them. We must [prepare] our school systems to help each child use his or her smarts to achieve at the highest levels possible. Each child is unique and uniquely smart. Today's world no longer accepts a one-size-fits-*all*. It calls for a one-size-fits-*one*.[3]

Never an Indistinguishable Fish in a School of Fishes

Each child has always been an incredible collection of so many and so much, an individual who can never be duplicated throughout unending time. Without a twin, he has no similar-looking reflection in the mirror, other than perhaps just enough of his parents to know to whom he belongs. That's *biology* operating. If the child has followed a different path, adopted perhaps, he will learn from consistent parenting his parents' preferences and learn with their guidance much about life. That's the *environment* operating.

Conception and Beyond

Each of us is a remarkable biological creature; our individuality begins at the moment of conception. If the chorus of things hums harmoniously, if no unwanted biological intruder touches the developing fetus, if the mother-to-be follows her doctor's orders, the fortunate newborn, now safely in Mom's arms, will begin to blossom and flourish right before her eyes, adding each day more promise to the preceding days.

Further, if all factors are in their proper nurturing place as the infant develops; if all basic needs are met abundantly; if a child experiences plentiful social, tactile, and linguistic interactions (caressing is a very big deal[4]); if a child's days are filled with active play and challenges from which to learn, chances are that with effort and a bit of good fortune, greatness in some fashion will be within the child's reach.

But Not for All Schoolchildren

For many American babies, such prosperity isn't so nearly assured. Through no fault of their own, these babies' potential for great accomplishments is *never greater* than at this first instant—their initial breath successful, their initial bathing pleasant, their initial wrapping in a warm blanket welcomed. With a world of possibilities on the horizon, the innocent infant's gradient leading toward any number of grand prospects may begin an immediate descent, gradually or steeply. Whether due to a poverty of affection, of finances, of applied intellect, of opportunities, of basic necessities, or of basic biology, the infant (and his experiences in life) remains the vulnerable part of the equation.

WE'VE LEARNED THIS MUCH SO FAR

All of what contributes to the developing child ensures measurable individual differences among youngsters of the same age regardless of culture, social status, gender, and financial means. These same measurable differences can be seen even among children raised in the *same* home environment by the *same* parents. Robert Plomin, psychologist and geneticist, wrote,

Some children no doubt inherit tendencies toward the same or similar behavioral predispositions as their parents: talkative, reclusive, hasty, bookish, intense, easy-going, disorganized, impulsive, forgetful, obsessive, energetic—and with a motor that rarely shuts down. Genes, after all, are transmitted from generation to generation—though everyday behaviors (phenotypes) are introduced, and selectively strengthened, weakened, and continually modified by an early active environment that extends far beyond the family's influence. The selective differentiation may, in part, account for the observations that, "Children in the same family are more similar than children taken at random from the population, but not much more. In terms of personality, we are similar to our siblings only about 20 percent of the time."[5]

Brains

At birth, a typical baby's brain contains about 100 billion neurons, roughly as many stars in our Milky Way.[6] At approximately age three, the average youngster's brain has about one quadrillion synapses (1,000,000,000,000,000).[7] A child's unique brain is especially responsive to what the environment provides during the youngster's first few years, capturing these valuable experiences more efficiently.[8] What most contributes to building a child's brain? A youngster's daily self-initiated active activities play a major role. Doing things. Lots of things.[9] "Whether the child rides a bike, plays chess, or bangs on drums, what the child does changes the structure of the brain forever."[10]

Off to Yale?

I wasn't able to find a respected authority who stipulated one activity was more beneficial to brain development than another, something like 20 minutes of jumping jacks per day when a child is four years old will prompt the admission department at Yale (with full scholarship in hand) to search out the brainy youngster. I did, however, find the following again and again, what points to the importance of *active* learning and *active* teaching, starting when the child is very young and continuing throughout all early school years. John Keith Brierley, author of *Give Me a Child Until He Is 7*, wrote, "A child does not learn from a passive kaleidoscope of experiences but from the outcomes of actions that he or she has initiated."[11] David Elkin stated, "The characteristics of learning readiness are developed rather than taught and only through numerous concrete interactions with the world can a young child prepare to benefit from formal instruction later."[12] And as Christy Adams wrote, "Child's play is not just all fun and games; rather the act of play is a crucial component in the growth and development of the brain, body and intellect."[13] Lastly, Alison Gopnik, a professor of psychology, explained, "What looks like just playing and messing around to parents is actually a very clever, experimental research program undertaken by the child."[14]

The Brain as Gardener

Thankfully, a child's brain is a smart organ. It takes it upon itself to prune weak and infrequently used synapses in the same manner that we trim unneeded or damaged tree limbs. These synapses are small pockets of space between two cells. They provide the opportunity for one neuron to "talk" to another and are thus responsible for the transmission of messages from the nerves to the brain and vice versa.[15] These synapses support learning, memory, and other cognitive abilities.[16]

The Ultimate Individual

Two biological operations known as "blooming" and "pruning" expressly *individualize* each child's cognitive, social, and behavioral strengths and weaknesses,[17] once more making one youngster measurably different from all other youngsters. This means that same-age children are certain to be differentially affected by their experiences, their genes, and their brain structure. Based on that fact, here's what's assured, 99.99% guarantee.

- Same-aged children's brain formation will differ.
- Same-aged children's school performance will differ.
- Not all children of the same age will be equally ready cognitively for the same teacher materials. Some kids of the same age will be ready for advance lessons well beyond what a teacher assigns; some kids of the same age will be ready for lessons well below what a teacher assigns.
- Placing all same-age children in the same classroom for instructional purposes simply because they share the same birth age is in direct conflict with what neuroscientists consider best practice.

Professor Anita Therese Kreide stated, "Humans will never be homogeneous as predetermined by their unique genetic makeup . . . and differing environmental stimuli. No two humans are alike, so why does graded education insist on uniformity?"[18] Similarly, Harvard psychiatrist Robert Berezin wrote,

> Somewhere along the line we have lost the understanding that kids come in all shapes and sizes. . . . Where did we ever get the notion that kids should all be one way? Every child matures in his own way, in his own time. Every child is different.[19]

Variations: Today's Pupil Population

American schools continue to see a dramatic increase in the number of schoolchildren with diverse curricular skills, with different school-related experiences, with varying language and communication proficiencies, and with parental involvement that spans the grid from zestful to zero. Few schools using today's educational format can avoid the challenge resulting from these discernable contrasts. All public, private, parochial, and public charter schools, even those who "cherry pick" their kids, need to program for all children who attend classes. If they fail to consider each youngster's skills, instead choosing to instruct them as if they are all ready for the same material, an untold number of children will be set back educationally.

We can honor the obvious that our same-age children differ from one another; we can insist that our educational system accepts that fact. We can reject the notion that all learners of various skills, histories, attitudes, and biologics—all assigned to one space within a school building—can be effectively taught in the same manner by the same teacher using the same lesson plan. We can do even better. We can use *our* brains to adopt an effective alternative approach, one that with effort and commitment is available.

A Surgeon's Relevant Lesson

The human brain doesn't come with a set of road maps or microscopic GPS navigational tools that pinpoints all locations. Dr. Paul Grundy was well aware of these missing travel guides when, as a neurosurgeon at a South Hampton, England, hospital, he set about to remove a brain tumor from a 30-year-old female patient. With the tumor projected to be dangerously near the woman's speech center, the experienced physician knew that the patient's language center might have its own relative designation within her brain. He knew as well that any mistaken insertion of his scalpel could render the patient unable to communicate verbally for the remainder of her life.

To aid the physician with his surgical invasion, the female patient was kept conscious during the procedure, providing her the opportunity to answer the surgical nurse's questions, which allowed Dr. Grundy, using electrical stimulation, to map the precise location of her speech center. Once he concluded the successful surgery, the physician divulged that the location of the woman's speech center surprised him: it was some two centimeters from where he expected it to be. In brain terms, that's a very significant three-quarters of an inch.[20]

It's easy to extrapolate the above situation to a school child who, too, might be figuratively two centimeters from where a teacher expects the child to be based on birthdate. In Dr. Grundy's case, he made no preconceived assumptions that might have wrongly directed his surgical incision. It would seem prudent for schools to do the same if they're to avoid a wrongful educational approach to a child's learning. Unlike the predictable musical note made by a piano's middle-C key, which is located in the same position on all standard piano keyboards, a child's age assures nothing that permits a teacher to predict the curriculum a youngster needs. Two centimeters' difference in what a child is expected to accomplish with what he's ready to accomplish might mean the difference between educational success and failure—the difference between a child who works to better himself and a frustrated one who tosses the towel.

A School's Map

We can develop a working map for each child who enters our schools. We can develop that map *before* any instruction begins, that prerequisite order important if the child's successful learning is our chosen undertaking. Unfortunately, the current format used by nearly every American school does not allow our quality teachers to be so progressive. At present, our instructional plan is developed long before any child takes his or her seat in the classroom; it is implemented only moments after the child nervously or otherwise settles into the classroom with eagerness or trepidation. Most distressingly, the teacher is rarely, if ever, afforded the time (or perhaps the training) to make adjustments to that curriculum either on the spot or over subsequent weeks or months. (FYI: I once consulted at a school where the principal made random visits into the classroom. *Not* to check on the kids' academic progress but to determine if the teacher was where she needed to be with her approved and submitted lesson plans, plans devised before the teacher knew anything about the incoming kids beyond their approximate age.) There's little strategic difference between a teacher who blindly presents to his or her pupils a lesson plan fabricated months before observing the youngsters, and a physician's decision to enter a patient's brain without being certain what exists directly at the point of his stainless-steel blade. Both professionals, with poetic license, are operating in the dark.

What's Rarely Considered

We need to look at how our schools group children. We need to look at how our schools choose curriculum for the children. We need to look at how our schools instruct children. We must design schools and prepare teachers to focus on each child's unique individuality. We must hire *only* those local, state, and federal administrators who agree on a format designed to provide teachers all the time and resources they need to serve all their kids.

Education's Blind Spot

The potential damaging effects resulting from improperly applied educational strategies are *entirely* preventable. Even if a child has a poor school history, if we catch the scholastic errors before the child turns his back on himself, the negative effects in almost every instance can be lessened. There's this complication, however. The longer a child is exposed to the negative experience of misapplied lessons, the more difficult it becomes to reverse the child's attitude toward schoolwork and himself.

While a large number of schoolkids struggle with assignments that are well beyond their skillset, and a sizable number of talented youngsters are required to suffer through previously mastered materials, education officials have shown their disinclination to make modifications to their educational model. Distracted by what we incorrectly believe are causes of school failures, we ignore what makes our educational system such an embarrassment: the format virtually all elementary schools have adopted to educate their assigned kids. We have enough data to order the education system to bring the current format's blueprints back to the drawing board to sketch out the changes that need to be made.

In the lull that follows, we'll fashion each classroom as if it were a one-room schoolhouse, teachers at the front of their rooms, sharing with their gathered children:

> We're all different, and that's good. To better teach each of you, we need to know what you know, what it is you can do well. No matter where you are along the curriculum continuum, we will build on your strengths. And we will both feel better having done so.

NOTES

1. Taken liberally from Popham, J. W. (1999). Why standardized tests don't measure educational quality. *Educational Leadership, 56*(6), 8–16. http://www.ascd.org/publications/educational-leadership/mar99/vol56/num06/Why-Standardized-Tests-Don%27t-Measure-Educational-Quality.aspx

2. Curriculum Development Institute (CDI). (n.d.) Catering for individual differences: Introduction. Retrieved January 22, 2022, from https://cd1.edb.hkedcity.net/cd/id/index_en.html; see also chapter 7 in this volume.

3. Bokas, A., & Rock, R. (2015, May 24). *Changing the mindset of education: Every learner is unique*. https://www.gettingsmart.com/2015/05/24/changing-the-mindset-of-education-every-learner-is-unique (emphasis added).

4. Thomas, L. (2021). *Importance of sensory stimulation for babies*. https://www.news-medical.net/health/Importance-of-Sensory-Stimulation-for-Babies.aspx

5. Spiegel, A. (2010, November 22). Siblings share genes, but rarely personalities. *NPR*. http://www.npr.org/2010/11/18/131424595/siblings-share-genes-but-rarely-personalities

6. Howell, E. (2018). *How many stars are in the Milky Way?* https://www.space.com/25959-how-many-stars-are-in-the-milky-way.html

7. Neuron (2022, January 18). In *Wikipedia*. https://en.wikipedia.org/wiki/Neuron

8. Urban Child Institute. (n.d.). *Baby's brain begins now: Conception to age 3*. http://www.urbanchildinstitute.org/why-0-3/baby-and-brain

9. Tierney, A. L., & Nelson III, C. A. (2009). Brain development and the role of experience in the early years. *Zero to Three, 30*(2), 9–13. https://www.ncbi.nlm.nih.gov/pmc/articles/PMC3722610

10. BBC & PBS. (2018). *The amazing human body*. https://www.pbs.org/show/amazing-human-body

11. Brierley, J. K. (1987). *Give me a child until he is seven*. London: RoutledgeFalmer.

12. *Research supports hands-on learning*. (n.d.). https://www.hand2mind.com/resources/hands-on-learning-manipulatives-enhance-literacy-instruction

13. Adams, C., Donnelly, C., Johnson, K., Payne, B., Slagle, A., & Stewart, S. (2017, November). *The importance of outdoor play and its impact on brain development in children*. https://www.casadeibambini.school.nz/wp-content/uploads/2017/11/The-Importance-of-Outdoor-Play-and-Its-Impact-on-Brain-Develpoment-in-Children.pdf

14. Gopnik, A. (2016). Nurturing brain development from birth to three. *Zero to Three* [Podcast]. https://www.zerotothree.org/resources/283-nurturing-brain-development-from-birth-to-three

15. Kumar, K. (2012). *What is synaptic function?* https://www.medicinenet.com/what_is_synaptic_function/article.htm

16. Johnston, M. V., Ishida, A., Ishida, W. N., Matsushita, H. B., Nishimura, A., & Tsuji, M. (2009). Plasticity and injury in the developing brain. *Brain & Development, 31*(1), 1–10.

17. Urban Child Institute (n.d.).

18. Kreide, A. (2011). *Literacy achievement in nongraded classrooms* [Unpublished doctoral dissertation]. Loyola Marymount University.

19. Berezin, R. (2015, March 17). *No, there is no such thing as ADHD*. http://www.madinamerica.com/2015/03/no-no-thing-adhd/

20. BBC & PBS (2018).

Chapter 4

Age, Grade Level, and Peers

AGE AND GRADE LEVEL: POOR PREDICTORS OF SCHOOL READINESS

The poorly considered practice of placing children in the same classroom for instructional purposes because they share the same birth year will produce what's termed a "curriculum mismatch" for any number of youngsters. A curriculum mismatch occurs when a teacher's assignments or lessons are not compatible with a youngster's academic entering (or receptive language) skills. Virtually nothing about a child's prominent skills or deficits will alter significantly what's scheduled on a teacher's calendar or what's scheduled within the teacher's lessons. Allowed to continue, the schoolchild with advanced skills long since mastered becomes bored or distant or a disruptive nuisance, whereas low-achieving youngsters lost in the instructional haze will find the school experience frustrating, if not agonizing, if not a waste of time. For the low-achieving pupil, these curriculum mismatches assume a particularly troublesome role. With the fewest of exceptions, low-producing youngsters have all the brainpower they need to greatly improve their skillsets. That hoped-for possibility, however, can be easily thwarted by the continued presence of these curriculum mismatches, what can occur at any grade level, including kindergarten. Failing to exercise the most minimal of assessments, a teacher will not know a curriculum mismatch is active and doing harm.

Egg Crates

This, too, must be said. The goal of effectively reaching and advancing all the children in the typical American classroom within education's current structure cannot be accomplished, not with the time constraints placed on teachers. Author and educator Marc S. Tucker, writing for the National Center on Education, expressed doubts about our schools' ability and willingness to ensure each child's academic success. He characterized today's school classrooms as "egg crates"[1] where sameness and symmetry are the rule, where teaching to the middle distribution of kids is most often the modus operandi. Will some pupils outside the center succeed academically under such conditions? Yes, those who possess an ongoing, independent drive to learn while surrounded by an interactive environment that encourages the children's learning. Will that be enough to maintain their success? That's a more difficult question to answer. Even the successful student will need the guidance of a quality teacher, one with time to impart his or her skills. Without time made available, we fumble miserably with excuses why neither the pupil nor the mentor succeeded. Imagine the public's uproar if surgeons or engineers or painters had to accomplish what's necessary under the unfriendly staring eyes of a taskmaster's clock.

A Terrible Practice

Daniel Lattier, writing for the Foundation for Economic Education (FEE), advised his readers,

> Segregating students by age is a terrible practice. It's a relatively recent phenomenon in the history of education [and] it's safe to say that the idea has been tried and found wanting. It assumes a uniform process of intellectual development that simply doesn't exist in reality.[2]

And it ignores the diversity of the majority of enrolled schoolchildren.

Advocating for his kids, 450 "bright" Baltimore 12–14-year olds who had knocked the ceiling off the mathematics portion of the Scholastic Aptitude Test (SAT), Dr. Lattier wanted the educational system to let his students join older equally accomplished youngsters who had access to more materials and advanced instruction. In today's rigid educational world, that translated to skipping grades, a policy that would require cooperation of teachers in an upper grade willing to take on more students as well as the approval of the school's often-pressured principal.

Supportive of Dr. Lattier's request, Vanderbilt psychologist David Lubinski insisted that advancing this small corps of talented students was a simple matter. "These kids often don't need anything innovative or novel; they just need earlier access to what's already available to older kids."[3] Call it individualized "curriculum accommodation," what today's stubborn educational system considers an unnecessary complication.

Irony

Dr. Lattier recounted, "In kindergarten, since I was the only student who could read, the teacher put me in a corner by myself to read books during many of the lessons." One can't help but ask, "What intractable rule's foundation would have suffered an initial (fatal) crack had Dr. Lattier's kindergarten teacher, with a colleague's cooperation, walked young Daniel to a first (or second) grade class to experience more challenging work suitable to his advanced abilities?" Would the educational system as it is have crumbled?

Early Decision

The decision to use age as the barometer for instructional placement began in the mid-19th century. "The publishing industry's success (in the 19th century) producing age-graded textbook series made it easier for teachers to manage their work."[4] If a book was titled "Second Grade," the teacher presumed the book suitable for *all* the children seated in a second-grade classroom. "Later, colleges produced teachers whose preparation assumed that each would work alone in a self-contained classroom with materials suitable for children of one age-group,"[5] a catastrophic presumption. Between book publishers and today's dubious teacher-prep college programs,[6] a beginning educator from day one could find herself in an untenable situation.

Today's Classrooms

Twenty-five (or more) youngsters find themselves assigned to the room and the teacher because most share the same birth year. The youngsters, then, by definition, are incorrectly viewed as "peers." Those "peers" have but *one* factor in common—their age.

- Do all these 25 or more same-age pupils enter the classroom with the same skills? They do not.
- Do they possess the same inherent cognitive abilities? They do not.
- Do they exhibit the same learning styles and preferences? They do not.
- Do all the children enter the classroom with the same experiences? They do not.
- Do they share the same attitudes toward school and learning? They do not.
- Do they enjoy the same level of familial support? They do not.
- Are their minds and bodies equally rested and nourished? They are not.
- Are the children equally prepared for schoolwork? They are not.

- Are all the children ready to read from the same book, ready to solve the same math problems, ready to speak and write of their life with equal thoroughness and confidence? They are not.
- Are all equally motivated to learn? They are not.
- Do they have the same positive histories with respect to school and learning? They do not.
- Have their young lives to date been equally pleasing and intellectually profitable? They have not.

The teacher facing these kids is compelled to ignore that within this one classroom of 25 or more same-age kids, there are fast learners, average learners, and slow learners. Added to that extraordinary variability, the children's learning style and learning speed can change abruptly and radically. Nearly as confounding, the teacher must likewise ignore that not all of the kids will arrive at the curricular destination at the same time, given the varied mile markers from which each started. Some of the same-age (same-grade) youngsters will finish the teacher's preplanned assignment lickety-split. Some will methodically complete what was asked though needing more time. Some even with more time won't have the skills needed to accomplish what the teacher had in mind. Though of the same age, same grade kids often have very little in common that matches what the teacher expects.

AN UNATTAINABLE GOAL

The current instructional format schools use is poorly equipped to accomplish the task many parents count on. If today's educational goal is to meet or exceed the educational needs of *each* enrolled student, that goal is not attainable. That's *not* school bashing. Consider the challenges quality general education schoolteachers face every day:

- the double-digit numbers of students in today's classrooms;
- the diversity of students in today's classrooms;
- the way children are assigned to today's classrooms;
- the differing attitudes toward education held by students in today's classrooms;
- the miserly numbers of teaching staff assigned to schools;
- the teaching staffs' often-inadequate range of skills;
- the degree of cooperation of children's parents;
- the pressures involving the ever-changing and often-contentious state and federal educational standards;
- the politicizing of today's schools to meet non-educators' agendas;

- the pressurized standardized tests that yield functionally worthless data as they pertain to an individual child[7]; and
- most deplorable, the Gregorian calendar (the same calendar that's attached to a refrigerator or found on a smart phone). It controls teachers' curriculum and lesson plans, thereby laying down foundations for educational failings that are wrongly interpreted as teacher inadequacies and children's educational disabilities.

Recently, I visited with a mom who has a challenging young son. Mother mentioned with clear disappointment that her boy exhibited classroom problems despite attending the finest (by reputation) suburban public school. I suggested the issue was not the school or its desirable geographic location. What mattered was very selective—what specifically occurred *within* the classroom.

I suggested that few general education teachers have the time, the support, the knowhow, or the administrative approval to develop personalized instructional strategies to accommodate the diversity of learners in the same classroom. Teachers, the good ones, need every instructional minute in a futile attempt to bring each child up to readiness for the next lesson. These teachers know that in late spring, the state's end-of-year exam will challenge the children to demonstrate what the teacher has *covered*—and what the children purportedly have *learned*, the two outcomes: "covered" and "learned" not always one and the same.

- *Fact*: A child can be seated in school and not learn what his teachers present.
- *Fact*: In many classrooms, without proper (non-standardized) assessments that reveal the effectiveness of the teacher's strategy, the teacher won't know if a child has learned the presented lesson.
- *Fact*: Since today's lesson often impacts tomorrow's learning, the lacking child will find himself further behind as the teacher presents new sets of lessons.
- *Fact*: Behind much of this rests the ever-present school calendar, what remains the teacher's and the schoolchild's worst enemy.

GRADE LEVELS: CONVENIENT FOR ADMINISTRATORS, NOT FOR KIDS

Kentucky educator Lois Adams Rogers once said that teachers are often mandated by district decree to "teach 1st graders *this* and 2nd graders *that*. So often [they] put walls up around a grade level, even though within those grade levels you have a whole range of abilities [and] strengths."[8] That means an unknown number of pupils' current competences are well *above* or well *below* Ms. Rogers' characterized "this" and "that." As a result, the school day begins and ends with no one in authority certain what the kids learned and what important acquisitions went missing. The consequences of such are significant. Consider the following, please.

John Goodlad and Robert Anderson explained,

> Children enter the first grade with a range of from three to four years in their readiness to profit from a "graded minimum essentials" concept of schooling. By the fourth or fifth year of school, more than half of the achievement scores in a class are above or below the grade level attached to the group. Any realistic attempt to approximate the readiness of these individuals for schoolwork must assume a four-year range in difficulty for what various children are to do: work levels must be geared for two years below first grade expectations as well as for two years above. There is, then, no such thing as a fourth-grade class or a fifth-grade teacher, regardless of the labels within our conventional graded system. . . .
>
> If what children are to learn is classified by grade [levels], some children because of their educational experiences will not be ready to profit from whatever a teacher or committee decides represents a year's worth of work. Others in the same graded class, however, might be ready to profit from a year's academic work that's pitched at a significantly higher level. Such disparity among kids should not come as a surprise. To expect [any] two children who begin their school careers several years apart in readiness for school tasks to be at the same place several years hence is to do an injustice to both. Not only is one child initially ahead but, in addition, he is traveling at an accelerated rate.[9]

Will the teacher advance all the enrolled youngsters? No.

MAJOR POLICY CHANGES

June Cox, former director of research at the Richardson Foundation, argued, "Students [need to be] instructed where they are at each stage of their educational experience, not where [age/grade level] suggests they 'should' be. Progress extends along a continuum. Students progress at the pace most appropriate for them." This continuous progress model where age and grade level are of little relevance offers a direct approach to matching a student's learning skills with the subject matter taught in a classroom.[10] The *Wall Street Journal* staff thought similarly. They wrote, "Schools are rewriting the rules on class time for students—and even ditching grade levels."[11] John Goodlad and Robert Anderson agreed, writing that the "abolition of grade barriers frees each child, whatever his ability, to move forward in his learning as rapidly and as smoothly as possible."[12] Quality teachers will likewise benefit.

IT'S HAPPENING

On windswept fields outside Fargo, North Dakota [in 2018], a bold experiment in education began. In a lone building flanked by farmland, the Northern Cass School District is heading into year two of a three-year journey to abolish grade levels. The goal is to stop tethering teaching to "seat time"—where students are grouped by age and taught at a uniform, semester pace. "Instead [we've] adopt competency-based education, in which students progress through skills and concepts by demonstrating proficiency. Some had finished all the material pegged to their grade level months ago and had moved on, while others were taking more time."

What makes Northern Cass notable is that very few mainstream schools, let alone districts, have set out to topple grade levels. "We can't keep structures that would allow us to fall back into a more traditional system," said Superintendent Cory Steiner. "If we're going to do this, we're going to have to manage without grade levels."

Teachers said, "If this is good for kids, why not bring it to all of them? . . . What if we tore the whole [graded] system down?"[13]

California's Lindsay Unified School District, which switched to competency-based education years ago, mentored Northern Cass. "Because Lindsay customizes learning to the individual learner, grade levels have been eliminated. The question is no longer 'Is Maria ready for the fifth grade?' but 'What learning outcome is Maria ready for now?'"[14]

Even the handful of schools that have successfully ditched grade levels, such as Waukesha STEM Academy, a charter school about 20 miles west of Milwaukee, still keep age-based groupings in the background to sort students for standardized testing. "We take the tests. But we don't think much about them, quite honestly," said James Murray, Waukesha's principal.

Northern Cass teachers and administrators have continued rewriting lesson plans and assessments, including those for "habits of work." They've also been visiting more-experienced competency-based districts such as Lindsay Unified. By 2020, Steiner wants Northern Cass to be the district hosting visitors, as a mentor to other schools mulling the idea of nixing grade levels. "On their way to visit Lindsay or another of these pioneering schools, they can stop in North Dakota," Superintendent Cory Steiner said, "because there's a school out in the middle of a cornfield that's doing this transformative work."[15]

"PEERS" REINTERPRETED

The phrase "jury of one's peers" dates back to the signing of the Magna Carta in England, created in 1215. The provision ensured that those of nobility who went to court were tried by fellow nobles, rather than the king or commoners. Money—not age—tied people together. A 20-year-old and a 40-year-old were peers if their bank accounts and positions in society were similar. If they weren't, they weren't.

This concept of peers holds considerable importance for the educational system—more importance than is either warranted or necessary.

Definitions

The American Psychological Association defines *peers* as "a group of individuals who share one or more characteristics, such as age, social status, economic status, occupation, or education. [They] exert influence on each other's attitudes, emotions, and behavior."[16] Boundless.com defines the term as follows: "A peer group is a social group whose members have interests, social positions, and age in common."[17]

Faulty Application

Educators often use the concept of peers to judge a school youngster's status by comparing his academic achievement (or behavior) against the achievement (or behavior) of other same-age youngsters. School "peers," then, are same-age children in the same classroom or same-age children from the same school or district or country. School "peers" are like-age youngsters interpreted to be equivalent to one another; they're expected/predicted to perform equivalently. When a "peer" doesn't perform equivalently, he or she is often seen as having a problem. That thinking is altogether flimsy, as you will see.

Exceptions: Developmental Milestones

Age-related peer comparisons work fine when considering early developmental milestones such as first steps, first words, first tooth, all that appear biologically influenced—with minimal if any effect imparted by the environment. Those genuine like-age peer comparisons are helpful, as they often initiate medical advice and timely intervention if development appears delayed—that is, if a child doesn't take a first step by about 15 months of age, "though the timeline is different for every baby." ("Walking is expected between 8.5 and

20 months, where 12–13 months is typical. Lots of variation with respect to time."[18])

Widening the Comparative Scope

Beyond those early milestones, a child's environment influences much about the youngster where age is irrelevant and the concept of "peer" is rarely if ever accurate or fitting. Dictionary.com deviates from other definitions in a fundamental way. It offers the following definition: [A peer is one] "who is equal to another in abilities, qualifications, age, background, and social status."[19] Notice that *age* is relegated to a third spot, altogether less important than a child's abilities and qualifications (i.e., skills, experiences, and education).

Comparisons

Consider the following classmates. Four boys, all 8 years old, all occupying the same Chicago third-grade classroom. At standardized test time, they are by age alone (wrongly) considered peers. Who are they? One was shuttled between multiple foster placements after being abandoned at birth by his mother, his father unknown. One helps an older brother sketch and construct by hand exquisite wooden seaworthy sailboats. One regularly joins his mother while she writes and produces elaborate videos for public television in a downtown Chicago studio. One is a remorseful former gang member who awaits a social services hearing for involvement with stolen merchandise. Despite their same ages, would you expect their acquired skills and attitudes toward school to be similar?

Consider these four girls each born in September of the same year, all raised in Chicago, all currently in the same third grade classroom: one from an affluent family with a summer home in Vancouver, BC; one who lives with her grandmother in a southside tenement often visited by drug dealers and local police; one with three siblings and one parent who holds down two minimum-wage jobs, and one whose parents are professors at Northwestern University, her mom's specialty mathematics, her dad's reading.

Consider the girls' talents and their status in the community or elsewhere (defining both anyway you wish). What might the youngsters have in common that would make them peers? Age? Yes, they're all the same age to the month. Grade level? Yes, they currently occupy the same grade level and enjoy the same teacher. On their own, however, neither age nor grade level provides any knowledge of their background, advantages, or hardships. Would we think it wise to use the mere dates of the girls' birth to predict their strengths and/or weaknesses academically and/or socially? Is it wise to use the year of the girls' birth to assign them schoolwork? Is it wise to compare them for any meaningful reason?

Picture now the above eight boys and girls, along with 18 other similarly diverse and similarly aged kids as members of the same third-grade Chicago classroom. They have one teacher who's conscientious and learned, dedicated, and—not insignificantly—by herself. In light of what we learned in the previous chapter about how biology and life experiences influence and differentiate kids, would we think it sensible to provide all the children with the same in-class lesson plan given their varied experiences and their special interests? Would we think it judicious to use the age of the boys and girls to predict what each is ready to do academically in the school classroom at any point in time during the school year? Would we think it smart to view the kids as each other's peers? To what possible end? Can we possibly justify providing all the children the same lesson plan? Probably not. Hopefully not.

Classmates

Why not call them "classmates" and leave it at that? We've buried (mostly) notable words like *dungarees* and *galoshes*. Why not *peers*? Wrap the little guy in a basket and send it out to sea. The friendly characterization *classmates* comes with no baggage, no expectations, and no comparative statistical or dire performance implications. It fits more honestly—it is or isn't true. The two same-age youngsters either did or did not attend the same school; they did or did not sit side by side in the same classroom; they either did or did not play on the same football team; they either did or did not do their best in the same school band. They may have had dramatically different impactful experiences, but they're still "classmates." They do have significantly different genes and environments. But they're still classmates. *Peers* has become a launching pad to suggest one is better or worse than another, even though the two may be as different to begin with as brim is to dregs. They're classmates. Period. *Peers* carries unnecessary (forced) implications and complications built on the shakiest of foundations.

A Celebrated Outlier and His Humor

Not all educators look on groups of same-age pupils who occupy the same classroom as a homogeneous body of learners—learners who are the same, thus comparable, thus peers. One such exception was Bill Bosher, a former superintendent of education for the state of Virginia. Thanks to UVA professor Carol Ann Tomlinson, we learn that Dr. Bosher was apt to suggest humorously, "The only time there was any such thing as a homogeneous classroom was when he was in the room by himself." Pausing long enough to slip on a boyish grin, Dr. Bosher added, "and come to think of it, I'm not even sure about that."[20] The educator-gentleman obviously believed in the integrity and uniqueness of every child and the need to accommodate educationally each youngster. One might safely presume he expected his teachers to follow his lead. For them, the term *peer* as a vehicle to compare kids had no place.

Peers

Peer is an umbrella term used to represent individuals with one or more shared attributes, age, signifying years lived, chief among those attributes. But those passing years neither assure nor reveal the full or partial experiences enjoyed or suffered by like-age youngsters. Predicting a child's character or future based on age or culture differs little from guessing the contents of a half-buried, soiled book whose hard cover has been weathered unreadable. If there's interest, the book, like the youngster, needs to be opened, considered, and the real meaningful substance within given a thorough look. From there, a gifted teacher *with time* can help the child take a step toward a worthwhile future—his classmates, those previously considered his "peers," not at all relevant to the youngster or the teacher's noble goal.

NOTES

1. Tucker, M. (2015). *Tucker's lens: On the use and abuse of evidence.* http://www.ncee.org/2015/12/tuckers-lens-on-the-use-and-abuse-of-evidence

2. Lattier, D. (2016). *Segregating students by age is a terrible practice.* https://fee.org/articles/segregating-students-by-age-is-a-terrible-practice

3. Clynes, T. (2016). *Nurturing genius.* https://www.scientificamerican.com/article/nurturing-genius

4. Anderson, R. H. (n.d.). *Nongraded schools: Brief definition, development of graded education, search for other models, research findings.* https://education.stateuniversity.com/pages/2297/Nongraded-Schools.html

5. Anderson (n.d.).

6. Merrow, J. (2017). *Addicted to Reform: A 12-step program to rescue public education.* The New Press, p. 226.

7. Layton, L. (2015, October 24). Study says standardized testing is overwhelming the nations' public schools. *Washington Post.* https://www.washingtonpost.com/local/education/study-says-standardized-testing-is-overwhelming-nations-public-schools/2015/10/24/8a22092c-79ae-11e5-a958-d889faf561dc_story.html

8. Quoted in Pardini, P. (2008). *The slowdown of the multiage classroom.* https://www.aasa.org/schooladministratorarticle.aspx?id=8720

9. Goodlad, J. I., & Anderson, R. H. (1963). *The non-graded elementary school.* Teachers College Press.

10. Cox, J. (1983). Continuous progress and nongraded schools. *Gifted Education International,* 2(1), 61–65. https://journals.sagepub.com/doi/pdf/10.1177/026142948300200118

11. Koh, Y. (2021). How schools are rewriting the rules on class time for students—and even ditching grade levels. *Wall Street Journal.* https://www.wsj.com/articles/how-schools-are-rewriting-the-rules-on-class-time-for-studentsand-even-ditching-grade-levels-11628517648

12. Goodlad & Anderson (1963).

13. Berdik, C. (2018, July). *Future of learning: What's school without grade levels?* https://hechingerreport.org/whats-school-without-grade-levels

14. Rooney, T. (n.d.). *Education reimagined.* https://education-reimagined.org/map/lindsay-unified-school-district/

15. Berdik (2018).

16. *Peer group.* (n.d.). Retrieved January 24, 2022, from https://dictionary.apa.org/peer-group

17. *Peer groups.* (n.d.). Retrieved January 24, 2022, from http://kolibri.teacherinabox.org.au/modules/en-boundless/www.boundless.com/sociology/definition/peer-groups/index.html

18. Schweizerischer Nationalfonds zur Foerderung der wissenschaftlichen Forschung. (2013, March 28). Child development: Early walker or late walker of little consequence. *ScienceDaily.* Retrieved February 18, 2022, from www.sciencedaily.com/releases/2013/03/130328075702.htm

19. *Peer.* (n.d.). Retrieved January 24, 2022, from https://www.dictionary.com/browse/peer

20. Tomlinson, C. A. (2017). *How to differentiate instruction in academically diverse classrooms.* https://files.ascd.org/staticfiles/ascd/pdf/siteASCD/publications/books/HowtoDifferentiateInstructioninAcademicallyDiverseClassrooms-3rdEd.pdf

Chapter 5

The Consequences of Lumping

The manner in which the educational system assigns youngsters to classes and curriculum hampers virtually all children's scholastic achievement in every traditional elementary school, even those that earn the signature "best" in the community. "All children" includes high-achievers, low-achievers, and every schoolchild in between. Neither can the quality teacher escape this arrangement that ultimately prevents her from exercising her full teaching talents.

What is it that we do? Professor James Delisle described it this way: We

> "Toss together several students who struggle to learn, along with a smattering of gifted kids, while adding a few English-language learners and a bunch of academically average students." Doing so, Delisle said, "causes even the most experienced and conscientious teachers to flinch, as they know the task of reaching each child is an impossible one."[1]

This casual "tossing together" of measurably diverse kids is termed *lumping*. Lumping is a cost-saving administrative convenience at the expense of the enrolled pupils and their teachers. The fact that it has remained in place since the invention of blue jeans (1873) tells us something about our educational priorities. If we're looking for a way to account for many of our schoolchildren's poor academic achievement, lumping captures the spotlight.

An Absence of Outrage

The absence of outrage from professionals who know the consequences of such a classroom arrangement is dumbfounding, of a teacher constrained to instruct (effectively, one might presume) 25–30 wildly disparate kids via a single lesson plan. Parents, too, have been noticeably silent about the arrangement. Perhaps those with advanced youngsters believe their youngsters aren't equally impacted. A mistaken perception, it turns out. It happens that the side effect of this forced parsimony is *increased* curriculum mismatching for both low-performing and advanced pupils, the latter group, in the words of Sally Reis, who are required to "wait around to January to learn anything new."[2] (Recall our Pasadena math prodigies.) Struggling youngsters (of all shades) are often forced to the sidelines, where it's easier to ignore them. This is our system.

Tricia Hedge in her book, *Teaching and Learning in the Language Classroom* said this:

> While each learner has their own unique way of learning coupled with different skills and an individual pace of learning, there is an overarching need for the instructor to apply methods that would engage all the students. A dilemma normally arises for the instructor on who to concentrate on. Should they concentrate on the advanced learners and neglect the weaker ones? [Or] the converse, [what] would be disadvantageous to the advanced learners.[3]

LUMPING

Lumping occurs when we configure same-age kids in the same classroom without regard to their individual skills or educational needs. Lumping is a throwback to the nineteenth century; it remains the exclusive approach throughout the United States. It works administratively—so long as we remove from the equation the advancement of all youngsters' achievement.

Not Everyone's on Board

The learned staff at *Education Week*, an independent news organization that has covered K–12 education since 1981, said, "Lumping students of all abilities together in one lecture-oriented class won't work; teachers must adopt new methods of instruction and flexible curricula to *cope* with these more diverse groups of students."[4]

The Approach's Many Serious Downsides

Lumping kids obscures a unique child's exceptionality. It likewise conceals what each child needs academically to progress toward more complex and necessary information. As a strategy, lumping kids with widely divergent readiness skills guarantees that an educator's predesigned lesson plan and any number of pupils' entering skills will be incompatible. The resulting negative effects on the child can extend far beyond the current day's class. Abigail Cox argued,

[We] lump our students together and teach them as if they are the equivalent of the same individual. This has only taught them to conform and not to learn. By ignoring the individual qualities, strengths, and interests of students, our society has failed to use schools to support students' strengths and passions and instead has forced them to rotely follow arbitrary tasks largely aimed at training students to pass [standardized] tests. The approach likewise has failed to provide great numbers of youngsters essential skills necessary to acquire other proficiencies, what represents schools' overall mission.[5]

Educator Clarissa Martinez summed up this situation adroitly: "Fair isn't everybody getting the same thing. Fair is everybody getting what they need in order to be successful."[6]

A Sense of Indifference

People who run the educational system seem indifferent to the injurious effects that accompany lumping all diverse kids together. That, or they are unaware of an available effective alternative that would benefit both schoolkids and their teachers. (See chapter 12.) Either way, they appear in no hurry to make the necessary changes where lumping is no longer practiced or needed. That doesn't sit well with everyone.

> One issue that a lot of teachers have been discussing more and more lately is the tendency to lump children with wildly different needs together in the same classroom. That often creates a situation where the teacher struggles with competing demands and frequently all the kids lose out. This tends to happen to disabled students, ESL [English Second Language] students, and students with "behavioural issues" in low-income schools in particular, and it does a huge disservice to both children and educators. Unfortunately, there's not a lot of traction on doing something about it.[7]

Educator Howard Gerber stated,

> A classroom teacher is expected to select educational methodology to best suit each student. This is a challenging goal for one teacher who potentially has more than 30 students in each of five to seven classes. [I]f you add special needs students to this mix, those who have severe learning delays, developmental issues, or who speak little to no English, this task can feel almost insurmountable.[8]

Dr. Matthew Lynch wrote,

> A class usually has about 30 students. These students, with different rates of assimilation and academic capabilities, are being taught the same thing at the same rate without due consideration to assimilation and brilliance. The clever

ones understand the concept quickly and become uninterested when the teacher stays too long on that topic, while others in the class would not have grasped the topic by the time the teacher moves on to another topic. A conflict of interest would arise should the teacher try to pay attention to this disparity.[9]

LUMPING: A CONVENIENCE THAT NO LONGER WORKS

Consider the setting: one teacher, 25–30 kids, all inherently different, all or most functionally different—different attitudes, interests, attentiveness, ranges of skills, learning strengths, and biological intelligence. The teacher has one lesson; the kids have 100 curricular needs. There's a clock on the classroom wall and a calendar on the teacher's desk, both visual reminders to move things along. There's a school year worth of curriculum that each day introduces new components. Some kids will be ahead of the day's curriculum, and some kids will be behind the day's curriculum; some kids will be *far* ahead; some kids *far* behind.

Good teachers understand the potential incompatibility between large numbers of pupils and every child advancing at their own pace. The good teachers know that without regard for the pupils' readiness, they still must cover curriculum materials in the limited time made available. The good ones know that every youngster in class differs from all others, that lumping them together in almost every instance is a poor choice, that the educational approach that requires the teacher to deliver a single planned lesson to the entire group of diverse youngsters is a doomed approach if, again, the goal is to advance them all—doomed not just for the kids but also for the teacher and colleagues, many who are markedly disillusioned by their chosen profession. Professor Richard Ingersol argued, "Teachers in schools do not call the shots. They have very little say. They're told what to do; it's a very disempowered line of work."[10]

This teacher with the 25–30 diverse kids, all of whom are important, remembers reading somewhere that to improve the quality of teaching and to keep teachers from leaving the field, we must "improve the quality of the teaching job." And reading further, "If you really improve that job you would attract good people and you would keep them."[11]

This teacher's been waiting for things to change for decades.

NOTES

1. Delisle, J. R. (2015). Differentiation doesn't work. *Education Week, 34*(15), 36. http://ew.edweek.org/nxtbooks/epe/ew_01072015

2. Reis, S., & the National Research Center on the Gifted and Talented. (1993). *Why not let high ability students start school in January? The curriculum compacting study.* University of Connecticut. See also Hertzberg-Davis, H. (2009). Myth 7: Differentiation in the regular classroom is equivalent to gifted programs and is sufficient: Classroom teachers have the time, the skill, and the will to differentiate adequately. *Gifted Child Quarterly, 53*(4), 251–253.

3. Hedge, T. (2000). *Teaching and learning in the language classroom.* Oxford University Press.

4. *Education Week* staff. (2004). Tracking. *Education Week.* https://www.edweek.org/leadership/tracking/2004/09, emphasis added.

5. Lynch, M. (2016). *5 keys to an effective school mission.* https://www.theedadvocate.org/5-keys-to-an-effective-school-mission

6. Martinez, C. (2018). *Individualizing to include all children.* https://teachingstrategies.com/blog/9-tips-responsive-teaching

7. Smith, S. E. (2012). *One of these things Is just not the same: Lumping kids with different needs together.* http://meloukhia.net/2012/12/one_of_these_things_is_just_not_the_same_lumping_kids_with_different_needs_together

8. Gerber, H. (2018). *Problems with inclusion in the classroom.* https://www.sunbeltstaffing.com/blog/problems-with-inclusion-in-the-classroom

9. Lynch, M. (2020). *Kids aren't failing school: School is failing kids.* https://www.theedadvocate.org/kids-arent-failing-school-school-is-failing-kids

10. Riggs, L. (2013). Why do teachers quit? *The Atlantic.* https://www.theatlantic.com/education/archive/2013/10/why-do-teachers-quit/280699

11. Riggs (2013).

Diagnostics, Strategies, and Formats

To be offered a fair chance at educational success, every school child, every school day, must be taught by a teacher who knows—*prior to instruction*—what the individual pupil can do educationally.

Chapter 6

Tailoring Instruction
Getting Started

An unnamed man (with provided facial photo) wrote the following post.[1] He asked the reader (you, please) to assume the role of the classroom teacher. The class is English. He *doesn't* mention the age or grade level of the intended students—as it should be given that you've learned what age and grade level *don't* tell us. You'll learn soon what rightfully takes their place.

He does, however, offer you the following instructions. You are to assign your pupils the task of writing an essay based on a text that you will provide. He also shared this much about your pupils: "Most students have not written a paper longer than two pages in length. Some are still mastering basic spelling and grammar. A few are naturally gifted writers."

Specifically, here's your class:

Twenty-five students. Five students are English language learners, i.e., limited English proficiency. Seven students have special needs and have IEPs (Individual Educational Program) though the educational needs aren't listed. (Again, as it should be. *You*, the classroom teacher, *will determine those educational needs*.) 12 students qualify for free or reduced lunch. 18 students read below grade level; 3 students read at grade level; 4 students read at an advanced grade level.

The gentleman poses the following questions for you to consider.

- How do you teach your lesson and support your students in ways that simultaneously ensure all students are being pushed academically while also ensuring that all students are receiving the support they need and are being taught in a way that speaks to their unique experience [and their unique capabilities]?
- If you stick to the curriculum, how many students are being left behind?
- If you slow down the curriculum, how many students are no longer being pushed?

- Do the benefits of heterogeneous [mixed ability] grouping [justify] their possible limitations?
- Wouldn't it be better to organize classes based upon student ability?

WHERE/HOW TO START?

Twenty-five kids. All different. One teacher—you. It does sound intimidating, particularly in the context of what you've learned: All same-age kids do not have the same readiness skills; all same-age kids do not learn at the same speed or with the same efficiency. In other words, your 25 kids' strengths and weaknesses are liable to resemble wind-blown dandelion seeds (i.e., all over the place). What can you possibly do? Advance each child's achievement—better skills tomorrow than today. That's what you can do.

ASSESSMENT I: ESTABLISHING PUPILS' ENTERING SKILLS

Your first task is to put to the side all of what's *unnecessary* for you to educate your 25 youngsters. Keep in mind professor James Kauffman's words:

> The differences [teachers] need to be most concerned about—maybe the only ones—are (a) what the student knows about whatever we're trying to teach and (b) what that student needs to learn next about whatever we're trying to teach. Then we need to find out how to teach that next thing most effectively and efficiently.[2]

Irrelevancies

Whether your youngsters qualify for free lunch or are English Language Learners matters little in the total scheme; the information simply isn't necessary for you to devise your teaching strategies. The same with the color of the kids' skin or the shape of their eyes or where they live or the status of their parents or caregivers. Information relayed by another teacher that a student is "at," "below," or "above" grade level in reading or math can be accepted with a "thank you" but it, too, isn't needed. As you'll discover, those descriptions convey nothing that you can use to assist your kids. Instead, you'll need to discover precisely what each pupil can accomplish academically with relative ease across all subject areas of interest. More, too, that you'll read about soon. We're talking about your students' "entering skills" or "readiness skills," information that tells you where within your curriculum the youngsters comfortably succeed, what will be their (and your) starting point.

> Regarding your "special needs" youngsters, those with IEPs, you do need to learn if any youngsters will come to class with visual and/or auditory modality issues. If so, they may influence their and your communication options. Since the gentleman said nothing about either, it's not likely that such challenges are involved with your student population. You can assume that the IEP students, not unlike *all* your youngsters, will need curriculum accommodations, what general education teachers historically have had no time (some no interest/desire) to consider.

Assessment: Standardized Tests

Standardized tests do not provide classroom teachers with anything they can use with today's or tomorrow's or next week's class assignments. They have no functional place in a child's education. The following should never have happened.

> It's almost midnight, and my daughter is calling to me. She went to bed hours ago, but she is so stressed—at age 10—that she can't sleep. She will do this nearly every night for two weeks until she finally takes the long-dreaded State English Language Arts exam.
>
> Pearson [Publishers] is a palpable presence in her education. The company developed much of the school's fourth-grade English curriculum as part of the Common Core standards. Pearson also designed the test for it. All of this in an education world where tests increasingly are the be-all and end-all.
>
> "Mom," she says, tears spilling onto her pillow, "why is one test so important?" She answers her own question with grim, distressing logic: "If I don't do well on the fourth-grade test, I won't get into a good middle school. If I don't get into a good middle school, then I won't get into a good high school, and if I don't do that, I won't get into a good college, and then I won't get a good job."
>
> I cringe, feeling that I have failed as a parent if this is what she believes. And yet she has a point. That test helps determine which middle school you get into. In her classroom, the pressure was so great that the teacher referred to the tests by aliases: the "waka-waka" and the "whablah." They were the elementary-school equivalent, it seemed, of Harry Potter's nemesis Voldemort, more commonly referred to as "he who must not be named."[3]

Standardized Tests: The Wrong Tools

W. James Popham wrote,

[Standardized achievement] tests contain too few items to allow meaningful comparisons of students' strengths and weaknesses. Although educators need to produce valid evidence regarding their [teaching] effectiveness, standardized achievement tests are the wrong tools for the task. These tests are not accurate measures of individual achievement, [and] are of little benefit to teachers. If educators accept that standardized achievement test scores should not be used to measure the quality of schooling, then [educators] must provide other, credible evidence that can be used to verify the quality of schooling.[4]

Authentic, performance-based assessment in the classroom should replace the overload of standardized tests currently being administered to our schoolkids. William Doyle, Fulbright scholar and lecturer at the University of Eastern Finland, stressed, "Don't waste time and money on mass standardized testing of children. Instead, test students correctly on a daily basis, with assessments and observations designed by their own classroom teachers and used for diagnostic purposes to improve learning."[5] That approach will allow teachers to better match their strategies to the children's accomplishments and deficiencies.

Linda Darling-Hammond wrote, "Standardized tests that were intended to inject more rigor into education are, instead, 'driving instruction away from the development of skills and thinking abilities.'" She added, "When standardized tests are too narrow a measure, they provide little concrete [timely] information that teachers and schools can use to improve teaching and learning for individual students."[6]

FYI:
Teachers in Finland spend fewer hours at school each day and spend less time in classrooms than American teachers. Teachers use the extra time to build curriculums and *assess their students*. [And they are provided] lots of special teacher help [in the classroom] to make sure no child really would be left behind. There are no mandated standardized tests in Finland, apart from one exam at the end of students' senior year in high school. There are no rankings, no comparisons or competition between students, schools or regions. "We prepare children to learn how to learn, not how to take a test," said Pasi Sahlberg, a former math and physics teacher who is now in Finland's Ministry of Education and Culture. "This is what we do every day, prepare kids for life," said Kari Louhivuori, a veteran teacher and a school principal.[7]

OTHER PROBLEMS PLAGUE STANDARDIZED INSTRUMENTS

Professor Jack Schneider wrote,

These [standardized] tests are written in standard English. Students may select phrases as the correct answer that are perfectly acceptable in their neighborhood but read as wrong on a test, the scoring machine unable to make that discrimination. Test writers often *assume* students are familiar with objects that though common in many homes, are not present in all of them, or [they] go my different names.[8]

Similarly, a district school superintendent shared, "Several years ago, a question on a state exam prompted elementary-level students to write a fictional story about a mysterious 'trunk' they had stumbled upon." The superintended reported, "We had English language learners writing about elephants, cars, and swimsuits. The state's intention was for students to describe what would be in a box."[9]

Dr. Schneider continued,

It is worth noting that even a question such as "What is the main event in the story" is not necessarily fair for all students. A student whose first language is not English, or who for some other reason has a limited vocabulary, may struggle to distinguish between [answers] despite being a perfectly good reader. . . . [More unsettling,] a student may respond with a right answer but still be marked wrong because it is not the *best* answer—the one the test publisher is looking for.[10]

Then there's this:

If the kids who score worse (generally low-income kids and students of color) actually score *better* on a question, that question often gets cut from the test and many questions are never included in tests because too many students answer them correctly.[11]

All in the name of statistics and its significance, not the kids—who are a sight more significant.

ASSESSMENT PREFERENCES: YOUR FIRST DECISION

Assessments are intended to provide a clear picture of the effectiveness of strategies and the outcomes resulting from those strategies. Medical doctors determine the effectiveness of medication; speech and language pathologists assess their therapies; bakers their tasty goods. In the case of good schools, quality teachers weigh the achievements of their pupils to learn about their own teaching effectiveness.

Choices

What might appear straightforward isn't quite so neat. When it comes to schoolkids and their performance, teachers (and parents) often hold two expressly different views of what they wish to learn from such measurements. Some teachers and parents are more interested in being informed how a child compares with a neighbor's child or a group of same-age kids within the classroom. The child's individual classroom performance is less valued. (FYI: When competing against six others in a foot race, if a youngster doesn't come in first, it's often viewed as a defeat. "You'll do better next time" is offered as consolation. That the youngster bettered her best time by 20% is often lost in the limited analysis. That's called improvement.)

Other teachers (and parents) are more interested in an individual child's current skills—that is, how the youngster's classroom achievements *today* liken to the youngster's achievements say last week or perhaps yesterday. The two differing preferences—how a child compares with others vs. the child's individual growth-over-time competencies—require different forms of assessment. Standardized tests focus on comparing same-age kids' achievements, whereas an alternative assessment strategy examines an individual youngster's classroom skills as they advance, what was meant by Dr. Popham's earlier call for "authentic, performance-based assessment in the classroom."[12] Imagine a child who struggles with reading who suddenly figures out keys that unlock that complicated process and makes a giant leap forward. His new reading skills may comparatively be less than those of his more accomplished classmates, but they are for him a breakthrough. Should he be evaluated down because he's behind his same-age mates, or evaluated up because of his individual improvement?

A Teacher's Decision

If a teacher is interested mainly in a child's standing in the classroom where such words like *better, best, equal to, worse than, above* (or *below*) *average* are important, the educator should opt for standardized tests. If, however, a teacher is more interested in a child's skill acquisition over time; his specific reading, writing, and mathematics proficiencies; and how those skills mesh with the teacher's current curriculum, then the teacher will want an alternative assessment strategy. This alternative compares the child against *himself* (i.e., his prior performance, what will tell the educator, the youngster, and the child's parents whether his skills have improved).

Norm-Referenced and the "Typical" Child

Standardized tests "are *norm*-referenced allowing a student's [scores] to be compared with [scores produced] by a national sample of students of the same age or grade level."[13] (Those pesky faux "peers" again.) Findings from those tests produce anemic statements such as: "Mary scored as well as the *typical* student in a national group in the spring of the 4th grade."[14] Not a lot of meat on that bone.

The problem centers on the ubiquitous term *typical*. It's hard to know who we're talking about. Actually, it's no youngster in particular. Rather, *typical* is a compilation of every youngster who shares the same attribute, like the average score of say a thousand nine-year-olds or a thousand foster kids or a thousand math majors who took the test. Considering today's extreme cultural diversity in the United States, however, nine-year-olds (or foster kids or fourth-graders or math majors) can differ hugely in everything *but* their age. Beyond the ranking of percentiles, the score on any standardized test doesn't tell an educator much about the individual 9-year-old sitting in his or her classroom (or his or her home living room) other than the youngster is on par or better or worse than the average of the thousand others. A statistician might get excited by that, but the info won't help a teacher provide the youngster with the best lesson.

Even being "on par with" or "better/worse than" is problematic. A child being assessed, though a minority or high school math major or a fifth-grader, may have unique experiences that rightly exclude him or her from the comparative group, like if he or she missed a year of school due to hospitalization or if he or she spent six weeks at Sal Kahn's[15] math camp just prior to taking the test. Each unique factor that's not represented within the comparative (normed) population separates the youngster further from the group and from the group's statistically manipulated average score. That can easily reduce the numbers' already-limited usefulness. A measured "above average" or "below average" pupil may be neither—and neither demarcation has much practical value from an instructional standpoint.

NAEP

Consider the National Assessment of Educational Progress (NAEP), again what's considered the nation's standardized report card. With the encouragement of President Reagan's secretary of education, William Bennett, "this excellent assessment was diverted from its original purpose of measuring what students at various grade levels actually know to a new goal: judging what students at various grade levels should know,"[16] what for a purported skill-driven assessment tool represents a huge change in the wrong direction.

How It Works . . . and Doesn't

The NAEP focuses on unique populations of American students, including those of different racial/ethnic groups, ages, grades, and those in different types of schools and geographic regions, *not* individual students.[17] Knowing *anything* about an individual from the reported scores is not possible. The kids taking the test are homogenized into a "nationally representative sample of students." Their culture, mores, traditions, familial history, uniqueness are so diluted by statistical averaging to be no longer identifiable. It's the same as taking one hundred distinct flowers and pressing them together to make one as a representative of all. What you're left with may be beautiful but it's not at all similar to what you started with. "In view of the nation's substantial curricular diversity, test developers are obliged to create a series of one-size-fits-all assessments. But, as most of us know from attempting to wear one-size-fits-all garments, sometimes one size really can't fit all."[18]

STANDARDIZED TESTS: ADVANTAGES AND SHORTCOMINGS

Professor Jack Schneider reminded us that standardized tests do "tell us something basic about [general] student achievement, and that information can be critical in advocating [dollars] for additional resources and supports." He contended that "the harshest critics are wrong when they claim that standardized tests are worthless." But, he added, "critics of [the] testing are right about a great deal else. Standardized tests are limited in what they reveal and are not entirely fair across social, ethnic, and economic lines." Former First Lady Michelle Obama said, "If my future were determined just by a standardized test, I wouldn't be [the former first lady]. I can guarantee you that."[19]

Dr. Schneider stated that standardized tests likewise "overlook most of what we value in schools."[20] (Perhaps how kids are doing day-by-day inside their own classroom.) Case in point: Author Ted Dintersmith wrote *What Schools Could Be.*[21] He reported on his nine months of travel though the 2015–2016 school year, which included an unexpected confrontation of sorts with standardized tests and a person who occupied a very high state-government position. He shared the following account.

> I went to all 50 states, visited 200 schools, and met thousands of people involved in education—students, teachers, administrators, parents, education policy makers, legislators, governors. You name it, I talked with them. I wasn't sure what to expect when I left, but this trip was flat-out inspiring. I saw the very best of U.S. education, and drew daily inspiration from remarkably innovative teachers.[22]

He then offered this unexpected example of an important person's startling view of what standardized testing can accomplish. (FYI: This woman's responsibilities included advising the governor and other state leaders on all things involved with educating the state's K–12 pupils, making her a singular VIP. Here's their conversation. "KM" were not her actual initials.)

> Mr. Dintersmith: "The meeting was short. I met with KM in her office at the state's capitol building. I tend to talk fast but after a couple of minutes, KM stopped me."
> "Look," KM said, "I know everything I need to know about education. You don't need to tell me anything. What can *I* explain to *you*?"
> Taking it all in stride, Mr. Dintersmith answered, "I believe that the more test-driven a school is, the more it puts kids at risk in a world of innovation."
> KM replied, "You're making this too complicated. Educating children is like fixing a car. You take a car to the garage and pay them to fix it. We pay our schools $7,000 per student and expect them to be educated."
> Mr. Dintersmith: "How do you know they're learning anything?"
> KM, the state's educational boss, answered, "That's why we have standardized tests."
> When I started to respond, KM stood up. She informed me, "Look, I'm important to the governor. Thank you for your time." And she left.[23]

The lady is woefully ignorant. That's not personal, and it's not pejorative. *Ignorant* means she's missing valuable information, not unlike all of us. When faced with something they know little about, people have the option to turn to someone who knows what they don't know—or, as happens in KM's case, conspicuously choose to remain ignorant.

Dr. Popham wrote,

> Standardized achievement test scores should be regarded as rough approximations of a student's status with respect to the content domain represented by the test [e.g., reading, mathematics, history, science, etc.]. But standardized achievement tests should not be used to evaluate the quality of education. Overall, standardized tests are poor measures of school success and educational quality.[24]

Physics professor Joseph Ganem explained, "Standardized tests compare groups of students from one year to the next, but they don't tell you about individual student progress,"[25] the information you need to gauge a child's school achievement.

Our children are not robots manufactured to comply with identical product specifications. Their diversity should be celebrated, not erased. Schools should be places of learning. Tests are an essential part of the education process, but they should be individualized to assess what a child has learned, not what he or she doesn't know. And all students should be challenged to learn, regardless of whether or not they meet the "standards." In our schools, learning should be the standard.[26]

ALTERNATIVE: DIRECT OBSERVATION OF CLASSROOM ACHIEVEMENT

A century ago, Iowa professor Everett Franklin Lindquist created the ACT (American College Test) and other popular standardized tests. That fact aside, he advised, "The only perfectly valid measure of [educational achievement] would be based on direct observation of the criterion behavior" (e.g., each child's reading or writing or math skills). In other words, professor Lindquist called for "assessments and observations [that are] designed by the individual's own classroom teachers and used for diagnostic purposes to improve [the youngster's] learning."[27]

Professor Koretz, Harvard Graduate School of Education, lamented,

> The more importance we attribute to standardized tests, the farther we have strayed from Lindquist's advice. Scores on a single [standardized] test are now routinely used as if they were a comprehensive summary of what students know or what schools produce. Taken by themselves, scores describe some of what students can do, but they don't describe all that they can do, and they don't explain why they can or cannot do it.[28]

SUMMARY

"Standardized tests are quite limited in what they can tell us about student ability," Dr. Schneider counseled. "All districts—and particularly urban districts which often have lower standardized test scores because of their makeup should be seeking to build better measures that more fairly capture academic performance."[29]

W. James Popham agreed:

> If we're going to argue against standardized achievement tests as a source of evidence for determining school and teacher quality, and if we're determined to hold our educational system accountable for what it does, then we need to ante up some other form of evidence to show the world that [we're] doing a good educational job. If the skills selected are also seen by parents and policymakers

to be genuinely significant, and if those skills can be addressed instructionally by competent teachers, then the assembly of evidence showing substantial student growth in such skills can be truly persuasive.[30]

Jack Schneider stated, "For years, parents and educators have been pushing back against the singular focus on standardized test scores in measuring school quality. Each time, however, they have been met by the same reply: What do you propose to do instead?"[31]

What should be used in place of standardized assessments to learn how schools and their kids are achieving? Next chapter, please.

NOTES

1. *To differentiate or to track?* (2019). https://www.relay.edu/article/to-differentiate-or-to-track

2. Personal communication, James Kauffman, December 1, 2014.

3. Reingold, J. (2015, January 21). Everybody hates Pearson. *Fortune.* http://fortune.com/2015/01/21/everybody-hates-pearson

4. Popham, W. J. (1999). *Why standardized tests don't measure educational quality.* http://www.ascd.org/publications/educational-leadership/mar99/vol56/num06/Why-Standardized-Tests-Don't-Measure-Educational-Quality.aspx. See also Perrone, V. (1991, Spring). On standardized testing. *Childhood Education, 67*(3), 132–142; Hilliard, P. (2015). *Performance-based assessment: Reviewing the basics.* https://www.edutopia.org/blog/performance-based-assessment-reviewing-basics-patricia-hilliard; American University School of Education. (2020, July 2). *Effects of standardized testing on students & teachers: Key benefits & challenges.* https://soeonline.american.edu/blog/effects-of-standardized-testing. See also Perrone, V. (1991, Spring). On standardized testing. *Childhood Education, 67*(3), 132–142; Hilliard, P. (2015). *Performance-based assessment: Reviewing the basics.* https://www.edutopia.org/blog/performance-based-assessment-reviewing-basics-patricia-hilliard; American University School of Education. (2020, July 2). *Effects of standardized testing on students & teachers: Key benefits & challenges.* https://soeonline.american.edu/blog/effects-of-standardized-testing

5. Strauss, V. (2016). *I have seen the school of tomorrow. It is here today, in Finland.* https://www.washingtonpost.com/news/answer-sheet/wp/2016/05/07/i-have-seen-the-school-of-tomorrow-it-is-here-today-in-finland/

6. Darling-Hammond, L. (2008). *How should we measure student learning? 5 keys to comprehensive assessment.* https://www.edutopia.org/comprehensive-assessment-introduction

7. Hancock, L. N. (2011). *Why are Finland's schools successful?* https://www.smithsonianmag.com/innovation/why-are-finlands-schools-successful-49859555 (emphasis added).

8. Schneider, J. (2017). *Beyond test scores: A better way to measure school quality.* Harvard University Press.

9. Schneider, J. (2017).

10. Schneider, J. (2017).

11. Schneider, J. (2017).

12. Hibbard, K. M., Pomperaug Regional School District 15 (Middlebury and Southbury, CT), & the Association for Supervision and Curriculum Development. (1996). A teacher's guide to performance-based learning and assessment. ASCD; Kelly, M. (2019). Authentic ways to develop performance-based activities. https://www.thoughtco.com/ideas-for-performance-based-activities-7686

13. Popham, W. J. (1999). Why standardized tests don't measure educational quality. *Educational Leadership, 56*(6). http://www.ascd.org/publications/educational-leadership/mar99/vol56/num06/Why-Standardized-Tests-Don't-Measure-Educational-Quality.aspx

14. National Council on Teacher Quality. *Standardized test: A definition* [PowerPoint presentation]. https://www.nctq.org/dmsView/Attachment_2_Standardized_Assessment_PWPT

15. Kahn Academy. (n.d.). *Impact.* Retrieved January 25, 2022, from https://www.khanacademy.org/about/impact

16. Strauss, V. (2018, April 26). "A nation at risk" demanded education reform 35 years ago., Here's how it's been bungled ever since. *Washington Post.* https://www.washingtonpost.com/news/answer-sheet/wp/2018/04/26/the-landmark-a-nation-at-risk-called-for-education-reform-35-years-ago-heres-how-it-was-bungled (emphasis added).

17. National Center for Education Statistics. (n.d.). *About NAEP: A common measure of student achievement.* Retrieved January 25, 2022, from https://nces.ed.gov/nationsreportcard/about/

18. Popham (1999).

19. Ershova, S. (2017, February 11). Standardized tests are inaccurate. The Sandbox News. https://sandbox.spcollege.edu/index.php/2017/02/standardized-tests-are-inaccurate

20. Schneider (2017).

21. Dintersmith, T. (2018). *What schools could be.* Princeton University Press.

22. Dintersmith (2018).

23. Dintersmith (2018).

24. Popham, W. J. (1999).

25. GreatSchools Staff. (2013, January 30). *State standardized test scores: What families should know.* https://www.greatschools.org/gk/articles/state-standardized-test-scores-issues-to-consider

26. Ganen, J. (2018). It's time to rethink the purpose of standardized tests. *Baltimore Sun.* https://www.baltimoresun.com/opinion/op-ed/bs-ed-op-1007-standardized-tests-20181004-story.html

27. Koretz, D. (2008). *Measuring up: What educational testing really tells us.* Harvard University Press.

28. Koretz (2008).

29. Schneider (2017).
30. Popham (1999).
31. Schneider, J. (2017).

Chapter 7

Authentic Performance-Based Assessment

OUR EDUCATIONAL SYSTEM'S MISGUIDED DECISION (2021–2022)

NEA *Today*'s John Rosales and Tim Walker wrote,

> As many students return to in-person learning for the first time in almost a year, states and school districts are also beginning to gear up for statewide standardized testing, as required by the US Department of Education (ED). . . . [Juxtapose this arbitrary imperative to the fact that] in April 2020, as the pandemic engulfed the nation and forced schools to close, the [same ED] department granted a "blanket waiver" to every state to skip mandated statewide testing for 2019–20. Last month, however, ED officials announced it was mandating schools to administer some form of statement assessment for 2020–21–22.

All of this occurred despite National Education Association (NEA) President Becky Pringle's voiced objections, "Every state should use flexibility from the new federal guidance to focus on students, not invalid, unreliable standardized tests."[1]

Rosales and Walker continued, "Many communities have suffered the most from high-stakes [standardized] testing—Black, Latin(o/a/x), and Native students, as well as students from some Asian groups." "We still think there's something wrong with the kids rather than recognizing [there's] something wrong with the tests," said Ibram X. Kendi of the Antiracist Research Center at Boston University. "Yet some organizations insist on more testing," noted Rosales and Walker, "arguing that the data will expose the gaps where support and resources should be directed." (That view is without merit if we're concerned about kids' school achievement. Please see later in this chapter:

"Money Issues? Or Something Else?") The two NEA authors observed correctly, "Standardized tests have never been accurate and reliable measures of *student learning and, one year into a pandemic, would be even less so now.*"[2]

CURRICULUM-BASED ASSESSMENT

In place of standardized tests, we have at our disposal an accurate, fair, and stress-free way to assess the skills all youngsters have acquired. The methodology fits today's classroom and all its diverse kids. It's professor W. James Popham's *authentic, performance-based assessment*, and it comes in the form of what's known as "curriculum-based assessment."[3] This planned, meaningful classroom assessment gathers evidence of student learning that

- helps a teacher adjust instructional strategies;
- lets the educator discover what a student knows and can accomplish with ease; and
- lets the teacher learn what within the curriculum interferes with the youngster's continued achievement.[4]

Curriculum-based assessments (CBAs) provide teachers all the above advantages. Authors and educators Drs. Jan Thomas, Carol Allman, and Marty Beech stated that CBA represents an

> on-going assessment methodology that involves periodic monitoring of a student's daily performance. It provides a measure of a student's progress through a teacher's chosen curriculum. CBAs are repeated [many] dozens of times throughout the entire school year. They are the basis for continual educational decision-making and student planning.[5]

Academicians and collaborative consultants Lorna Idol, Ann Nevin, and Phyllis Paolucci-Whitcomb wrote, "Curriculum-based assessment helps teachers build more effective instructional programs to increase and enhance student achievement."[6] Without such assessments, a teacher won't know if his or her strategies are effective. If they're not effective, kids do suffer—most often in silence.

PROBES: MEASURING WHAT A TEACHER TEACHES

Curriculum-based assessments measure precisely what teachers teach, the curriculum they've selected for their pupils. These CBAs inform teachers of both student progress and challenges by means of probes that assess skills the teacher wants the kids to learn. These probes are *brief* diagnostic tests, quizzes, worksheets, or oral queries applied to class projects. Examples include asking a pupil to read aloud a short passage, writing or editing a three-to four-sentence grammar exercise, solving a half-dozen math problems, writing a 100-word story about a provided topic, or identifying alphabet letters and/or their phonetic sounds.

> The probes are easy to monitor and evaluate, making CBA a form of ongoing assessment of student performance over time, what provides the teacher, the youngster, and the youngster's parents a clear picture of the youngster's growth. The teacher can tell quickly if a youngster is on track with emerging skills, can see the characteristics of errors the student is making, and can learn what skills are in need of remediation. CBAs is a child-centered approach to evaluating and documenting [scholastic] progress that provides teachers with a valuable tool for planning, delivering, and assessing instruction.[7]

CBAs tell a quality teacher if he or she needs to adjust the curriculum or the instructional method used with an individual child or group of youngsters. CBAs inform a teacher where within his curriculum each youngster has progressed to date, as well as revealing how well a youngster can apply the knowledge she has acquired. Standardized tests aren't designed to do the above.

CRITERION-REFERENCE TESTS (CRTS)

Curriculum-based assessments collect their data by means of *criterion-referenced tests* (CRTs), those probes previously mentioned. CRTs are constructed by the classroom teacher, not by a publisher that doesn't know the child, the child's teacher, or the child's curriculum. CRTs focus on an individual youngster's current skills with no relationship to the performance of any other classmate.[8]

CRTs and Diverse Children

Some professionals and some in the general public seem content to judge the effectiveness of schools/teachers/kids by comparing standardized percentile rankings of pupils that public schools often provide. They'd be better served by learning if a youngster's skills are stronger today than they were yesterday. Does the youngster read better, write better, calculate numbers better, problem-solve better? This is all best monitored and verified often with weekly, brief CRT assessments, not standardized tests administered once or twice a year.

While essential for all pupils, including our most advanced kids, nowhere is this change from standardized achievement instruments to these pragmatic CRTs more critical than with our diverse populations of low-functioning kids, kids specifically with limited opportunities, limited parental support, and limited exposure to life's circumstances that promote general learning. The latter particularly includes a child assigned to a poorly funded school, taught by a poorly trained teacher, who is guided by a poorly trained administrator. CBAs will instantly pinpoint the lack of academic progress. Administered a second time *after* a teacher's lesson, they will show if that lesson raised the youngster's skills. A few days later, after multiple lessons and exercises, the CRT will tell interested parties whether the child improved further, shedding light on the teacher's strategies. From the previous chapter, Jack Schneider counseled, "All districts—and particularly urban districts which often have lower standardized test scores because of their makeup should be seeking to build better measures that more fairly capture academic performance."[9] CRTs will serve that purpose. And more. Consider the following.

Money Issues? Or Something Else?

Recall what we learned in chapter 2. "Incredibly, even at the government-funded charter school being touted as a model of progress, less than 15 percent of [minority] students were proficient in math . . . [and] . . . nine out of ten black boys are not reading at grade level."[10] With all that despairing news, an essential piece of information goes missing, what, shockingly, may not be known even by the youngsters' teachers. The answer ranks as perhaps *the* most important strategic piece of information yet to be divulged. I'll share in a moment. First, though, a brief detour.

As suggested, one argument offered in favor of standardized tests claimed that they help educational administrators know where to invest their funds. The earlier phrase suggested, "The data will expose the gaps where support and resources should be directed." I'd argue that "added resources [money] will have little to no effect on the kids' achievement if nothing changes at the classroom instruction level." Baltimore city kids come from a district that has "some of the highest spending per pupil in America."[11] Pouring more money on top won't budge the achievement needle one millimeter. Dollars are not the problem. More likely, we have

- a reading strategy problem;
- an indifferent instructor problem;
- a textbook supply problem;

- an inflexible system format problem; and
- an administrative "look the other way" problem.

This from language literacy specialist Susan Bishop Zirpoli:

A child who reads poorly may be a "curriculum casualty." Low scores on a comprehensive reading evaluation may be due to a lack of adequate instruction. Proper assessment of the child's current reading skills is essential. Running records, reading decodable word lists, sight word assessments, fluency measures, as well as comprehension measures both reading and listening will reveal the child's many strengths. Instruction must be based precisely on those strengths—what a child *can* do. Names, labels and/or proposed biological deficiencies change none of that. How a child's reading compares with another child's reading is not relevant. Learning to read is an individual goal; it is not a race.[12]

Missing Essential Information

An accomplished reading specialist with proper training would never solely report to classroom teachers (or parents) that youngsters aren't reading at grade level. Nothing within that utterance puts anything useful in the hands of a teacher or parent. Something invaluable is missing.

What's missing is CRT documentation that reveals what the youngster can read—even if only a few letters of the alphabet. Irene C. Fountas and Gay Su Pinnell have provided teachers and others with a list of reading behaviors that clearly indicate what a reading child can do. These behaviors are divided into levels from A to Z that spell out what youngsters "should exhibit at each reading level."[13] For example, a beginning level A youngster "reads words from left to right," "locates both known words and new words," and "relates the book to his/her experience," among other basic skills. A more advanced reader at level E "figures out some longer words by taking them apart," "recognizes many words quickly and automatically," and "remembers details and uses them to clarify meaning," again among other skills. It would have been most helpful (a necessity) for a quality teacher to have learned at what level the Baltimore boys *succeeded* rather than only being told they read below grade level.

It's essential that teachers know precisely what a youngster *can* do to know where within the curriculum materials they must begin their reading instruction, regardless of a child's age, grade level, location of school, the financial status of the child and family, his culture, color, height, weight, politics, or background. Determining what the youngster can read successfully requires direct observation and direct assessment, what Ms. Zirpoli outlined a moment ago: Running records, reading decodable word lists, sight word assessments, fluency measures, as well as comprehension measures (both reading and listening). Some form of teacher-made CRT involving any and all of those factors is essential.

Summary

CRTs are simple to devise, a cinch to administer, and easy to evaluate. Because they can be administered weekly if not more often, the scores can be plotted on graph paper to show parents (and the child) growth curves that eliminate unpleasant surprises at parent-teacher conferences.

> [CRTs] are better suited to measuring learning progress than norm-referenced [standardized] exams, and they offer educators information they can use to improve teaching and school performance. [CRTs] are fairer to students than norm-referenced [standardized] tests because they don't compare the relative performance of students; [instead] they evaluate [a youngster's achievement] against a common and consistently applied set of criteria.[14]

CRTs measure progress toward goals and objectives established for an individual youngster.[15] Not to be overlooked, CRT results help teachers evaluate the effectiveness of their own instructional methods.

Diminishing Achievement

In addition to conveying to the teacher where within the curriculum the child succeeds with ease, CRTs can tell a teacher where within that curriculum a child's successful behavior begins to break down. That, too, stands near the pinnacle of importance. The latter information provides on-the-spot vital information for the well-prepared quality teacher who can adjust his or her strategy to include targeted examples and helpful explanations to aid the child over the troubling hurdle. (Please see "Error Analysis" in the next chapter.)

Standardized tests don't approach that benefit. Michael Casserly, executive director of the Council of the Great City Schools, stated:

> In a U.S. Department of Education study, 40 percent of the districts surveyed, [standardized] test results [weren't] available until the following school year, making them useless for teachers who want to use results to help guide their work in the classroom.[16]

More to the point, and more urgent for today's diverse schoolkids, nothing within a standardized test's data can guide even the finest of teachers how best to teach any individual child. That requires discovering the particulars of the intimate relationship between the youngster, the teacher, and the teacher's curriculum. That requires our CRTs.

Sidebar: Parental CRTs

We know the benefit of engaging parents in their child's education. Teaching them how to administer a CRT can be enlightening. A parent can get a first read on what his or her child knows in two–three minutes. A few questions targeting a particular skill constitutes a CRT. Reading a few words, solving a few math problems, and revealing what's missing in a picture are all examples of quick preliminary CRTs.

Involving the Parent

Let's assume a parent expresses an interest in working with their child's reading. The teacher might inquire if she'd like to practice with a popular set of exercises that involve vocabulary, spelling, word choice, word naming, word/letter phonetics, word use, synonyms, and antonyms. Easy to do and often done in relative minutes. If the parent's willing, direct her to http://www.kidzone.ws/dolch. Have her select a certain number of words just below her child's assigned grade level, 5 to 10 words to begin with. In the unlikely event the child's school has adopted an ungraded approach, you can use the child's own books to select words. Have the parent decide what she wants to focus on: spelling, vocabulary, synonyms, or antonyms. If spelling is the criterion area, have the youngster spell (or define, pronounce, or suggest one synonym or antonym) for each of the 5 or 10 words.

If the child answers all the parent's queries in a snap, advance to the next level, words slightly more difficult. If the child makes errors, drop back a grade level (and perform an "error analysis"—to be explained soon). You can ask the parent to share what she finds. Explain that what she shares will provide you with important information relating to the youngster's skill level.

Teachers can do the above with their entire class, or a small group of youngsters, if that's the teacher's preference. Making notes of what words are commonly missed, the teacher can develop strategies to introduce the words in sentences to help a struggling child build understanding, what will improve youngsters' spelling, reading, communicating, and writing.

CRTs can do all of that. And more. The following scenario represented an emotional time in the life of a youngster and her parents. All of what happened could have been avoided.

88   Chapter 7

CASE: PRACTICAL CRTS

Consider yourself the general education teacher with the following girl in your classroom. What would *you* have done as this girl's teacher in a similar situation? If you're a student in education, give yourself moments to formulate your ideas or get together with classmates and have a group discussion that ends with specific, easily replicable strategies to be used in the girl's behalf. If you would, do so *before* you read the critique.

Keep this in mind, please. The young person was a general education pupil when she first arrived at school. That status changed because of the school's view that bright youngsters who aren't achieving as expected are most likely impeded by a neurological (and/or genetic) impairment. (You might remember that point from discussions regarding "learning disabilities." You don't have to accept that conclusion. Non-neurological school-related issues are most certainly involved.) Even with the unnecessary label imposed, a well-trained general education teacher who assumed responsibility for this young girl would have known immediately the corrective strategies. He or she would have needed maybe a dozen minutes to have resolved this issue.

One last related point. Every child is unique, with needs and abilities specific to himself or herself. Special education labels obscure that fact.[17] Special education teachers (and school psychologists) are mandated to use these obscure, arbitrarily created disability labels. That's a system problem, not a child problem. (See "Finland" below.)

Real-Life Situation

As you read, keep in mind professor Jack Schneider's penetrating maxim:

> Schools are places where we make the future—for our children as well as for our society. If we remember this truth, we might concern ourselves less with the status of schools and more with what actually happens *inside* them.[18]

We're now heading *deep* inside—in this instance, the aforementioned intimate relationship between the teacher, the schoolchild, and the curriculum the teacher delivers to the youngster. After the critique, I'll share what the girl's parents chose to do. At this moment, the girl's mother is speaking.

> I am in hell—or its equivalent. Specifically, I am in an IEP meeting [Individual Educational Plan] for my daughter, a special-education student. My daughter's reading comprehension and vocabulary skills are ranked as "very superior"; her learning issues center on math. Some teachers assume that a child who is smart in one area is simply being lazy or obstructionist by not being smart in another.

After three years at an elementary school with the county's highest standardized test scores where she was constantly told that she "just needed to *focus*," my daughter collapsed to the floor one night sobbing. She'd spent two hours on (math) homework (that might have been done in 30 minutes). The school's institutional culture regarded kids with learning disabilities as impediments to their goal of keeping those standardized scores high. The emotional toll exacted on a child who is told that his repeated failures are his own fault can be high.

An educator sitting close to me [at the IEP meeting] says she has a great (new) place for my daughter: a program at one of the county's lower-performing schools for kids who have emotional disabilities or autism. . . . [Or], a school for kids with a variety of learning disabilities, where kids' brains are wired differently, [or one] for kids with autism and emotional disabilities; [or], a school [with] kids with dyslexia [and/or] ADHD.[19]

(This is not the forum to discuss the medical model and the errors it creates with purported educational disabilities such as dyslexia, LD, and ADHD. Just know that not all psychologists, psychiatrists, otherwise physicians, and educators interpret the three "conditions" [and others similar] as real disorders.[20] The book *The Medicalization of America's Schools* has addressed the topic more thoroughly.)

Critique

What should the educators have done in behalf of this struggling youngster? It's not complicated. The first time the girl exhibited *any* difficulty with her in-class math assignments, the ready teacher would have performed two exercises. First, using CRTs, the teacher would have assessed the girl's present entering skills with regards to the mathematics being taught. The information provides a reliable measure that would tell the teacher where the girl succeeded at or near 100% proficiency and where within the curriculum the girl began to experience math difficulties. These entering skills are unrelated to age or grade level. They represent the girl's starting point, where within the curriculum she is successful—no matter where that point lies, no matter how it compares with the other kids' starting points. Remember Ms. Zirpoli's early statement: "Learning is an individual goal; it is not a race." Though the young lady was unable to complete her mathematics homework as assigned by her teacher, rest assured this gal possessed solid math skills. The CRTs would have highlighted those proficiencies.

Second, knowing where within the math curriculum the girl succeeded reliably at or near 100% proficiency, the teacher would have provided the girl with additional math exercises to *intentionally* produce consistent errors. Discovering consistent errors, the teacher would have conducted an error analysis, what would have uncovered critical cognitive deficiencies. Once discovered, a quality teacher would immediately know what the youngster needed.

As it turned out, little effort was spent by the teachers or the school in behalf of the young lady. It was easier to assign the young student any number of special education labels and let someone else worry about her future. In all of what was done, no one in a position that mattered consider the following basic tenet. Jim Wright, school psychologist and school administrator, stated,

> The measurement of a child's school [academic proficiencies via CRTs] is just as important as the teaching of those skills. Only by carefully testing what a child has learned can an instructor then draw conclusions about whether that student is ready to advance to more difficult material.[21]

Homework and Specifics

Further, the girl's teachers would have (should have) verified her mathematic skills and knowledge prior to assigning any homework. An interested teacher would have asked the *relaxed* young lady to do her best with 10 to 20 different math problems, some easy, some more difficult, all that covered a wide range of multiple grade-level math skills. No pressure. None. Zero. That's a probe; that's our CRTs. The CRT exercise would have provided the teacher with a good estimate of the girl's entering skills. (Mom could have done the same, had she known what to do.)

As it was, no one at the school took the time to see what math skills the youngster had mastered. That's gross incompetence. The school seemed more interested in their standardized test scores and its reputation than the girl's learning or her state of mind. The teachers involved assigned the same homework to all the kids based on the false assumption that because the kids were in the same class and the same age—"peers," wrongly judged—the same homework assignment would suit them all. (Please, *classmates* rather than *peers*. The kids in class were the former; they were not in an stretch the latter.)

For this girl, the teachers played the same apathetic record over and over: "You just need to focus more." That's worse than incompetence. A vigilant, accountable principal would have (should have) pulled the plug. With the results of the 10–20-problem CRT analyzed, the teachers' assigned homework would have served to build on the girl's already-acquired strengths and would easily and gradually have introduced more challenging concepts during future mathematical instruction and future homework.

CRTs permit a teacher to instantly observe and record a student's performance and gather information used to make immediate instructional decisions.[22] Using CRTs, a teacher assesses a child's responses and based on the results "decides whether to continue instruction in the same way, or to change it."[23] These efficient assessments leave more time for the teacher to instruct the skills she's targeting.[24] Remember, please, CRTs are generated by teachers themselves. They are made up of academic material taken from the child's own school curriculum.[25] Not to be forgotten:

- An able youngster whose teachers assessed recurrent entering skills to help make instructional adjustments would never *ever* reach seventh grade and not know his alphabet.
- An able youngster whose teachers assessed readiness skills to help make instructional adjustments would never *ever* collapse to the floor thoroughly devastated by her math homework.

What Did Her Parents Do?

The parents removed their daughter from the public system and enrolled her in a school with a different attitude and a different instructional methodology, the young lady the beneficiary. The public educational system has no one to blame but itself. The following information was not sealed away in a secret vault intentionally hidden from teachers and school administrators. It reads: "Students whose quality teachers used curriculum-based evaluations to monitor academic progress and to make adjustments in instructional programs when [they are needed] significantly outperformed comparable students whose teachers did not use curriculum-based evaluations."[26] That says a lot.

End-of-School-Day CRT

By administering and later examining a three-or four-question "exit" CRT just prior to the closing of a school day, a teacher will have a better idea of what he or she accomplished during the class session. If students' deficiencies are noted, the quality teacher writes a reminder of what needs to be done to further help those students the following day. Often, a quick "error analysis" and subsequent written or oral practice session is all that's needed to move the youngsters forward. Which youngsters would benefit from this approach? Better yet, which youngsters wouldn't?

Probes Summary

The more practical information a teacher can discover about a youngster's acquired skills and curriculum challenges, the more likely the teacher will help the youngster succeed with his or her studies. This holds true for those youngsters overwhelmed by classroom work that exceeds their entering skills, and youngsters excessively bored who are required to face yet again schoolwork they mastered last year.

A teacher asking a youngster to describe the location or setting of a story is a probe. A teacher asking a youngster to tell the time by looking at a clock is a probe. Every time a teacher asks a youngster to write a sentence or two, she has conducted a writing probe. A teacher who asks a child how many dimes are in a quarter has presented a multifaceted numerical probe. A teacher working with a youngster on how to do puzzles who has inserted all but one piece in place in a six-piece puzzle has presented a probe. Requesting that the youngster place the final piece is a probe of multiple skills, including the youngster's ability to understand what was said.

A weekly test of a dozen words based on a spelling list or preferred word list is a CRT probe; it won't be graded when the teacher has a higher purpose in mind. Sentences (or words) within a paragraph reading assignment are a CRT probe. A selection of questions regarding a world map is a CRT probe. A mini test that includes a grouping of 5–15 math problems all assessing what a teacher has just reviewed is a CRT probe. All of these CRTs reveal valuable information a teacher can use to determine a child's entering skills—where within the math curriculum, the reading curriculum, map-reading curriculum the child succeeds at or near 100% proficiency. Such measures tell a teacher if a particular child is leaps ahead of her curriculum presentations, several steps behind, or right on target.

No-Fault System

Probes work best within a no-fault system of education. Probes are used to determine what to do, *not* who to blame for the youngster's academic difficulties. As you've read, accusatory fingers should never be pointed toward teachers, indifferent parents, or hypothesized dysfunctional neurological systems. Those are lazy answers. Inadequate strategies (that may involve inadequate teachers) are always the culprits. Inadequate strategies can be changed immediately. The new ones can be evaluated to measure their effects. If the new strategies improve achievement, fine. If not, back to the drawing board. Always. The problem is never the youngster.

Once more, teachers use probes to discover if they need to change their own instructional methods. By monitoring the effectiveness of the instruction a child receives,[27] good teachers are better able to make educational decisions and develop positive plans to assist students.[28] Recall our Pasadena math wizards from an earlier chapter who suffered through a major curriculum mismatch. A simple CRT probe would have told the Pasadena folks, teachers, principal, superintendent, and parents all they needed to know to assist the math prodigies. Nice for everyone involved.

YOUR (EARLIER) 25 DIVERSE KIDS

You, our teacher, have work to do. If a yard stick were used to represent where your 25 youngsters were along the districts' predetermined curriculum, the distribution of your kids, in all shapes, sizes, and colors, would cover from one end of the 36-inch measure to the other. On this, your first day, after closing your classroom's door, after welcoming the youngsters, after introducing yourself, and after reminding them of a few rules that speak to respect and consideration for others and coming to class on time, you might have directed them, "Let's get started. . . . [In the absence of personal laptops] get your pencils and open your schoolbooks to the first chapter, page 3, and we will begin." *You might have.* No one would know you did, other than you.

Even with personal laptops, you remember reading educator James Lewis Jr's incisive question: "How can [I] consider using identical textbooks [and materials] for individualized pupils whose learning approaches differ, whose retention differs, and whose interest levels run the gamut from intense to indifferent?"[29] You do remember. You don't have the kids open their books/computers first thing. Instead, you gather the youngsters close. "I need to know what you know, what you can do well," you begin, as would the teacher in the one-room schoolhouse.

> Not all of us have had the same experiences; not all of us have learned the same things. Once I discover what you can do, I will help each of you do more. Because we haven't experienced and learned the same over the years, many of you will be asked to work on different exercises and read different materials, some from books, some from material I will assembled for you after I see what you need.
>
> If I ask you to do something that you're unsure of, something that seems difficult, you are not to worry. You let me know and I will make myself a note and together we will work on a positive next step. If you're itching to do more that I ask, again let me know. I will write myself another note and match you with your interests and skills. If you're smarter than me, a definite possibility, I will find someone who is smarter than both of us to move us both along.
>
> For the next couple days, I will challenge you with some exercises. Quizzes that are not graded. They are diagnostic. That means I will use them to learn what you know, what you can do, and what you need help with. They also tell me what I must do. Remember always, all of us need help with many things. Never be ashamed of what you don't know. If it's important, dedicate yourself to learn what you can.
>
> And I will meet with each of you individually to learn about your reading skills. Again, just do your best. I have some exercises for the rest of you to do

while I meet individually with others. Remember this: no answer is without merit. Even wrong ones help us do better.

THE DEFEATING "WAIT AND SEE" ATTITUDE

In 2016, a Texas special education teacher at a federal hearing committee in Houston stood up and informed the U.S. government representatives,

> Oftentimes when it was very, very obvious that children needed services, I would go through the steps required and they [the school eligibility committee] would say, well, "Let's wait six weeks, eight weeks and see how they do." . . . So by the time [the children] do get tested [six-, eight-weeks later,] they've lost all that time for support.[30]

Yet another speaker stood, her pleas as imperative, as passionate. "The schools are not meeting [the children's] needs. You need to change that. You really do. This just cannot keep going on."[31]

Timeline

A young child's deficiencies—his limited skills—may go unnoticed for several early years. If those delayed skills are observed by a quality teacher in the public school and special education assistance is considered, a "wait and see" period often kicks in. It's an administrative decision. This "waiting" often results in many months passing before extra services are provided to the youngster and his teacher.[32] *Maybe* provided. There's no guarantee assistance will be forthcoming. In America, eligibility for extra school services can be a slippery issue—when it should be immediately forthcoming. It's all about the money.

Here's the hard truth about how the system often operates, thanks to Drs. James Ysseldyke, Bob Algozzine, and Martha L. Thurlow:

> Being declared eligible for special education services [has] less to do with the difficulties the child [is] experiencing with his or her school work, and more to do with the state and school district in which the youngster live[s]. When school districts have plenty of money to spend on educating students with disabilities, diagnostic personnel are encouraged to locate and identify as many students with handicaps as possible. When funds are limited, concerns grow about the large numbers of students being declared handicapped.[33]

The latter reality drew a dreary warning from a 1990s special education director who had spent her professional life fighting for kids.

Special education is often the only available program for students needing some kind of classroom help. However, we must keep in mind that only students who are handicapped and in need of special education can be placed. Any student who does not meet the criteria is illegally placed and when we are monitored, we will have to payback any funds collected for an ineligible student. . . . We cannot afford inappropriate placements, nor should we be labeling students as handicapped who are not.[34]

Finland

Our colleagues in Finland see this issue differently; they're more progressive. Carol A. Kinlan, middle-school director of learning resources, stated:

Finland's educational structures are very flexible, with teachers enjoying high levels of authority and autonomy. Diagnostic labels for students struggling with learning disorders are rarely used and students receive immediate support when they begin to experience academic difficulty. A formal diagnosis is not a prerequisite to receiving extra help.

In contrast, special-education policies in the U.S. are bureaucratic [i.e. unbending]. Our policies for determining eligibility and services—based on the medical model—are rigid, complex and prescriptive. Navigating the special-education system can be downright nightmarish for parents. Most important, the U.S. educational system does a poor job of identifying weak students in the earliest grades and supporting them effectively. The result is a time-consuming and frustrating process for parents who struggle to determine exactly why their child is faltering in school—and what they can do to help them.[35]

Curriculum mismatches and improper instructional strategies most often underlie the youngster's struggles.

An Inexcusable Waste of Time

In the United States, we continue to debate the validity of educational disabilities rather than provide services to children who need the extra help. Again, money stands at the center of the contest between parent and school officials, what often produces crushing acrimony and little chance for any compromise. It invites expensive lawyers—each certain their side is in the right—while parents look on and abide the agonizing futility of it all. Somebody pays those lawyers.

Disability Names Do Not Explain

The field of special education has been plagued for decades by its insistence that educational disabilities—that is, "LD"—are (a) real and (b) easily diagnosed. In the late 1960s and the decades that followed, debates percolated throughout the field supporting or discounting the veracity of special education labels. It culminated with this pointed play on words:

> A "Rumpelstiltskin fixation" [coined by Alan Ross] characterizes the preoccupation of some [professionals] with whether a given child is or is not brain damaged. That question and related questions of etiology and classification often dominate evaluations and staff conferences as if everything depended on that one answer. In a well-known fairy tale, the chance for the princess to live her life happily ever after depends on her discovering the name of an ill-tempered dwarf. As a result, she goes to great lengths to learn his name, and upon doing so, earns her salvation. Many clinicians and educators seem to engage in similar fairy-tale behavior. They act as if, could they but give the condition a name, the child would be saved.[36]

Disability names serve little purpose beyond providing an umbrella under which kids who exhibit similar characteristics are grouped. Labels do not tell anyone what specific interventions to use. For that, we need a superb teacher ASAP to help the involved youngsters, what we needed *before* we spent so much time creating, debating, and paying for those names. Finland and its kids do fine without the labels; so could we.

INTERVENTION

As soon as any child demonstrates difficulty with skill acquisition, reading, mathematics, writing, communication, even attention-to-task, we must assign a quality teacher to the youngster to administer brief CRTs to discover what the youngster can do educationally with relative ease and where within his teacher's curriculum the youngster's academics run into problems. From data collection to instruction will require a small portion of an hour. Subsequently, the "wait and see" mentality will be buried deep within a history book's unread appendix.

NOTES

1. Busser, C. (2021). *Every state should use flexibility from the new federal guidance to focus on students, not invalid, unreliable standardized tests.* https://www.nea.org/about-nea/media-center/press-releases/nea-president-becky-pringle-every-state-should-use

2. Rosales, J., & Walker, T. (2021). *The racist beginnings of standardized testing.* https://www.nea.org/advocating-for-change/new-from-nea/racist-beginnings-standardized-testing

3. Curriculum-based assessment is also known as "curriculum-based measurement." Both are forms of "curriculum-based evaluations." Which term is used depends mostly on which university one attended.

4. Alberta Education. (2008). *Purpose of classroom assessment.* https://www.learnalberta.ca/content/mewa/html/assessment/purpose.html

5. Thomas, J., Allman, C., & Beech, M. (2004). *Assessment for the diverse classroom: A handbook for teachers.* Florida Department of Education, Bureau of Exceptional Education and Student Services. http://www.fldoe.org/core/fileparse.php/7690/urlt/0070083-assess_diverse.pdf

6. Idol, L., Nevin, A., & Paolucci-Whitcomb, P. (1996). *Models of curriculum-based assessment* (2nd ed.). Pro-Ed.

7. University of Pittsburgh School of Education. (n.d.). *Curriculum-based assessment.* Retrieved January 25, 2022, from https://mosaic.pitt.edu/curbasedassess.html

8. Spinello, S. (n.d.). *What is a criterion-reference test?* Retrieved January 25, 2022, from https://classroom.synonym.com/what-criterionreferenced-test-4586617.html

9. Schneider, J. (2017). *Beyond test scores: A better way to measure school quality.* Harvard University Press.

10. Newman, A. (2017). *33% of Baltimore schools have NO students proficient in math.* https://freedomproject.com/the-newman-report/427-33-of-baltimore-schools-have-no-students-proficient-in-math

11. Newman (2017).

12. Personal communication.

13. Fountas, I. C., & Pinnell, G. S. (2011). *The continuum of literacy learning: Grades preK–8.* Heinemann; Fountas, I. C., & Pinnell, G. S. (2011). *Scholastic guided reading program: Teacher's guide.* Scholastic.

14. Great Schools Partnership. (2015, July 22). Norm-referenced test. In *Glossary of Education Reform.* https://www.edglossary.org/norm-referenced-test

15. Great Schools Partnership. (2014, April 30). Criterion-referenced test. In *Glossary of Education Reform.* https://www.edglossary.org/criterion-referenced-test

16. Layton, L. (2015). *Study says standardized testing is overwhelming nation's public schools.* https://www.washingtonpost.com/local/education/study-says-standardized-testing-is-overwhelming-nations-public-schools/2015/10/24/8a22092c-79ae-11e5-a958-d889faf561dc_story.html

17. Job, J. (n.d.). *Changing the focus from label to need.* http://www.learnnc.org/lp/pages/7196; See also Lauchlan, F., & Boyle, C. (2007). Is the use of labels in special education helpful? *Support for Learning, 22*(1), 36–42.

18. Schneider (2017).

19. Thompson, T. (2016, January). The special-education charade. *The Atlantic.* https://www.theatlantic.com/education/archive/2016/01/the-charade-of-special-education-programs/421578

20. Morrison, N. (2014, February 27). "Dyslexia" is a meaningless label and should be ditched. *Forbes.* https://www.forbes.com/sites/nickmorrison/2014/02/27/dyslexia-is-a-meaningless-label-and-should-be-ditched/?sh=20092e28f55e; Mental Health Empowerment Project. (2016). *Harvard psychologist reveals ADHD doesn't really exist.* https://mhepinc.org/harvard-psychologist-reveals-adhd-doesnt-really-exist

21. Nisbet, J. (2019). *Curriculum-based measurement: Top benefits and examples.* https://www.prodigygame.com/main-en/blog/curriculum-based-measurement

22. Shinn, M. R. (1989). *Curriculum-based measurement: Assessing special children.* The Guilford Press; Fuchs, L. S., Deno, S. L., & Mirkin, P. K. (1984). The effects of frequent curriculum-based measurement and evaluation on student achievement, pedagogy, and student awareness of learning. *American Educational Research Journal, 21,* 449–460.

23. Kegsunflowersutra [username]. (2011, March 25). *What is CBA, CBM, and CBE?* [Blog post]. https://kegsunflowersutra.wordpress.com/2011/03/25/47

24. Trachok, M. (2011, March 22). *CBA, CBM, CBE* [Blog post]. http://megansblog23.blogspot.com/2011/03/cba-cbm-cbe.html

25. McLane, K. (n.d.). *What is curriculum-based measurement and what does it mean to my child?* The National Center on Student Progress Monitoring, American Institutes for Research. Retrieved January 25, 2022, from https://www.readingrockets.org/article/what-curriculum-based-measurement-and-what-does-it-mean-my-child

26. Stecker, P. (2003). *Monitoring student progress in individualized educational programs using curriculum-based measurement.* National Center on Student Progress Monitoring. See also Fuchs et al. (1984).

27. McLane (n.d.).

28. Thomas et al. (2004).

29. Lewis Jr. (1969).

30. Wright, P. (2017). *Waiting to fail instead of teaching a child to read.* https://www.wrightslaw.com/info/read.wait.fail.htm

31. Rosenthal, B. M., & Barned-Smith, St. J. B. (2016, December 12). Angry parents in Houston and Dallas turn out at forums, demanding end to special education target. *Houston Chronicle.* https://www.houstonchronicle.com/news/houston-texas/houston/article/Angry-parents-in-Houston-and-Dallas-turn-out-at-10792247.php

32. Siegel, L. S. (1989). IQ is irrelevant to the definition of learning disabilities. *J Learn Disabilities, 22,* 469–478.

33. Ysseldyke, J. E., Algozzine, B., & Thurlow, M. L. (1992). *Critical issues in special education.* Houghton Mifflin Company, p. 350.

34. Personal communication: memo from executive director of special education and pupil services to school psychologists (1992), Tucson, AZ.

35. Kinlan, C. (2011). Rethinking special education in the U.S. *The Hechinger Report.* https://hechingerreport.org/rethinking-special-education-in-the-u-s

36. Smith, R. M., & Neisworth, J. T. (1975). *The exceptional child: A functional approach.* McGraw-Hill.

Chapter 8

Error Analysis

ASSESSMENT II: ERROR ANALYSIS

CRTs expose where within a teacher's curriculum a youngster makes either an error of omission (overlooking something important) or an error of commission (adding a component that's not needed). Both types of missteps are reasons for quiet celebration. *Good* teachers welcome them. It's from these errors that accomplished educators can learn much about how a child thinks, plans, and problem solves. There's little that's more illuminating than listening to a child explain how he or she arrived at an *incorrect* answer. A young boy years ago completed a math problem the following way:

$$\begin{array}{r} 99 \\ +\ 23 \\ \hline 1112 \end{array}$$

The youngster's heady teacher could have put an *X* through the above answer and moved on. Instead, she valued the youngster's attempt and responded, "That's a good answer, Jimmy. Tell me how you got it."

The youngster, with an "it's *so obvious*" look on his face, answered without hesitation, "You add the first column, 9+3, and then you add the second column, 9+2. Everybody knows that." The educational value of such errors is priceless. When such errors occur, they provide teachers the information they need to help the child work through the correct solution while assisting his understanding of each component. Lots of active learning involved.

RED Xs AND SAD FACES

Not all teachers are inclined to take this valuable step. Because of a lack of time to work with all the youngsters in the classroom, pressed teachers often move on without asking each youngster to explain his or her incorrect answer. (Asking a youngster to explain how he or she arrived at a *correct* answer often reveals a shaky foundation. A quick error analysis and a new strategy could supply a more stable underpinning.)

Some teachers simply want the school day done and gone. In those instances, when children make errors on exercises or exams, the errors are marked, a score is reduced, and the matter ends. The child later learns he did something wrong, though often without a clue about what was wrong, ensuring the error will be repeated unless a different type of teacher steps in. Exploring a child's errors, immediately or shortly after their occurrence, provides opportunities for new strategies and learning. The following is a true (personal) story.

Home from the university, I found my younger daughter scrunched in the corner of the couch. All signs pointed to a state of distress, what was most unusual for this normally bubbly youngster. Guessing the source, I asked her how things went in school. Reluctantly, she removed a scrunched-up paper from her backpack and handed it to me. I couldn't help but see two *large Xs* on the bottom of the assignment's page, the "–2" in red ink on the top of the page, and the *stamped* "sad face" in the paper's upper-right corner. (I admit the stamped "sad face" got me. How about impersonal?) She curled next to me when I sat beside her.

The assignment involved vocabulary words in sentences. At the top of the page, 10 words were listed, and 10 sentences, each with a blank space, covered the paper's remainder. (It was a CRT probe, and a nice one. Kudos to the teacher. Lots of possible learning opportunities.) My daughter was to place each correct vocabulary word within the correspondingly correct sentence.

A quick check disclosed that my youngster had difficulty with *zebra* and/or *bait*. The ninth sentence read: "The fisherman uses the ____ to help him catch fish." For reasons known only to my daughter, she completed the sentence with *zebra*. (Probably obvious, but under such an arrangement, if a student misses one answer, she'll miss two. Unless she uses the same word twice; a slim possibility.)

Exploring her rationale for the answers she chose, I supportively asked, "What were you thinking about when you answered the question?"

She paused briefly. "I didn't know what the word *bait* meant. I never heard it before." (Ouch! Dad's oversight, growing up in Florida with *bait* fish everywhere.) "So, I thought the fisherman took the zebra down to the river, and the zebra looked for the fish and showed the fisherman where they were."

Wrong answer. Great logic. Unknown to the teacher, my daughter had watched (with me) a National Geographic special on Alaska a few weeks earlier. You can't watch a documentary on Alaska without seeing bears at the riverside, spotting and catching airborne salmon. From the child's viewpoint, there was little difference between a zebra and a bear. Hands/paws with claws vs. hoofs were not factored in. We chatted and looked at pictures of both animals. Before the week ended, I took her to a sporting goods shop and showed her a *bottle* of bait. Ugh! That summer we went fishing using live bait. *Bait* was no longer a problem.

"HOW DID YOU ARRIVE AT YOUR ANSWER?"

Imagine a classroom teacher making notes of children's incorrect responses and spending a few minutes that day or the following class period asking the kids to help out with definitions or problem solutions. "Hey, a couple of you had problems with the word *bait*. Can anyone help us out? A story you wish to tell?" Imagine teachers using pupils' errors to develop curriculum; imagine teachers meeting with children and asking them, "Great answer. How'd you get there?" Could children learn to ask themselves the same questions? Could parents do the same? Absolutely. (Caution: While the parent [or teacher] may experience the urge to tell the child, "Here, let me show you," please refrain, at least until after discovering the high hurdle over which the youngster stumbles. By the parent/teacher doing the work, the child may learn a correct answer but not the mental roadmap necessary to make the journey on her own.)

ERRORS: THE RIGHT ATTITUDE
FOR PUPILS AND TEACHERS

Many youngsters have learned that errors are bad, to be avoided whenever possible. Adaptively, many are reluctant to try an answer if they think there's even a small chance they'll be wrong. (Some accomplished college kids experience this as well.) It's important to change the youngsters' attitude. It's best if a youngster feels comfortable making errors and admitting areas of confusion and difficulty; best if a youngster knows that errors are not only acceptable but also welcomed; best if a youngster knows that all answers, even those that are incorrect, have value. A teacher asking the youngster to share—"How did you arrive at your answer?" "What were you thinking about when completing the problem?" "What steps did you use to answer the question?"—may provide the educator exactly what he or she needs to help the child work through a perplexing assignment.

Error Types

For convenience, errors can be either mechanical, motivational, conceptual, or a combination of those. The common *b/d* reversal is a mechanical error (not a brain problem). Few kids have problems discriminating the letters *E* and *F* and *m/n*. The letter *E*'s *bottom line* and the extra "hill" with *m* designates the difference between the two printed letters. Remove either *E*'s bottom line or *m*'s soft, rounded second protuberance, and most every child (and adult) will be confused. Regarding the *b/d* challenge, had the architects added a dot in the half-circle of either letter (not both, of course), or a short-angled line from the tip of either letter, the inclusion would have spelled an end to 99.9% of *b/d* reversals. (Please see Marie Rippel.[1])

Thinking the Atlantic Ocean is off the coast of California is a mechanical error. Mechanical errors require little complex thinking. Mechanical errors are corrected by providing cues and prompts and reminders with lots of practice using *spaced* practice, particularly with brief practice sessions spread over several days or weeks. ("Spaced practice" means you practice, then stop for a minute or two, then return to the practice sessions before briefly stopping again. This facilitates long-term retention, particularly if the process is repeated with spacing in between sessions under multiple conditions, e.g., dinner table, walk in the park, spread over a couple weeks.)

Motivational Errors

A child who consistently repeats the same errors (and suffers the embarrassing consequence therein) may feel intimidated and choose not to try any longer. That can likely appear to be a motivational error. Although such is possible, a youngster's achievement shutdown often occurs when he or she experiences a curriculum mismatch that involves *conceptual* difficulties. A strategically asked question, or a brief CRT, might reveal the real problem: A *conceptual* component is missing.

Conceptual Errors

Conceptual errors occur in part when a child lacks knowledge of important *attributes* associated with the concept involved. An attribute is a characteristic. It's what makes one concept different from another concept (e.g., dogs bark, cats meow). Concepts have attributes and nonattributes. A concept is understood when a child can correctly identify examples *and* nonexamples of the concept. A "meow" is a nonattribute of a dog, cow, bird, or high-jumping salmon. Just about all of us can tell the difference between a dog and a cat but not a finch and a Carolina wren. Why? Because we're not altogether certain of their distinctive attributes: colors, body shape, feathers, beak, or unique trill.

If a student struggles with an assignment, there's a good chance he or she lacks knowledge of the topic's distinctive attributes. An error analysis will help. Discuss with the youngster what attributes are specific to the topic that's creating difficulty. What attributes help differentiate subtraction from addition (e.g., more, less, bigger, smaller, all concepts in themselves)? What attributes signify a story's "main idea"? What's different about literal and inferential comprehension? What attributes would help a youngster make that distinction? Geometry issues? What attributes distinguish a square from a rectangle? What are *nonattributes* of a square?

IDENTIFYING TROUBLESOME CONCEPTS

Teachers will want to identify what concepts a child is missing and those that confuse the youngster. A quick check of a youngster's homework, with an error analysis, can provide examples. Discovering during class discussions that a child is having difficulty with a troubling concept can prompt a teacher to make a note to meet with the youngster and administer a brief CRT (oral or written) to clarify what underlies the youngster's confusion.

Teachers hurried by their district or school's insistent and imposed curriculum deadlines often omit important conceptual components in their lesson plans, the absence of those components easily threatening a pupil's performance and progress. Every day, teachers talk concepts (i.e., *constructs* that are words that represent other words). But a teacher's *expressive* language and a pupil's *receptive* language aren't always compatible. That can easily pitch a youngster off-kilter.

A child doesn't have to be classified as an "English Language Learner" to have problems with understanding the English language. Likewise, the uniqueness of the English language can play absolute havoc with a child who is learning to read. The following will tease a neurological synapse or two.

A poem attributed to Lord Cromer[2] that was published in *The Spectator* magazine in 1902 eloquently illustrates the quirks and complexities of the English spelling system. Baffling at best. Funny if you're of a mind to think so. The beginning reader might not think so.

Our Strange Lingo
When the English tongue we speak.
Why is break not rhymed with freak?
Will you tell me why it's true
We say sew but likewise few?
And the maker of the verse, Cannot rhyme his horse with worse?
Beard is not the same as heard. Cord is different from word. Cow is cow but low is low. Shoe is never rhymed with foe. Think of hose, dose, and lose, And think of goose and yet with choose. Think of comb, tomb and bomb, Doll and roll or home and some.
Since pay is rhymed with say Why not paid with said I pray?
Think of blood, food and good.
Mould [British] is not pronounced like could.
Wherefore done, but gone and lone—Is there any reason known?
To sum up all, it seems to me sound and letters don't agree.[3]

It's amazing most of us read as well as we do.

COMMON CORE: CONCEPTS

Common Core's curriculum *will* snag many youngsters assigned to a grade level by age who are not ready for what's demanded of them. The potential problem lies with the teacher's ability to fashion his or her language to match the conceptual skills youngsters need to work through an assigned task. It's a sure bet that a one-size-all-language approach will be insufficient for the diverse receptive skills that characterize our diverse pupils. Not using CRTs to assess what the kids learned from listening to the teacher's lesson is a recipe for missed errors and conceptual confusion. A pre-CRT would alert the teacher to language difficulties.

(I went online and found examples of Common Core's early standards. Notice the following Common Core exercises, the number of concepts that could cause difficulties.)

- *Creates*, reads, and solves problems using a picture graph, bar graph, and line plot.
- *Partitions* circles and rectangles into halves, thirds, and fourths.
- Uses correct spelling *patterns* for unknown words.
- Expresses ideas in *complete* sentences using *proper* grammar. Knows and applies grade level *phonics*.
- *Circles* words that best describes picture.
- Name and tell *value* of coins.
- Name each word and list *ending* sound.

- *Match* fractions to pictures.
- *Balance* addition equations.
- *Estimate* sums.
- Understands *concepts* of grade level science units.
- Listens for information in *science*.
- Uses maps *effectively*.

Once again, we're talking about public school classes filled with diverse kids whose receptive and cognitive entering skills vary tremendously, many youngsters with unfamiliar words and unknown concepts aplenty. (See the reference to Todd Risely and Betty Hart's work in chapter 11, suggesting that many kids, because of a lack of exposure, come to school with many fewer words in their active repertoire, which is certain to impact their conceptual understanding of much in the world that surrounds them.)

The classroom teacher shoulders the responsibility to help all the kids be successful, surely those youngsters who enter classrooms without a firm language and/or concept base. At the same time, educational administrators shoulder the responsibility to make significant changes to the system under which teachers must operate, one that provides those valued individuals with all the time and resources they need to reach today's diverse youngsters.

An educational system that neglects both its young charges and its professional mentors is a poor system. As you'll see, such neglect unfortunately defines our current educational system for many teachers and their pupils.

NOTES

1. Rippel, M. (2015). *How to solve letter reversals*. http://www.allaboutlearningpress.com/how-to-solve-b-d-reversal-problems

2. Owen, R. (2004). *Lord Cromer: Victorian imperialist, Edwardian proconsul*. Oxford University Press.

3. Oxford Royale Academy. (n.d.). *Why is English so hard to learn?* https://www.oxford-royale.com/articles/learning-english-hard

Chapter 9

Formative Assessment

ASSESSMENT III: FORMATIVE ASSESSMENT

While formative assessment as a strategy has only existed since the 1960s, educators have been using "formative assessments" in various forms since the invention of teaching. Designed to improve the educational accomplishments of all schoolkids, formative assessment "is now widely considered to be one of the more effective instructional strategies used by teachers."[1] Formative assessment's simplicity is its calling card. "Any teacher who adjusts his or her teaching during instruction on the basis of evidence of student understanding and performance is employing formative assessment."[2]

Formative assessment refers to a variety of options that teachers use to conduct evaluations of student comprehension *during* a lesson, unit, or course.[3] The assessment helps teachers identify concepts and skills students are having difficulty acquiring. It provides feedback that is used by instructors to improve their teaching and used by students to improve their learning. Teachers use formative assessment to conduct evaluations of a child's learning needs and academic progress so that adjustments can be made to lessons, instructional techniques, and academic support.[4] Formative assessment is the hallmark of quality educators.

Spotting Curriculum Mismatches

Since formative assessment is designed to be used at the time of a lesson, the methodology allows teachers to spot immediately what deficiencies threaten pupils' continued achievement progress. Ideally, once noting the difficulty, a teacher can schedule a timely CRT to determine where within the curriculum a youngster succeeds and where related skills have broken down. With a brief error analysis targeting the latter, a corrective strategy will become evident.

Used daily as part of class lessons, formative assessment can identify any curriculum mismatch a youngster is currently experiencing. It can provide teachers the information they need to modify the pupil's curriculum before the mismatch takes hold, before it spreads and creates serious deficits. In addition to providing students feedback that allows them to improve their performance, "[formative assessments] check for understanding along the way and [help] guide teacher decisions about future instruction."[5] Educator Hans Mundahl stated,

> Teachers know many things: we are experts in our field, we have a plan for the structure of our course, we know what we are teaching today and how it fits into the bigger picture. But here's something we don't always know: what do our students know? The goal of [formative] assessments is for teachers to see how they are doing and to adjust [what they're doing] if needed.[6]

Time: A Precious Commodity

A teacher's vital exploratory question, "What did my teaching accomplish today?" often goes absent in today's classrooms. It's not that current quality teachers are without the tools to assess the essential question, "Did my teaching methods help the students learn their alphabet or improve their math sense or advance their reading skills?" The tools to answer such essential questions are available to all teachers—if those teachers are provided the opportunity to use them. Available time is a precious commodity often denied teachers. That's a serious system problem, one we will scrutinize in the book's final chapter. While the big losers are the schoolkids, as educational consultant Judith Dodge acknowledges below, quality teachers also feel the frustration from being unable to help all the youngsters advance forward in their studies.

Hurried Along the One-Way Track

The above hinderance is the educational system's own doing. Because of its calendar standards and predetermined lesson plans, most American teachers are forced to ride the one-way educational train with departing and arrival times already scheduled, already printed, and already disseminated. The educational train leaves the station sometime in August or early September with a full complement of kids. It has its destination, its timetable, and its preset miles to cover; and cover those miles it will, the following mentioned shortcomings notwithstanding.

The rush to finish within the school hour, while new, more complex curriculum is in queue for the following school day, presents the educator with multiple problems. The process gives the teacher little opportunity to step back to discover what if anything during the current lesson the kids missed, what if anything was confusing—more still, if any kids were overlooked or left wanting. The educational engineer (the teacher) has little option but to watch the clock and the calendar, not the passengers—the school youngsters—leaving quality teachers scant moments to measure the outcomes of their labors.

In this daily (forced) haste, what goes missing? First and foremost, time to conduct formative assessments. Why is that so essential? Because the methodology has shown its ability to *substantially* improve educators' efforts and kids' learning. "Formative assessment works! [It's] a process used by teachers and students during instruction that provides feedback to adjust ongoing teaching and learning to improve students' achievement of intended instructional outcomes."[7] In their *Kappan* article, Paul Black and Dylan Wiliam maintained, "Formative assessment, properly employed in the classroom, will help students learn what is being taught to a substantially better degree."[8] Considering America's currently administered school system, rightfully embarrassed by a plethora of disappointing achievement test results, the phrase *substantially better* should get some administrators' undivided attention. Verified now, formative assessment practices, including checks for understanding, have been shown to have a significant effect on student learning.[9]

Nearly Twice the Gains

Professors Black and Wiliam have confirmed that when teachers regularly use formative assessment practices in their classroom, students make *almost twice as much progress* over a year as students whose teachers do not use formative assessments. Formative assessment provides feedback to students that helps them learn what the teacher intends, just as it helps that teacher modify his or her teaching and learning activities.[10] As researchers point out, "Formative assessments should be low stakes and used for information gathering only (not for grading)."[11]

Time: The Pervasive Villain

As Judith Dodge shared,

> [While] formative assessments provide feedback to help [teachers] differentiate instruction and thus improve student achievement, teachers during staff development often tell me they don't have time to assess students along the way. They fear sacrificing coverage and insist they must move on quickly. *Yet in the rush to cover more, students are actually learning less.* . . . Without time to reflect on

and interact meaningfully with new information, students are unlikely to retain much of what is "covered" in their classrooms.[12]

Within some instructional systems, formative assessment is inextricably woven. In the Wilson Reading System®, for example, formative assessment is part of every single lesson.

> During the lesson, a teacher is assessing how the student is responding to instruction, that is, how the student's skills and understanding of concepts are progressing. The teacher tracks this by maintaining a progress chart for each student. For all students, the errors identified during the wordlist charting help to pinpoint trouble spots and patterns. *The next lesson is written based entirely upon the student's understanding of concepts and skills taught in the current lesson.* In a small-group setting, a student will be charted at least once during each substep. This progress monitoring allows teachers to diagnostically plan for the following lessons and to pace the group appropriately. The teacher progresses to the next substep when the majority of the students in the group have achieved mastery. Additional practice is provided to students not reaching benchmark.[13]

Exit Cards Revisited

To allay her teachers' expressed fears about sacrificing coverage as justification for not using formative assessment, Ms. Dodge told her teacher-audience,

> One of the easiest formative assessments is the Exit Card. Exit Cards are index cards (or sticky notes) that students hand to you, deposit in a box, or post on the door as they leave your classroom. On the Exit Card, your students have written their names and have responded to a question, solved a problem, or summarized their understanding after a particular learning experience. In a few short minutes, you can read the responses, sort them into groups suitable for
>
> - students who have not yet mastered essential skills;
> - students who are ready to apply the skill; and
> - students who are ready to go beyond the skill,
>
> and you can "use the data [you've collected] to [modify] the next day's . . . instruction."[14]

Notice please that as a result of your exit cards, you can divide your class into (at least) three groups, each with relatively *similar entering skills*, an arrangement that makes a teacher's effort easier and considerably more productive. Keep that in mind, please, as we proceed. It has earned its important place.

Individual Pupil Progress

Formative assessment is not concerned with how a child compares to his or her classmates (not "peers," thank you). The assessment concerns itself with how well each individual youngster succeeds with the teacher's curriculum. Educators at the Eberly Center within Carnegie Mellon University reminded us that "formative assessment represents a method to monitor student learning that provides ongoing feedback used by instructors to improve their teaching."[15] Charlotte Danielson—professor, curriculum director, and consultant—made that latter point more personal (necessitating that we recall our previously mentioned young lady and her dreadful math struggles). "Let's say you teach 4th grade mathematics," Dr. Danielson began.

> From reading the standards [Common Core, appendix A], you can see that there's a premium on mathematical reasoning. So you would want to be both teaching and formatively assessing kids on [mathematical reasoning]. Do the students understand the processes they are using? Can they apply them in varied situations? . . . I consider formative assessment to be an integral part of instruction, something that is assimilated into lesson plans and instructional decision-making. It's ongoing monitoring done by the teacher, not just of the group as a whole but of individuals as well. Formative assessment, a skill you learn how to do, has to be part of teaching. [The teacher asks:] What kind of responses am I getting from [my students]? What kind of evidence do I have that [my students] understand [what I am teaching], and what they are learning? In mathematics, for example, you're expected to focus on a few key concepts for 3rd graders. But suppose you've got some students who never mastered the 1st grade skills. Say I'm a 4th grade teacher but I've got some 4th graders who don't understand place value. [e.g., "369"—means 3 hundreds, 6 tens, 9 ones.] In that case, my own personal inclination would be to ensure that my students develop conceptual understanding of place value at that point—because that's what they need. I don't see how you can responsibly say anything other than that you have to be flexible and teach students what they have the background to learn at that point. Otherwise, you're setting them up for failure.[16]

EDUCATIONAL ALTERNATIVES

Some in America believe that our public schools should receive a daily free pass, that accountability is beneath them. Frankly, public schools *have* been given such a pass since their early beginnings, educational authorities unwilling to admit that their system needs a significant overhaul. Recent secretaries of education, regardless of their politics, made no move to revamp the bare-bones essentials of the elementary classroom. They either promoted their own causes or preferences, or they closed and reopened schools with new *unproven* staff, thinking fresh faces and a replaced light switch on the recently painted wall would satisfy what needs to be done. Within short order, the new schools were indistinguishable from the old.

Social Critics

Social critics at the extreme have accused parents of committing a treasonable offense when they've pulled their endangered youngster from the public-school system hoping to provide the school child a better educational experience. Allison Benedikt, then senior editor at *Slate* magazine, said of a parent who made that difficult decision,

> You are a bad person if you send your children to private school. Not bad like murderer bad—but bad like ruining one of our nation's most essential institutions in order to get what's best for your kid bad. So, pretty bad.[17]

Ms. Benedikt informed today's moms and dads *and* grandmas and grandpas, "If every single parent sent every single child to public school, public schools would improve." Then she added astonishingly, "This [improvement] would not happen immediately. It could take *generations*. Your children and grandchildren might get *mediocre* educations in the meantime, but it will be worth it, for the eventual common good."[18]

DIFFICULT DECISIONS

The major contributor to the alleged downfall of public education is not the parent who accepts responsibility for his child. The major contributor is *what* drives the parent to make that tough decision. Change the source of the ruination, and the inevitable flight will end. Accountable teachers do understand the difference between a good education and one that's *mediocre* or worse. Some of these accountable teachers make a very personal (and difficult) choice. Public-school teacher Michael Godsey confessed publicly on the internet that he had chosen a private school for his children, even though he said he "loathe[d]" the school for its elitism. But the private school, he said, "promotes 'personal character' and 'love of education,' and the tangible difference between this environment and that at the public school in the area was stunning to me—even though I'm a veteran public-school teacher."[19]

Parents do have the option to search out a new school, one that

- matches instruction to a child's entering skills;
- holds little concern how one child compares with others;

- is directed at helping a child become academically stronger each passing day;
- is more concerned with each individual youngster's achievement than the school's standardized test score rankings; and
- practices formative assessment and error analysis throughout every instructional class.

Summary

Formative assessments occur during the lessons the teacher teaches, not at the end, the latter referred to as "summative assessments."

> Formative assessments are a form of two-way communication providing valuable information for both the student and instructor; formative assessments support pupils' learning during the learning process; formative assessments can serve as practice for students; formative assessments help instructors differentiate instruction and thus improve student achievement; and, formative assessments can be done using individual, partner, small group, or whole class models.[20]

Results

Employing the strategy produces exceptional results:

> The achievement gains realized by students whose teachers rely on formative assessment can range from 15 to 25 percentile points, or two to four grade equivalents, on commonly used standardized achievement test score scales. In broader terms, this kind of score gain, if applied to performance on recent international assessments, would move the United States' rank from the middle of the pack of 42 nations tested to the top five. . . . [More significant,] an additional outcome common among the studies researchers Paul Black and Wiliam Dylan analyzed showed that certain formative assessment practices greatly increased the achievement of low-performing students, in some cases to the point of approaching that of high-achieving students.[21]

TODAY'S DISTANCE LEARNING

Many school districts had planned on offering only in-person learning in the fall of 2021, hoping for a more normal school year with fewer pandemic concerns after a tumultuous year of remote and hybrid learning. The delta variant forced some school administrators to reconsider plans. Currently, however, Chicago's top doctor, Allison Arwady, said the delta variant "has been out competed by omicron." While young children are less likely to get seriously ill from the virus, many children are not yet protected by vaccines. While vaccinations and a decline in COVID-19 cases could drive more in-class and in-person learning during the 2021–2022 school year, it's likely some form of virtual or online learning will still be in play.[22]

Choosing to Stay at Home

Anna Saavedra, Amie Rapaport, and Dan Silver wrote,

> For the 2021–2022 school year, data collected from 1,510 parents reveals that 9.5% reported they plan to continue with remote education in the fall and 13.5% are unsure about sending their child to in-person learning. Stated another way, a full 23% of families expressed either tentative or concrete plans to keep their children learning remotely in the fall.[23]

Adding more pressure to school district administrators,

> the sheer level of school hesitancy among some subgroups is worthy of immediate attention. Almost 40% of Black families and more than one-quarter of Hispanic families are expressing hesitation about sending their children back to school in the fall, significantly higher proportions than white families. Nearly 20% of Black families report they are not planning to send their children back, with another 20% unsure, citing the view that schools had not provided their children with a strong education before the pandemic, plus fears of COVID-19, and the unpleasant thought of returning to dilapidated school buildings. Lower-income groups and those with less-formal education also prefer to continue remote education at higher rates.[24]

Robin Lake, the CEO of the Center on Reinventing Public Education, which has been monitoring schools' responses to the pandemic, wrote,

> Everyone wants to get back to normal. But snapping back to normal when we know that didn't work well for too many kids, that's a real danger. . . . Are districts really going to force families to bring their kids back? That's a bad look.[25]

Formative Assessment Online

"COVID-19 brought a distinctive rise of e-learning, whereby teaching is undertaken remotely and on digital platforms."[26] Changes beget challenges, many that were easily predicted and easily ignored. "Major differences [exist] among schools in their access to different kinds of educational technology. Students attending poor and high-minority schools have less access to most types of technology than students attending other schools."[27] According to the University of Illinois, Springfield, "Before any online program can hope to succeed, it must have students who are able to access the online learning environment. This is a significant issue in rural and lower socioeconomic neighborhoods."[28]

Kirsten Weir, writing for the American Psychological Association reported,

> Regardless of ZIP code or family background, schools are, in theory, places where all students can receive education and support. But the coronavirus shutdown has emphasized (and widened) existing disparities in education. Teachers and parents have reported that some kids are thriving with fewer social distractions or have been energized by their newfound independence. Yet many other children lack devices or reliable access to the internet. And while some families have parents who can oversee their children's remote learning, many youths are caring for younger siblings while their parents work in essential jobs or living with the chaos of unemployment or homelessness.[29]

In her article, Ms. Weir provided additional troubling perspectives. "It's a question of privilege," attested educational psychologist Michele Gregoire Gill. Ms. Gill continued, "Some families are just in survival mode." Avi Kaplan, a professor of educational psychology at Temple University, added,

> When kids come to a classroom, it's easy to imagine they're all the same. But we can't expect the same outcomes from a kid learning on his own computer at his family's vacation home and a child who doesn't even have a table to sit at.[30]

Reality

Victoria Collis and Emiliana Vegas wrote,

> Children living in households where food is sometimes or often in short supply lack access to the technology needed for distance education compared with their . . . [more fortunate classmates, scarcely "peers"]. Fully 26.5 percent of children living in homes where there is often not enough food to go around—more than 1 in 4—are rarely or never able to get online to learn. While just 0.1 percent of white respondents in Los Angeles say a device is rarely or never available for learning at home, 13.2 percent of Black respondents surveyed in the same city reported rarely or never having access to a device for learning. In Detroit, this form of educational disadvantage affects children in almost 1 in 5 households that identified as Black.[31]

To deal with those issues, the authors suggested,

First, extra support will be critical for students whose family circumstances have made it difficult or impossible to continue learning during the pandemic. This means supporting teachers with tools to [educationally] diagnose students' [strengths and weaknesses] as well as [evaluating] the materials and pedagogical approaches [used] to serve the learning needs of what is certain to be an even wider range of student skills.

Second . . . some communities may need to adopt policies such as giving preferential access to school-based learning for the most disadvantaged, since more privileged students will be better equipped to study online. It also means designing and resourcing initiatives to improve poor children's access to technology, either through equipment loan programs, capital investment in better internet access in relevant neighborhoods, or both.[32]

Ideas

The message is repeated often. Assessing student learning is an essential component of effective teaching and learning in the online environment.[33] "Formative assessments have been shown to be particularly valuable with lower performing students. Learning deficiencies can be identified early in the learning cycle, allowing instructors to make teaching modifications before lower performing students are left behind."[34]

Andre Miller, director of teaching and learning at Singapore American school, argued,

> It remains crucial that teachers find ways to see what students are learning. Whether we call it distance or virtual learning, we're all challenged to provide meaningful education experiences at a distance as the education world grapples with the impact of Covid-19. Formative assessment at a distance is challenging but possible and we still need to check for understanding and provide meaningful feedback.[35]

Since it's important to have routines and still have variety, consider from the following what might work well for you and your students. Collect data overtime: work with students to have them document their learning along the way, what amounts to assessing growth over time. Focus on feedback: When checking for understanding, it's important to provide feedback to students, the feedback can be written and/or oral or through videos or sound recordings. Check for understanding in which a group of youngsters are engaged in learning at the same time: Those in-the-moment checks for understanding [via formative assessment] allow us to adjust instruction and meet students where they are. Leverage personal conversations: Conversing with students remains the most powerful and meaningful way to check for understanding. In our distance learning environment, we run the risk of being further isolated. By scheduled individual sessions with students, we can assess their learning and provide feedback what a real human connection. Check on social emotional learning. In addition to checking on academic learning, be sure to check in on students' well-being and their overall distance learning experiences. Simple questions can prompt students to share their feedback: What's working? What's not working? What would you recommend? Make it useful. Data are useless unless we use them. When we collect and examine formative assessments, we need to use what we learn when considering our instruction. We might find that a session didn't go so well, and thus a reteach needs to be offered in a different way.[36]

Nora Fleming offered,

Finding out what your students are really learning remains indispensable for teaching. . . . To help students synthesize important takeaways from a lesson, ask them to take one to two minutes during live class time to summarize everything they learned on a particular unit by typing into a Google Doc, in a chat box, or on a virtual message board like Padlet. Also, ask for student volunteers to share their "elevator pitch," or a verbal summary of what they learned with the class in 60 seconds or less. As a 21st century spin, Matt Levinson, principal in Seattle, Washington, suggests having students summarize the lesson in a tweet or Instagram post, staying to character limits.[37]

Ms. Fleming also described "Virtual Exit Tickets." She suggested,

Using exit tickets, or students' responses to prompts or questions on a slip of paper at the end of class, is a popular formative assessment practice that easily transfers online. . . . To get a wider view into students' thinking, use open-ended prompts like these:

- What I found most interesting today was . . .
- Today was hard because . . .
- What do you understand well?
- What's something that's still shaky?
- What's something I (teacher) don't realize?
- What takeaways will be important three years from now?
- How does this relate to (something learned before)?
- How would you have done things differently today?
- [Again] Today was hard because.[38]

WHAT HASN'T CHANGED

Quality teachers rely on formative assessment like an electrician relies on his wire cutters—may as well not show up for work without it. Formative assessment reveals a pupils' strengths and weaknesses. In all instances, if the pupil demonstrates any weakness, the assessment suggests to the teacher what modifications in directions, language, and/or concepts are needed.

Formative assessment must be a part of teaching, something that is assimilated into lesson plans and instructional decision making. And all teachers must be provided in-class time to conduct the assessment. How often must we hear "education is not a race" before twenty-first-century educational decision-makers begin to believe it. "Race to the top" may be the worst catchphrase ever pinned on education. Dr. Tony Wagner wrote, "Kids only have to 'race to catch up' in an assembly line class where everyone must finish at the same time. Kids need an individualized mastery-based approach instead, where students become proficient at their own pace."[39]

DUBIOUS GOAL

If a school's goal is to rush through materials to announce proudly to parents and state officials that they've covered everything required of a state or national standard, that affected school won't allow its teachers sufficient instructional/query time to assist kids who need a helping hand—*or*, for that matter, allow teachers to support those advanced youngsters who sit on the highest rung on the school ladder and need to be challenged. By default, those schools *will* experience large numbers of struggling (and/or dissatisfied) pupils.

WHEN LEARNING DOESN'T OCCUR: CLOSE SCHOOLS OR INITIATE ACTIVE INTERVENTION?

What to do when data show that a large number of public-school youngsters are not learning. There's more than one choice. A few years back, Michigan named 38 schools that could close over poor academics. In addition, the state's reform office released a list of 35 schools that were at risk if they [the youngsters] failed to show improvement. In Cleveland, 18 schools were scheduled to close "as part of transformation plan that aims to raise academic achievement."[40] In New York, over 100 schools were on the chopping block. Since 2002, Chicago closed or shook up 200 schools. Across the United States, 1,522 schools—1,204 traditional public and 318 charter schools—closed because of poor performance, "the most common reason given"[41] for the decision to shut the front door. It's not surprising to learn that "Black and Hispanic students were more likely to be in closed schools. Among regular public schools, low-performing schools with higher poverty rates were more likely to be closed than low-performing schools with fewer low-income students."[42] Professor Linda Darling-Hammond was quick to point out that "educational outcomes for minority children are much more a function of their unequal access to key educational resources, including skilled teachers and quality curriculum, than they are a function of race."[43]

Researching the decision to close schools due to their poor performance, Gail L. Sunderman, Erin Coghlan, and Rick Mintrop suggested the practice was not the best choice:

> School closure as a strategy for remedying student achievement in low-performing schools is at best a high-risk/low-gain strategy that fails to hold promise with respect to either increasing student achievement or promoting the non-cognitive well-being of students. The strategy invites political conflict and incurs hidden costs for both districts and local communities, especially low-income communities and communities of color that are differentially affected by school closings. It stands to reason that in many, if not most, instances, students, parents, local communities, district and state policymakers may be better off investing in persistently low-performing schools rather than closing them.[44]

Parents

The closure practice was not without serious parental concerns.

> Parents are ambivalent about the practice. They recognize the inconvenience and disruption of searching out new school options for their children. They fear their children will find the transition difficult, further hindering their academic progress. Worse, some parents and students fear the reaction they might receive when students' deficiencies are realized at the next school they attend. Moreover, they have a legitimate concern in many cases about the quality of the alternatives they will be offered.[45]

The "Root" Contributor

The following critique offered much to consider. "Closing schools without finding out why they're struggling 'isn't a viable long-term strategy,'" said Steve Cook, president of the Michigan Education Association, the largest teachers' union in the state. "For many years, Michigan Education Association (MEA) has advocated for rigorous educational audits of struggling schools to get to the bottom of why they aren't succeeding," Cook said. "Simply closing schools and up-ending the lives of students [and their families] won't fix any problems if the root causes aren't adequately addressed."[46]

While each school differs in various respects, all of the schools shared this one commonality: the kids significantly underperformed. And while the teachers and administrators within the schools also differ in multiple ways, there's this certainty: all the schools were burdened by the current problematic educational system within which faculty were required to operate, a system unfriendly to the kids, the teachers, and to those administrators who wanted their schools to be better. (See chapters 11 and 12.)

When to Close, When Not To

We should close schools for health reasons—when it's necessary to bring in crews to replace windows and warped doors, to remove ugly and dangerous black mold, to fix an ailing roof that leaks and threatens to come down, to replace faulty plumbing and ensure safe drinking water, to service furnaces, to update faulty building wiring, to fumigate when faced with a pandemic. But to close schools without first expertly retraining the school's staff—while offering them the option to go elsewhere if they don't wish to be retrained—is a foolish kneejerk reaction. We do know many of the essentials needed for youngsters to succeed with their studies; the targeted schools' remaining staff need to know them as well.

Active Intervention

Recall the worst elementary schools mentioned in chapter 2; their percentile numbers for reading and mathematics were horrific. Candidates all for immediate closing. Unless one acknowledges that

- It's certain the schools' teachers *did not* use formative assessment to gauge the youngsters' learning or its absence.
- It's certain they *did not* administer CRTs to determine where within the curriculum the youngsters were successful thereby knowing where their instruction needed to begin and be focused.
- It's certain they *did not* run any error analyses to ascertain what skills the schoolkids were missing that prevented them from making progress.
- It's safe to conclude their principals *were not* involved; it's safe to conclude their state educational officials *were not* involved.

Should we close schools on Monday only to open them on a subsequent Tuesday to the same nineteenth-century model that assigns kids to classrooms and teachers and curriculum on the basis of age? Only to treat all the diverse same-age kids as if they were the same, as if they knew the same, as if they were ready for the same? As if a one-size-fits-all lesson really fit all?

We can do better. Much better. If we finally make that choice. For the children's sake, how can we not?

NOTES

1. Great Schools Partnership. (2014, April 29). Formative assessment. In *Glossary of Education Reform.* http://edglossary.org/formative-assessment
2. Shepard, L. A. (2005). *Formative assessment: Caveat emptor.* The Future of Assessment: Shaping Teaching and Learning ETS Invitational Conference, New York; see also Popham, W. J (2008). *Transformative assessment.* ASCD.
3. Great Schools Partnership (2014).
4. Eberly Center, Carnegie Mellon University. (n.d.). *What is the difference between formative and summative assessment?* Retrieved January 27, 2022, from http://www.cmu.edu/teaching/assessment/basics/formative-summative.html; Great Schools Partnership (2014).
5. Dodge, J. (n.d.). *What are formative assessments and why should we use them?* Retrieved January 27, 2022, from https://www.scholastic.com/teachers/articles/teaching-content/what-are-formative-assessments-and-why-should-we-use-them
6. Mundahl, H. (2017). *4 ways to use formative assessments in your classroom.* https://k12hub.blackbaud.com/blog/4-ways-to-use-formative-assessments-in-your-classroom
7. Popham, W. J. (2008), *Transformative assessment.* ASCD. http://www.ascd.org/publications/books/108018/chapters/Formative-Assessment@-Why,-What,-and-Whether.aspx
8. Black, P. J., & Wiliam, D. (2014). *Inside the black box: Raising standards through classroom assessment.* Learning Science International.
9. Black, P. J., & Wiliam, D. (1998). Assessment and classroom learning. *Assessment in Education: Principles, Policy & Practice, 5*(1), 7–73; Black, P. J., & Wiliam, D. (2009). Developing the theory of formative assessment. *Educational Assessment, Evaluation and Accountability, 21*(1), 5–31; Black & Wiliam (2014).
10. Ainsworth, L., & Viegut, D. (2006). *Common formative assessments: How to connect standards-based instruction and assessment.* Corwin.
11. The Colorado Coalition of Standards-Based Education (2012). *The standards-based teaching/learning cycle* (2nd ed.). https://www.cde.state.co.us/fedprograms/dl/ti_a-ti_sstmembers_standardsbased
12. Dodge (n.d.), emphasis added.
13. Wilson Language Training. (n.d.). *Student assessment.* Retrieved January 27, 2022, from https://www.wilsonlanguage.com/programs/wilson-reading-system/implementation/screening-assessment (emphasis added).
14. Dodge (n.d.).
15. Eberly Center, Carnegie Mellon University (n.d.).
16. Pipkin, C. (2013, March 4). Charlotte Danielson on teaching and the Common Core. http://www.schoolimprovement.com/common-core-360/blog/common-core-standards-charlotte-danielson
17. Benedikt, A. (2013, August). If you send your kid to private school, you are a bad person. *Slate.* https://slate.com/human-interest/2013/08/private-school-vs-public-school-only-bad-people-send-their-kids-to-private-school.html
18. Benedikt (2013), emphasis added.

19. Peterson, P. E., & Barrows, S. (2016). *Teachers more likely to use private schools for their own kids.* https://www.educationnext.org/teachers-more-likely-to-use-private-schools-for-their-own-kids/

20. Sessions, D. (2016, June 15). *What is formative assessment?* https://cole2.uconline.edu/courses/333119/pages/what-is-formative-assessment

21. Black & Wiliam (2014).

22. Class Technologies Inc. (2021, Summer). *What K–12 virtual learning looks like in 2021 and beyond.* https://www.class.com/blog/what-k-12-virtual-learning-looks-like-in-2021-and-beyond

23. Saavedra, A., Rapaport, A., & Silver, D. (2021, June 8). Why some parents are sticking with remote learning—even as schools open. *Brookings* [Blog]. https://www.brookings.edu/blog/brown-center-chalkboard/2021/06/08/why-some-parents-are-sticking-with-remote-learning-even-as-schools-reopen

24. Saavedra et al. (2021).

25. Gewertz, C. (2021, Summer). Forbidding remote learning: Why some schools won't offer a virtual option this Fall. *Education Week.* https://www.edweek.org/leadership/forbidding-remote-learning-why-some-schools-wont-offer-a-virtual-option-this-fall/2021/06

26. Li, C., & Lalani, F. (2020). *The COVID-19 pandemic has changed education forever. This is how.* World Economic Forum. https://www.weforum.org/agenda/2020/04/coronavirus-education-global-covid19-online-digital-learning

27. Coley, R. J., Cradler, J., & Engel, P. K. (n.d.). *Computers and classrooms: The status of technology in U.S. schools.* Retrieved January 27, 2022. https://www.ets.org/Media/Research/pdf/PICCOMPCLSS.pdf

28. *Strengths and weaknesses of online learning.* (n.d.). https://www.uis.edu/ion/resources/tutorials/online-education-overview/strengths-and-weaknesses/

29. Weir, K. (2020). What did distance learning accomplish? *Monitor on Psychology, 51*(6), 54. https://www.apa.org/monitor/2020/09/distance-learning-accomplish

30. Weir (2020).

31. Collis, V., & Vegas, E. (2020, June 22). Unequally disconnected: Access to online learning in the US. *Brookings* [Blog]. https://www.brookings.edu/blog/education-plus-development/2020/06/22/unequally-disconnected-access-to-online-learning-in-the-us/

32. Collis & Vegas (2020).

33. Teachology. (n.d.). *How do I assess student learning online?* Retrieved January 27, 2022, from https://www.teachology.ca/knowledgebase/how-do-i-assess-student-learning-online

34. Athanases, S., & Achinstein, B. (2003). Focusing new instructors on individual and low performing students: The centrality of formative assessment in students: A pilot study. *Instructors College Record, 105,* 1486–1520.

35. Miller, A. (2020). *Formative assessment in distance learning.* https://www.edutopia.org/article/formative-assessment-distance-learning

36. Miller (2020).

37. Fleming, N. (2020). *7 ways to do virtual formative assessment in your virtual classroom.* https://www.edutopia.org/article/7-ways-do-formative-assessments-your-virtual-classroom

38. Fleming (2020).

39. Wagner, T. [@DrTonyWagner]. (2021, July 25). *Kids only have to "race to catch up" in an assembly line class where everyone must finish at the same* [Tweet]. https://twitter.com/DrTonyWagner

40. Chen, C. (2020). Why public schools across the country are closing their campuses. *Public School Review* [Blog]. https://www.publicschoolreview.com/blog/why-public-schools-across-the-country-are-closing-their-campuses

41. Chen (2020).

42. Superville, D. R. (2017, August). Closing failing schools doesn't help most students, study says. *Education Week.* https://www.edweek.org/leadership/closing-failing-schools-doesnt-help-most-students-study-finds/2017/08

43. Darling-Hammond, L. (1998). Unequal opportunity: Race and education. *Brookings.* https://www.brookings.edu/articles/unequal-opportunity-race-and-education

44. Sunderman, G. L., Coghlan, E., & Mintrop, R. (2017). *School closure as a strategy to remedy low performance.* National Education Policy Center, p. 4. http://nepc.colorado.edu/publication/closures

45. Han, C., Raymond, M. E., Woodworth, J. L., Negassi, Y., Richardson, W. P., & Snow, W. (2017). *Lights off: Practice and impact of closing low-performing schools.* Center for Research on Education Outcomes. https://credo.stanford.edu/sites/g/files/sbiybj6481/f/closure_final_volume_i.pdf

46. Higgins, L. (2017, January 20). Michigan names 38 schools that could close over academics. *Detroit Free Press.* https://www.freep.com/story/news/education/2017/01/20/michigan-schools-close-reform/96805844

Chapter 10

Tailored Education for All Schoolkids

Peter Greene wrote,

> In the midst of a staggering assault on public education, with their integrity, judgment, reputation, and ability under attack, millions of teachers went to work and did their jobs. In environments ranging from openly hostile to merely unsupportive, teachers went into their classrooms and did their best to meet the needs of their students. . . . Teachers helped millions of young humans become smarter, wiser, more capable, more confident, and better educated. Millions of teachers, caught in a storm not of their own making, under fire, under pressure, under the thumb of people with far more money and power still stood up and did their job.[1]

A DEMANDING CAREER

Quality public school teaching is among the most difficult of all essential professions. It may well be the most arduous and exhausting career when done properly. Teaching calls for an exceptionally talented, committed, ceaselessly focused, tireless individual who understand that the workweek scarcely ends when the weekend rolls around.

Demanding as it is, the job today is even more grueling than it was just a few decades ago. Consider the following revealing snapshot provided by professor Carol Ann Tomlinson and the late Susan Demirsky Allan, former assistant school superintendent whose specialty areas were curriculum and instruction:

> Look inside almost any classroom today and you'll see a mirror of our country. You'll find students from multiple cultures, some of whom are trying to bridge the languages and behaviors of two worlds. Students with very advanced

learning skills sit next to students who struggle mightily with one or more school subjects. Children with vast reservoirs of background experience share space with [classmates] whose world is circumscribed by the few blocks of their neighborhood. All these students have the right to expect enthusiastic teachers who are ready to meet the students as they are, and to move them along the pathway of learning as far as fast as possible. . . . The reality, however, is that many of these students will encounter a teacher who is enmeshed in a system geared up to treat all 1st graders as though they were essentially the same, or all Algebra I students as though they were alike.[2]

By any measure, the policy of treating all youngsters as copies of one another will fail many pupils. Yet that unsound, uninspired, antiquated representation is sanctioned and maintained by the U.S. educational system that includes the out-of-touch U.S. Department of Education, what amounts to a political vehicle rather than one dedicated to improving the educational futures of all schoolchildren.

A VARIETY OF YOUNGSTERS

Expecting a single teacher to adequately instruct such a wide variety of youngsters as described above would be challenging enough. But the whole story has yet to reveal itself. Add to the diverse mix of kids the reality that programming for each youngster is made more time-consuming by the common fact that "an individual pupil's readiness can vary across subjects, with considerable skills in one subject, reading, for example, but limited skills in mathematics."[3] It's apparent that to best assist any individual youngster with such varied abilities, a teacher would need to be ready and willing to accommodate the classroom's curriculum to fit any child's readiness to learn. (Otherwise we set the kids up to fail, warned consultant Charlotte Danielson.[4]) What would seem obvious doesn't always materialize.

A proactive school's principal requested that I observe a young boy who was creating problems for himself and his teacher. Quietly entering the classroom, and without introductions, I easily spotted the youngster. He was placed alone at a large table in the very back of his classroom, some five paces from his closest classmate. Our eyes instantly met, almost as if he expected me—or had visited before with others like me. When I stealthily reached him, he asked me in a soft voice if I was a cop (his word). I told him I wasn't.

At his side, and after a few moments of light talk, I asked him to show me his teacher's assignment. He had turned the paper on its face. His math problems had gone unanswered; I guessed unseen. No sense staring at a ladder you know (or believe) you can't climb.

We played a little with a new set of math problems (several that he verified were well within his skillset). He worked to answer a handful of problems including a couple his teacher had assigned, finding them not as difficult as he had predicted. Succeeding with those two from his teacher, his eyes brightened, his frown slipped away, and his small body relaxed as it might with any child who felt a positive glimmer. I congratulated him on his good work; he seemed to relish my brief expressed appreciation for his efforts. I stood up to leave and told him I hoped to see him again soon. (I knew that decision was not in my hands.) He showed a hint of a sweet, youthful (though guarded) smile. I had no preconceived notion that he and I would be able to establish a trusting relationship. Experience had taught me to wait for the cards to fall into place. I didn't have to wait too long.

I approached his teacher feeling good about the towhead boy; he had so much going for him. I waited for the educator to give me a sign that she had time to talk. When at last she turned toward me, she glared as if I had trespassed on her privileged ground. I guess I had, though I was sure the principal had alerted her to my visit. Politely, I shared what the bright-eyed pupil had done and suggested that a slight modification of the curriculum might help the youngster regain confidence and motivation, thereby improving his attitude and his classroom behavior—what might make her job a little easier. Before all my words reached her, her face flattened as she stared through me. Arms folded against her tight chest, she declared, "I teach second grade. Second grade!" she repeated like a hammer against a nail. She turned and huffed away.

Implicit in her words and actions was that she had one lesson for all the children. If it missed their readiness mark, it was not her business. I returned to the principal. We talked frankly. I'm not shy when it comes to kids and their best interests. The principal assured me she would meet with the teacher. That doesn't always produce change. The teacher stood her ground, and I was not welcomed back.

Cognitive Differences Among Schoolkids

Research on children's cognitive development "demonstrates big differences *between* age groups as well as substantial differences between individuals *within* age groups."[5] Both pieces of information diminish the value of age and grade level as predictive variables that tell a teacher what curriculum to assign; both argue steadfastly against treating all kids the same; both insist on individualized accommodation.

These common recurrent variations challenge even the best teachers in today's schools where time restraints and calendar mandates significantly limit teachers' efforts to personalize instruction, what qualifies as helpful if not necessary. Professors John Goodlad and Robert Anderson wrote,

> A single child does not progress in one piece: he surges ahead more rapidly in some areas than others. Consequently, a one grade difference between his reading skills and his arithmetic skills at the end of the second-grade classification may be extend to a three-or four-year difference by the end of fifth grade. A prodigy at math, he will struggle with reading. Or vice versa. A fifth-grade teacher, then, in spite of the classroom designation, is not a teacher of children all suited to fifth grade work. With respect to skill sets and subject readiness, the educator teaches several children who are more aptly prepared for third, fourth, fifth, sixth and even up to ninth grade work—even though all the pupils in his room are labeled "fifth grade." Any attempt to deal with these children as fifth graders, providing them only fifth grade curriculum, enforces uniformity and conformity without regard to natural variation or the youngsters' individuality.[6]

Without assessing pupils' curriculum readiness *before* delivering a lesson, a teacher won't know if his or her level of teaching fits with the child's level of learning, often leading to a decidedly undesirable outcome. Lilian Katz, education professor emeritus at the University of Illinois at Urbana-Champaign, predicted the following when teachers provide a lesson without being aware of the youngsters' curriculum readiness. "Chances are, one-third of the kids already know [what's being taught], one-third of the kids will get it, and the remaining third won't. So, two-thirds of the children are wasting their time."[7] The teacher likewise, if that matters.

Today's Diverse Classrooms and Pupil Entering Skills

Let's take a look at a newly arrived (basically same-aged) group of youngsters who fill the classroom this first day of school. All pupils will display an incredible range of enthusiasm, confidence, interest, cooperation, history, egocentrism, kindliness, academic preparedness, introversion, fickle attitudes, and acquired disruptiveness. This much is undeniable: The children are not tightly bunched checkers on a checkerboard.

- *Q*: Do all the children enter the classroom with the same skills; the same inherent cognitive abilities; the same learning styles? *A*: They don't.
- *Q*: Do they enter the classroom with the same experiences? *A:* They don't.
- *Q*: Do they enter the classroom with the same attitudes toward schooling and schoolteachers? *A*: They don't.

- *Q*: Do they enter the classroom with the same energies? *A*: They don't.
- *Q*: Do they enter the classroom with the same home support systems? *A*: They don't.
- *Q*: Do many teachers have a prepared set of lesson plans for the entire group of enrolled children? *A*: They do.
- *Q*: Do many teachers repeat lesson plans that were used the previous years with different groups of same-aged children? *A*: They do.
- *Q*: Does this practice present a problem for some children? *A*: Yes.
- *Q*: Is the teacher *solely* responsible for this counterproductive predicament? *A*: With the fewest of exceptions, *no!*

Quality teachers know the greater the range of classroom entering skills, the greater the challenge to meet the needs of all their students. While today's teachers need a flexible system to effectively educate the diverse kids coming to class, the educational system has provided them an entirely inflexible format to work within. Not much chewing on a piece of gum that's set like stone. (See chapter 11.)

This unyielding system has built first-grade/six-year-old curriculum and standards, second-grade/seven-year-old curriculum and standards, and so forth. This, even though three first-grade classes or three second-grade classes situated in the same school building may have different curricula, different objectives, and different teacher styles[8]—not to mention decidedly different kids. With time restraints along with administrative pressure related to upcoming standardized tests, a classroom teacher's lesson plan is likely designed to target the *average* child's entering skills. Within the traditional classroom setting, even for the most exuberant and dedicated educator, the options to such are slim bordering on none.

Average Kids

Average in this instance is more a figure of speech than a measured reality. Like the "typical" child we spoke of earlier, the average child is a statistical compilation of multiple children; recall the 100 blended flowers that end up looking nothing like the original. This approach assures any number of curriculum mismatches affecting an unknown number of underperforming *and* advanced youngsters. Authors/educators Char Forstein, Jim Grant, Betty Hollas wrote,

> One size does not fit all; however, many current classrooms teach all students using the same methods and materials for all children. Often called teaching to the middle, a one-size-fits-all curriculum does not meet the needs of the growing diverse populations in classrooms.[9]

Kristen Canning, elementary instructional director for Frederick County, Maryland, wrote, "[Teaching] to the middle [of a classrooms' entering-skill distribution] only meets the needs of one-third of students. What does that mean for the remaining two-thirds of students who are not receiving instruction geared to their needs?"[10] Carol Ann Tomlinson and M. L. Kalbfleisch answered, "Some students may fall behind or lose motivation if they are continually unsuccessful, while other students may become bored if not challenged."[11]

TIME TO GIVE THE (OVERWHELMED) TEACHER MORE WORK

Few (if any) public school teachers have the time to adequately factor the following into their lesson plans. Please know, however, the teachers' *lack* of opportunity doesn't *eliminate* the presence of the following variability.

Inter-Pupil Variability

Up to this point, we've been talking mostly about *inter*-pupil variability: how a schoolchild's skills *compare* with the skills of his/her classmates. As suggested earlier, this inter-child variability is the basis of classmate comparisons that produce words like *best* and *brightest* and *slowest*. ("Classmates," please, not "peers.")

Intra-Pupil Variability

We know even more than the above. Academic readiness skills in reading, mathematics, writing, and so on vary *within* each individual school child enrolled in the classroom. The first-grader, just like most of us, is better skilled at some activities than others. The same can be said about all the kids who share a child's classroom. This intra-pupil variability requires teacher attention, what little of it remains available.

Consider the following. As suggested by Drs. Goodlad and Anderson, a child enters first grade with excellent reading skills but mostly rudimentary math skills. Best practice tells the graded-formatted teacher that the child will need curriculum and instructional modification in both math *and* reading—to push the child to become an even better reader, and to aid the child in improving his math skills.

Reality

The astute teacher knows that the single struggling schoolchild is one of many children; the educator knows as well that other children will need equal (*intra*-child) curriculum and instructional accommodations if she's to do her best job. Exceptional teachers take on that challenge every day despite the impossible odds against succeeding. That, once again, is a system problem (see chapter 11)—with a good chance at a solution (see chapter 12).

Time: The Pressure Cooker

"Your students: no two are alike."[12] Teachers know their curriculum. They know what they must cover. They know the number of school days in the school calendar year. They do the math: they must cover a specific amount of material each day or fall behind—with scant chance to catch up.

This pressurized process to cover material in its slotted time begins in kindergarten. Even this early, an enrolled child's cognitive deficiencies may go unnoticed or more likely unattended to. With a teacher's single lesson plan, the enrolled children as years pass will become more academically diverse: some will advance, and some will fall further behind. Confident children whose parents have taught them to seek out a teacher's help when puzzled by an assignment may approach the educator and request additional assistance. Less confident children, often marginalized youngsters, will adapt, though not similarly. They'll let the moment—and their lack of understanding—skip by without comment. The declining children will fall further behind, worsening the mismatch. Advanced students likewise caught by the mismatch, those who keep to themselves, will quietly sit around and wait for what may seem a very long time. For a brief moment in history, it wasn't like this.

> [British teacher Joseph Lancaster] developed an instructional system that migrated to the United States. Between 1806 and the 1830s, Lancaster's system dominated classrooms in the U.S. This early 19th century school run on the Lancaster principle came with a special look and feel. The children, instead of being grouped into different classrooms by age or grade, *were grouped by their mastery of subjects.*[13]

They were taught more individually with different materials rather than as a whole group with the same materials. Such personalized instruction became customary when American community fathers hired an educator to instruct their children, most often a woman. The perceptive lady quickly discovered that some of the gathered children knew written words, while others had no sense of what purpose book-words served. Aligning herself with what Joseph

Lancaster brought to the United States, she told those gathered, "I need to know what each of you can do."

Before she met each youngster individually and soon grouped and instructed them, it's likely this insightful educator told her pupils, "Don't you worry about what the other children are doing. Focus on bettering yourself. I'm here to help you." She had in mind to develop different instructional strategies that suited the different children for whom she accepted responsibility. For many of the kids who were brought to her, those who wanted to learn as much as they could, along with those who were curious about what she called "book learning," she was a godsend. A century and a half later, her approach would earn the name "differentiated instruction."[14]

DIFFERENTIATED INSTRUCTION

Educators Scott Willis and Larry Mann optimistically suggested,

> Every child is unique. Although we may rejoice in this fact, it poses a dilemma for educators. When students are diverse, teachers can either "teach to the middle" and hope for the best, or they can face the challenge of diversifying their instruction. Today, more and more teachers are choosing the second option.[15]

Not unexpectedly, the two professionals hinted at the difficulties involved. They acknowledged,

> Determined to reach all students, teachers are struggling to tailor their instruction to individual student needs. They are working to deliver instruction in ways that meet the needs of [all] learners. And they are trying to tap into students' personal interests. In short, these teachers are differentiating instruction.[16]

"Doing their best at it" would be a suitable postscript.

METHODOLOGY

Dr. Raymond L. Hatfield wrote,

> To differentiate instruction is to recognize students varying background knowledge, readiness, language, preferences in learning, interests, and to react responsively. Differentiated instruction is a process to approach teaching and learning for students of differing abilities in the same class. The intent of differentiating instruction is to maximize each student's growth and individual success by meeting each student where he or she is and assisting in the learning process.

Initial and on-going assessment of student readiness and growth are essential. Incorporating pre and on-going assessment informs teachers how to better provide a menu of approaches, choices, and scaffolds for the varying needs, interests and abilities that exist in classrooms of diverse students.[17]

Shane Lockhart stated, "Teaching isn't differentiated when a teacher sets the same task for every student, provides little variation, assesses all students against a general criterion, applies differentiated teaching techniques only for gifted students, and consistently establishes inflexible teaching groups." He explained,

> Differentiated teaching occurs when a teacher plans a lesson that adjusts either the content being discussed or modifies the product expected from students to ensure that learners at different starting points can receive the instruction they need to grow and succeed. A good differentiated teaching program means high quality, evidence-based instruction that meets students' needs within their zone of proximal learning development and has clear SMART (Specific, Measurable, Achievable, Realistic and Time-based) goals. By adjusting content, you deliver different parts of the curriculum to different students depending on their starting level and what you expect them to learn in that lesson.[18]

Educator Carol Ann Tomlinson wrote,

> Kids of the same age aren't all alike when it comes to learning, any more than they are alike in terms of size, hobbies, personality, or likes and dislikes. Kids do have many things in common because they are human beings and because they are all children, but they also have important differences. What we share in common makes us human. How we differ makes us individuals. In a classroom with little or no differentiated instruction, only student similarities seem to take center stage. In a differentiated classroom, commonalities are acknowledged and built upon, and student differences become important elements in teaching and learning as well.[19]

According to Tomlinson,

> At its most basic level, differentiation consists of the efforts of teachers to respond to variance among learners in the classroom. Whenever a teacher reaches out to an individual or small group to vary his or her teaching in order to create the best learning experience possible, that teacher is differentiating instruction. Teachers can differentiate at least four classroom elements based on student readiness, interest, or learning profile:
>
> - Content: what the student needs to learn or how the student will get access to the information;

- Process: activities in which the student engages in order to make sense of or master the content;
- Products: culminating projects that ask the student to rehearse, apply, and extend what he or she has learned in a unit; and
- Learning Environment: the way the classroom works and feels.[20]

Differentiated Instruction's Purpose

The concept is not complicated; the intent to tailor instruction to the needs of all the enrolled pupils. *Tailor* means to personalize if not individualize. The approach served as the foundation adopted by our godsend eighteenth-century wunderkind schoolmarm who had in mind to fashion for her multi-aged, multi-cultured, multi-skilled kids a worthwhile set of lessons that matched their readiness to benefit. Fortunately, twenty-first-century educators Scott Willis and Larry Mann thought the same when they shared,

> Differentiated instruction [embraces] the premise that teachers should adapt instruction to student differences. Rather than marching students through the curriculum in lockstep, teachers modify their instruction to meet students' varying readiness levels, learning preferences, and interests. They are striving to provide the right level of challenge for gifted students, for students who lag far behind and for everyone in between.[21]

Lumping Rejected

Willis and Mann's methods stand in robust opposition to the practice that we spoke about in chapter 5, what we termed "lumping"—assigning kids to classrooms and curriculum without considering their skills. It's what professor James Delisle railed against when he said, "[We] toss together several students who struggle to learn, along with a smattering of gifted kids, while adding a few English-language learners and a bunch of academically average students."[22]

Recall your 25 kids. It's what you were asked to do with your assigned youngsters who were expected to write a paper, the group that included some kids who hadn't composed anything longer than two pages in length, some who were still mastering basic spelling and grammar, and a few who were naturally gifted writers. This much at least is certain:

> Given that different students have different learning styles, have different strengths and weaknesses, and receive varying amounts of parental support at home, does it make sense to throw all students onto the same "conveyor belt" of education and expect the same outcomes?[23]

Conveyor Belt

That "conveyor belt" metaphor represents lumping in its rawest form, an approach without any consideration for who the kids are or what they can do. In place of that indolent tactic, other educators found a better way to teach the youngsters: "Whenever a teacher reaches out to an individual or small group to vary his or her teaching in order to create the best learning experience possible, that teacher is differentiating instruction."[24] A decade-plus ago, that mindset produced the following experiment consistent with differentiating instruction.

NYC's Crusade Against the "Conveyor Belt"

Education has traditionally been approached using a "one-size-fits-all" model, wherein students are subjected to the same teaching styles and evaluation methods irrespective of their ability or interest.[25] In 2010, New York City's Department of Education launched iZone, a community of over 300 schools to test innovative classroom methods and technologies with the goal of "designing schools around the needs, interests, and motivations of individual students, by personalizing rather than standardizing the model of schooling and learning."[26] One of the most well-known initiatives that emerged from iZone was the School to One program.

Under School to One, students were placed in a classroom of 80 youngsters all supervised by four teachers, four graduate students, and two high school tutors. In contrast to the traditional model of listening to a teacher lecture at the front of a classroom, students received a personalized "playlist" curriculum that they worked on laptops to complete individually and in small groups. Students were given quizzes, games, and worksheets throughout the day. *They ended each day with a quiz that was used by staff to determine the following day's "playlist."* Teachers monitored student performance in real time and intervened and supported when needed.[27] The staff differentiated their instruction.

Studies on the School to One model for mathematics found a 47% increase in student achievement relative to the national average in the second year of the program. The largest gains came from the lowest-performing students.[28]

Maximize Each Student's Growth

> Differentiated instruction is a process to approach teaching and learning for students of differing abilities. The intent is to maximize each student's growth and individual success by meeting each student where he or she is rather than expecting students to modify themselves [to fit] the curriculum.[29]

"Differentiated teaching occurs when a teacher plans a lesson that ensures that learners at different *starting points* can receive the instruction they need to grow and succeed."[30] Professor Carol Ann Tomlinson wrote, "While I know of no aspect of education on which all studies are in total agreement, this one comes close . . . that teachers are obliged to ensure that each learner moves forward consistently *from his or her starting point*."[31]

Putting this in perspective, picture for a moment a curriculum ladder with a dozen rungs. In a typical classroom today, each of the kids' starting points might be on any one of those 12 rungs: a few kids on the upper rungs, a few kids on the lower rungs, and the rest distributed on all the remaining middle rungs. Imagine the results if a teacher's lesson were designed for only the middle rungs. Professor Geoff Masters wrote,

> Typically in our schools, we deliver the same year-level curriculum to all students of the same age. The assumption underlying this practice is that individuals' learning needs generally can be inferred from the group to which they belong—primarily their age . . . but gender, Indigenous status, and socioeconomic background also shape assumptions about individuals' capabilities and learning needs. The problem is that very able students can disengage when material is so easy that it fails to challenge them—just as students can become disengaged when given difficult material on which they have little chance of success.
>
> Schools tend to be organised on an assumption that the vast majority of students of the same age are at broadly similar points in their learning and development. In reality, students at the beginning of each school year are spread over a wide range of achievement levels. In subjects such as reading and mathematics, the least advanced 10 per cent of students commence each school year about five to six years behind the most advanced 10 per cent of students.
>
> The solution is to meet all students at their points of need with personalized, targeted teaching.[32]

That's differentiated instruction.

Writer/editor Geri Coleman Tucker wrote,

> Collectively, teachers tailor their teaching approach to match their students' learning styles. Instead of using a one-size-fits-all approach, a teacher uses a variety of methods to teach. This can include teaching students in small groups or in one-on-one sessions.[33]

That's differentiated instruction.

Ginny Osewalt, elementary/special education teacher, stated,

> Teachers change and switch around what students need to learn, how they'll learn it, and how to get the material across to them. When a student struggles

in one area, the teacher creates a plan that includes extra practice, step-by-step directions, and special homework.[34]

That's differentiated instruction.
Carol Ann Tomlinson argued,

> It is the teacher that adapts to the specific learning needs of the student. She 'modifies content, process and product,' to fit the students' current readiness skills, interests and learning profiles.[35]

That's differentiated instruction.
Welda Consults wrote,

> The description of good lessons which "start with a clear, curriculum-based objective and assessment, followed by multiple cycles of instruction, guided practice, [and] checks for understanding instruction" [i.e., formative assessment]. That's a great nutshell definition of differentiated instruction![36]

Amy Struntz, supervisor for employee induction and professional learning in Frederick County Public Schools, stated, "Differentiation is knowing your students, knowing where your students are, understanding their strengths and weaknesses, and then adapting your instruction to move them forward from where they are."[37]

Kristen Canning, elementary instructional director, wrote,

> Teachers must work from an "ability model" rather than a "deficit model" to ensure they are focusing on the capabilities [and present skills] of their students. All students have individual abilities, strengths, and weaknesses. Students need to be met where they are in order to "fill in gaps or missed skills" that they may have, which will lead to continued progress and building from their current level.[38]

Kristen Cole, education writer, stated,

> Each student works at a different pace for different reasons. This is why differentiated instruction is important. Differentiating instruction meets each individual student's needs. The first part of differentiating instruction is figuring out what students know so teachers can help them learn. There are a variety of ways to do that through a pre-assessment of some sort.
>
> After figuring out what each student knows, the challenging part begins. Creating different lessons and activities to meet each student's level and interests can be daunting, but it is necessary to help students learn. For instance, one student may struggle to identify what a noun is while another student has no problem identifying them. They are each ready for a different lesson. The first

student needs an activity to help them identify nouns, and the latter might be ready to write sentences with different types of nouns. Both can achieve success on their own terms and based on their own goals.

The last part of differentiating is to assess each student's growth. Assessments can be created to see if the first student is now able to identify nouns. Can the other student write sentences with different types of nouns? If they've found success with that goal, then, consequently, they've learned something. This allows students and teachers to be able to celebrate success no matter their academic level or individual strengths.[39]

Differentiated Instruction and Flexible Grouping

Recall from the last chapter when we discussed "Exit Cards." It was suggested, "You can divide your class into three groups each with relatively *similar entering skills*, an arrangement that makes a teacher's effort easier and considerably more productive."[40] Differentiated instruction is frequently applied to groups of youngsters within the same class. (These groups have been named "clusters"). In such cases,

> Flexible grouping is at the heart of differentiated instruction. It provides opportunities for students to be part of many different groups based on their readiness, interest, or learning style. These groups may be homogenous or heterogeneous. They may be student-selected or teacher-selected. Group assignments may be purposeful or random. Groups may work together for a day or a month. Flexible grouping also provides opportunities for independent work.[41]

These clustered groups may be homogeneous or heterogeneous. Homogeneous groups are composed of kids with similar entering skills and similar instructional needs where the focus is on skill-building. Heterogeneous groups are composed of kids with different entering skills and different educational needs where varied points of view are desired.

> [This] mixed-ability classroom was born from a desire to promote greater equity among students. Too often, tracking and grouping fall along racial and socioeconomic lines creating disparities between students that exacerbate achievement gaps. The mixed-ability classroom, in theory, creates equal expectations for all students and provides them with the same resources. It eliminates the possibility that lower-income and racially diverse students will miss out on hearing academic talk and engaging in higher-order thinking.[42]

The hesitant learner who observes classmates and schoolmates using their know-how can serve as a powerful platform to model.

That said, supporters of mixed-age and mixed-ability grouping agree some curricula are most effectively taught to children of similar experience and achievement and readiness skills. Basic reading and mathematical subskills are principal examples. Cooperative projects (with multiple student input) lend themselves to heterogeneous grouping where youngsters have different entering skills and thus provide different interpretations.

The ideal group size is "usually no more than six youngsters."[43]

Malleable Groups

Educational expert Janelle Cox stated,

> The key to making flexible grouping effective is making sure the groups are not static. It's important that teachers continually conduct [CRT] assessments and move students among the groups as they master their skills, [movement based on their assessed entering skills]. Grouping students according to their ability at the beginning of the school year then forgetting to change the groups based on accomplishment is not an effective strategy. It will hinder students from progressing.[44]

Instructional technology specialist Ryan Miller wrote,

> Flexible grouping is a teaching "best practice" that allows your students to team up according to their learning level. It gives you [the teacher] the opportunity to focus and zero-in on certain skills and objectives according to student need, making differentiated instruction possible. Ultimately, with increasing classroom sizes and a broader spectrum of student needs, flexible grouping and differentiated instruction can be a game changer for teachers. Active learning in groups means every member of the group is participating and makes a contribution which can be assessed.[45]

Frederick County, Maryland, principal Amy Routzahn argued,

> Based on prior formative assessment, teachers can create flexible groups on a day-by-day basis. These groups will address specific skills that may need extra support to reach mastery. Flexible small groups will also be created for students who are excelling with content and need an additional challenge. Flexible small groups may be created on the spot if a teacher notices several students with a specific need during whole group instruction. Then, during one of their rotation activities, students could meet with the teacher to receive "time specific feedback" that will propel students forward on their "individual continuum."[46]

Professor Raymond Hatfield added,

> within flexible groupings, learners are expected to interact and work together as they develop knowledge of new content. Teachers may conduct whole-class

introductory discussions of content's big ideas followed by small group or pair work. Student groups may be coached from within or by the teacher to complete assigned tasks. Grouping of students is not fixed. Based on the content, project, and on-going evaluations, grouping and regrouping must be a dynamic process as one of the foundations of differentiated instruction.[47]

Janelle Cox wrote,

Many teachers who differentiate instruction in their classroom find flexible grouping an effective method of differentiation because it provides students with the opportunity to work with other students who may have a similar learning style, readiness, or interests. Depending on the purpose of the lesson, teachers can plan their activities based on a students' attributes, then use flexible grouping to group students accordingly.[48] [This flexibility is necessary because] everyone learns differently and at a different pace. With flexible grouping, teachers can use these differences to better accelerate learning in the classroom. Depending on the activity, some educators prefer to mix the groups so that students of all levels are represented in each group (heterogeneous grouping of students), while others prefer organizing the students by ability levels (homogeneous grouping of students). Each approach has its strengths and drawbacks, and the decision whether to form instructional groups with students of similar or mixed ability depends on the purpose of the learning activity at hand.[49]

A Cautionary Word About Clusters

In today's educational world with its diverse school population, grouping kids together who possess similar entering skills offers educators a better chance to meet the educational needs of all the kids. It's been said that with clustering, the focus in principle changes from individualization of instruction for each youngster to instructing them in groups. Professor Tomlinson offered her perspective why group/cluster instruction was necessary:

Individualized instruction proposes that each learner have materials and tasks based on the very particular needs of that student. It's likely that (a) we could never generate enough lesson plans to address the needs of each individual we teach, and (b) we really don't know how to make such precise distinctions between each student so that we could "slice the onion that thin"—even if time were not an issue. Differentiation suggests we look at "ballparks" or "zones" so that on a particular day, depending on our students and their needs we might offer two or three or four routes to a goal—not 23 or 30.[50]

Influenced by Dr. Tomlinson's point of view, differentiated instruction took on a new look. *Education Week* said it this way:

Differentiated instruction is a teaching approach in which educational content, process, and product are adapted according to student readiness, interest, and learning profile. In place of individualized instruction, in which teaching is directed toward the specific needs and skills of each *individual* student, differentiated instruction addresses the needs of student *clusters*.[51]

A Necessary Clarification

The above perspective is not entirely accurate; the misstatement warrants a closer look. To say that differentiated instruction addresses the needs of student *clusters* is really to say that the teacher's strategy addresses the needs of all the individual youngsters placed within the cluster. The "cluster" is merely an umbrella under which the gathered youngsters sit. Five or six kids under the umbrella represent five or six individual kids. Consider what was said by the innovative educators associated with RELAY Graduate School of Education: "Even when students are in groups of similar abilities, teachers who have earned their stripes know that they still have classrooms of individual learners that need to be understood [and] valued" as the individuals they are.[52] More on that point in a moment.

How Many Clusters?

As you've learned, preassessing kids prior to instruction to determine their entering skills is essential. Disseminating one lesson plan without knowing the pupils' readiness skills is equivalent to spinning an educational roulette wheel. The same is equally important when considering clusters. Data drawn from the preassessment that's administered to an entire class will tell a teacher roughly how many clusters will be needed for the instruction the teacher intends. Setting the maximum or minimum number of clusters *without* this preassessment will almost always configure clusters incorrectly.

Keep in mind the following caution. Typically, the educator needs to avoid a cluster with schoolkids who possess widely diverse readiness skills—with this exception: when the teacher wants a breadth of ideas and perspectives with all diverse youngsters having the opportunity to offer their differing viewpoints. Cooperative projects (with multiple student input) lend themselves to such heterogeneous grouping[53] where youngsters have different entering skills and experiences and thus provide different interpretations. Such a heterogeneous group of kids can provide quality learning time for all.

The above granted, if *skill improvement* is the teacher's goal, the educator is urged to avoid a cluster composed of kids with highly diverse entering skills. Say one student-cluster is composed of five or six kids, the recommended number. If those five or six youngsters possess nearly the *same entering skills and make many of the same conceptual and/or mechanical errors*, the teacher's prepared (focused, i.e., narrowed) lesson plan intended to enhance skill-building will more than adequately cover the five or six youngsters. All the youngsters will participate, and *all will benefit*.

But if the entering skills and committed errors *deviate significantly* among those five or six kids, and the teacher (without preassessing the kids' skills) opts to use his or her one pre-planned lesson, one of two outcomes is likely. The teacher might maintain her lesson plan resulting in two or perhaps three of the five or six kids gaining less than is optimal from the experience. Or the teacher might attempt to accommodate all the kids. If so, the teacher's prowess and energy would be spread quite thin among the five or six kids due to their highly varied entering skills. Under such a condition, not all the youngsters would benefit equally, what a cluster approach dedicated to skill-building should guarantee. The teacher can avoid most if not all of these issues by deciding prior to setting up the cluster what he or she intends as the goal for the instructional hour: is it to be skill-building or group discussion of a topical issue? Once done, she can decide if she wants a homogeneous cluster (very similar entering skills) or a heterogeneous cluster (highly variable entering skills). A quick CRT will reveal the students' readiness skills, what the teacher should administer prior to presenting the lesson.

DIFFERENTIATED INSTRUCTION IN TODAY'S SCHOOLS: A MAJOR PROBLEM

With all of what differentiated instruction seems to be, with all its apparent promise to provide a fertile field for educational growth for all of America's diverse kids, the fact remains there exists a sharp protruding thorn in the rose, what in part we will look at in chapters 11 and 12. For the moment, think about this, please:

> Differentiation consists of the efforts of teachers to respond to variance among learners in the classroom. Whenever a teacher reaches out to an individual or small group to adjust his or her teaching in order to create the best learning experience possible, that teacher is differentiating instruction. It sounds lovely. But actually, start imagining it. It quickly gets messy and above all incredibly difficult [especially when the teacher has 25 or more highly diverse students in his or her classroom].[54]

There is a reason why teachers target their instruction to the average or middle distribution of kids: "Everyone open your books to page X" is easier.

The mediocre teacher can ignore most everything beyond the youngsters' attentive or lackluster eyes and still complete the instructional hour.

Teacher Reality

Teachers as a group do not stand and applaud when hearing the term *differentiated instruction*, especially those who know what the approach requires when done properly. Faced with the task of instructing differentially their *large* group of school youngsters, it's easy to imagine the knowledgeable ones grabbing large megaphones and shouting back, "There's *no time* to do it *right*!" attempting to convince an oblivious educational system that operates schools as if the calendar read 1860 instead of 2022.

Differentiated instructional lessons and their analyses are time consuming. Teachers understandably worry that what's asked of them cannot be done effectively within the instruction period school districts provide.[55] Their point is spot on, and I'd ask that you keep it in mind in advance of the upcoming chapters on format. But there's this to consider as well, something I'd likewise ask you to look at closely. As if desperate (and determined) to bolster their argument that differentiation represents a *failed educational approach*, some educators offer as evidence the following statistical narrative: 83% of teachers interviewed nationwide and reported in 2008 by the Fordham Institute[56] stated that differentiation was "somewhat difficult" or "very difficult" to implement.[57]

Troubling Lexical Semantics

While the percentile number is substantial, the two descriptors—*difficult* and *ineffective*—are semantically unrelated—the flow from one to the other doesn't serve the skeptics' argument. Brain surgery is "very difficult," but that's not grounds for suggesting it's ineffective. It's only ineffective if the surgeon or other medical-team members in attendance fail to adhere to best practice, which includes the decision to even try it. That a sizable group of teachers find differentiated instruction "very difficult" doesn't make the methodology a failed effort. Some of the same group of educators find formative assessment very difficult, assessing entering skills prior to instruction very difficult, analyzing errors very difficult, accommodating curriculum for a second-grade boy *too* difficult. But none of the aforementioned strategies are unsuccessful or useless.

What of the Other 16%?

Knowing that 83% of teachers tallied stated that differentiation was "somewhat" or "very" difficult to implement, the math tells us that 16% of the teachers who were asked about differentiation's classroom application answered that it was "somewhat easy" to "very easy." The pie chart shows exactly that. (With 1% "unsure.")[58] When trying to distinguish between those 16% of educators who described differentiation as "easy" from those 83% who assessed the strategy as "difficult," we may be talking about several factors, including some teachers having little to no preparation on how best to use differentiated instruction, some teachers working for administrators who fail to support the strategy, some teachers having many more kids in their classrooms; some teachers being poorly skilled; and not all teachers sharing the same commitment to their jobs.

Any one or more of the above factors may have influenced teachers' responses to the questionnaire. Additionally, whether a school's staff enthusiastically embraces differentiated instruction depends in large measure on the school's principal. He or she is authorized to set the instructional tone for the staff. The principal may prefer the administrative ease a "one-size-fits-all" method offers his or her teachers, thereby eliminating differentiated instruction altogether.

Other Voices With Similar Claims

It seems human nature guarantees a shower of opposing arguments to virtually any claim that touches recipients' personal emotional buttons. The "Flat Earth" folks have their own society and founder, and their members *circle* the globe they believe resembles a dinner plate. They won't hear arguments to the contrary. Likewise, it's an absolute certainty that several naysayers told Orville and Wilbur Wright to go back to their bike shop and forgot their foolish notion that they could fly a winged contraption that was heavier than air. Thankfully, the boys' stick-to-it-iveness won out.

Too, it would be totally disappointing if no one voiced exception to Sally Reis and her colleagues, who said of differentiated instruction, "Taken at face value . . . differentiated instruction is hard to argue with. *Who* wouldn't agree that students learn more efficiently and effectively when learning tasks are geared toward their individual needs?"[59]

Administrator, teacher, and coach Mike Schmoker came through: he took such exception to Sally Reis's gracious view of differentiated instruction. In a commentary published by *Education Week*, Mr. Schmoker asserted that, "in every case, differentiated instruction seemed to complicate teachers' work, requiring them to procure and assemble multiple sets of materials . . . and it dumbed down instruction."[60]

Though his comments are welcomed, something about them seems curious at best. This is the same Mike Schmoker who wisely pointed out that the consistent delivery of lessons that include multiple checks for understanding may be the most powerful, cost-effective action we can take to ensure learning. Solid research demonstrates that students learn as much as four times as quickly from such lessons.[61]

Four times. That's a wow. Beginning teachers might want to put to memory what Mike Schmoker just said. His words are worthy of all teachers' attention, words that speak to the last chapter's formative assessment, what provides teachers information used to evaluate (and perhaps modify) their own teaching strategies. Given that, consider the following, please.

What if through these "multiple checks" that Mr. Schmoker highly recommended, a teacher discovered that several youngsters weren't learning what was being taught. What's the teacher to do? One option: Don a football helmet and pads and plow through the educational line teaching the same way with the same lesson without thought extended to the struggling kids. Would Mike Schmoker champion that approach? Not likely. Perhaps this option then: After noting the kids struggling, and after a quick CRT assessment and a thorough error analysis that would take maybe five minutes, the quality teacher chooses to modify his or her lesson to correspond with the pupils' readiness to learn. Sounds good, right? Question: What do we call the educational approach where a teacher adjusts their instruction, including content, to fit a pupil's acquired readiness skills and experiences, where information is disseminated based on a youngster's verified starting point rather than their age or grade level? The answer: differentiated instruction.

Maybe, However . . .

But perhaps Mr. Schmoker had a point worth further consideration. "The right level of challenge for all students" was the way educators Scott Willis and Larry Mann presented the approach earlier; that's what differentiated instruction is all about, they said. That's a lot to ask of a teacher, accurately challenging *all* the schoolkids in a large class of diverse kids. Maybe that undertaking was what riled Mr. Schmoker. It's obvious that not all teachers think in terms of multiple clusters of five or six kids; they're more likely to envision instructing an entire class of diverse youngsters, 20 to 35 or more, all assigned to the room and the teacher based on their shared age and likely not much else. That's the futility of lumping once again, what we do as a matter of practice in today's schools. Maybe that's what really earned Mr. Schmoker's dismissiveness. If so, he's got company.

Remember professor James Delisle's words:

> We toss together several students who struggle to learn, along with a smattering of gifted kids, while adding a few English-language learners and a bunch of academically average students and expect a single teacher to differentiate for each of them. . . . That is a recipe for academic disaster if ever I saw one. Such an admixture of students with varying abilities in one classroom causes even the most experienced and conscientious teachers to flinch, as they know the task of reaching each child is an impossible one.[62]

Twenty to thirty-five *diverse* kids in one classroom waiting for the teacher to reach them, maybe energize them? It's a tough job, this teaching game. Maybe more than just tough. It seems professor Delisle thought the same.

DIFFERENTIATED INSTRUCTION AND TODAY'S REALITY

James Delisle titled his January 7, 2015, opinion piece in *Education Week Commentary* "Differentiation Doesn't Work." He wrote, "Although fine in theory, differentiation in practice is harder to implement in a heterogeneous classroom than it is to juggle with one arm tied behind your back." Dr. Delisle picked his next words carefully; he said more as if more were even necessary:

> Differentiation is a failure, a farce, and the ultimate educational joke played on countless educators and students. [It] is a promise unfulfilled, a boondoggle of massive proportions. When it comes to differentiation, teachers are either not doing it at all, or beating themselves up for not doing it as well as they're supposed to be doing it.[63]

(FYI, a boondoggle is "a waste of both time and money yet is often continued due to extraneous policy or political motivations."[64])

And he said still more. Much more. He provided an explanation for differentiated instructions' troubles: "The biggest reason differentiation doesn't work, and never will, *is the way students are deployed in most of our nation's classrooms.*"[65]

That last statement represents Dr. Delisle's forceful swipe against the practice of lumping, and a thorough condemnation of those administrative authorities who for their own convenience give no thought to how we group kids in classrooms, much less how we instruct them.

The Professor Wasn't Finished

Professor Delisle took the argument to an explicitly higher level and provided those same authorities information they needed to hear, assuming they had our schoolkids' futures at heart. Pay close attention, please. This is *your* profession we're talking about.

> Differentiation might have a chance to work if we are willing, as a nation, to return to the days when students of similar abilities [similar entering skills] were placed [or grouped flexibly] in classes with other students whose learning needs [and entering skills] paralleled their own. Until that time, differentiation will continue to be what it has become: a losing proposition for both students and teachers, and yet one more panacea that did not pan out.[66]

Formats

Professor Delisle's incisive argument brings us closer to our two final chapters. He's talking about formats, what schools use to guide their operations. In the current format, the lumping format, what constitutes our current educational system, we cannot accomplish academically what we want for all our schoolkids. It simply is not possible. The root cause for this impossibility is known, though it's almost always overlooked by very smart people, Mr. Schmoker one of them.

Mike Schmoker made the claim that differentiated instruction "dumbed down instruction." He was expressly wrong. What currently dumbs down our classroom instruction?

- What throttles the efforts of quality teachers?
- What stifles schoolkids' academic progress?
- What maintains the gap between privileged and underprivileged youngsters?
- What allows kids to proceed through years of schooling without learning important basic skills?
- What impedes the ability of youngsters to learn to self-evaluate and self-correct, to problem-solve, to think objectively, to assume more control over their lives, to prepare for the future?
- What hinders if not prevents good teachers from helping all schoolkids advance?

Answer: The inhibiting nineteenth-century format that rules today's educational system. Rethink that format, modify it *finally*, and we provide teachers and all kids the time and setting both need to learn in leaps and bounds and along the way enjoy the process of becoming smarter and more able. It's not an easy assignment, admittedly, somewhat like manually digging out from under 15 decades of rubble before one can see a clear sky—too much for some, a challenge for others.

Conversely, if we choose to duck our responsibility, what we've been doing for well over 150 years, if by our inaction we leave our educational system's format in its current repressive form, Julian Stanley's hope for the educational future of America's youths—"some such plan as a continuous progress model where a pupil's [work] is assessed continually, and his/her personal curriculum is adjusted accordingly"[67]—what amounts to differentiated, personalized, respectful, and altogether effective instruction, will have to wait for another time. Those youngsters, the group of them lost in the wake of our apathy, might look at us and wonder why.

NOTES

1. Greene, P. (2014, December 31). *The biggest ed win of 2014* [Blog post]. http://curmudgucation.blogspot.com/2014/12/the-biggest-ed-win-of-2014.html

2. Tomlinson, C. A., & Allan, S. D. (2000). *Leadership for differentiating schools & classrooms.* ASCD.

3. Morin, A. (n.d.). *Flexible grouping: What you need to know.* https://www.understood.org/en/school-learning/for-educators/universal-design-for-learning/what-is-flexible-grouping

4. Danielson, C. (2007). *Enhancing professional practice: A framework for teaching* (2nd ed.). ASCD.

5. Fischer, K. W., & Silvern, L. (1985). Stages and individual differences in cognitive development. *Annual Reviews Psychology, 36,* 613–648. http://www.psychology.sunysb.edu/ewaters/552-04/slide%20sets/steph_sohl/fischer.pdf (emphasis added).

6. Goodlad, J. I., & Anderson, R. H. (1987). *The non-graded elementary school.* Teachers College Press.

7. Katz, L. (n.d.). *Defining differential instruction.* https://iris.peabody.vanderbilt.edu/module/di/cresource/q1/p01/#content

8. Cuban, L. (2010, January 15). *Breaking news! In the same subject in the same school, teachers teach differently!* [Blog post]. https://larrycuban.wordpress.com/2010/01/15/breaking-news-in-the-same-subject-in-the-same-school-teachers-teach-differently/

9. Forsten, C., Grant, J., & Hollas, B. (2002). *Differentiated instruction: Different strategies for different learners.* Crystal Springs Books. https://www.researchgate.net/publication/234752993_Differentiated_Instruction_Different_Strategies_for_Different_Learners

10. Fachler, A. (2021). *Differentiated instruction in the elementary classroom.* https://mdsoar.org/bitstream/handle/11603/21365/Differentiated%20Instruction%20in%20the%20Elementary%20Classroom.pdf?sequence=1

11. Cited in Subban, P. (2006). Differentiated instruction: A research basis. *International; Education Journal, 7*(7), 935–947. https://files.eric.ed.gov/fulltext/EJ854351.pdf

12. Dyck, B. (2014). *Your students: No two are alike.* https://www.educationworld.com/a_curr/voice/voice061.shtml

13. Blakemore, E. (2018, August 22). *In early 1800s American classrooms, students governed themselves.* https://www.history.com/news/in-early-1800s-american-classrooms-students-governed-themselves (emphasis added).

14. Hatfield, R. (n.d.). *Differentiated instruction.* https://www.dr-hatfield.com/educ342/Differentiated_Instruction.pdf; Allan, S. D., & Goddard, Y. L. (2010, October). Differentiated instruction and RTI: A natural fit. *Educational Leadership: Interventions That Work, 68*(2). http://www.ascd.org/publications/educational-leadership/oct10/vol68/num02/Differentiated-Instruction-and%20RTI@-A-Natural-Fit.aspx#content

15. Willis, S., & Mann, L. (1999). *Finding manageable ways to meet individual needs.* https://www.chinuchoffice.org/templates/articlecco_cdo/aid/987495/jewish/Finding-Manageable-Ways-to-Meet-Individual-Needs.htm

16. Willis & Mann (1999).

17. Hatfield (n.d.).

18. Victoria State Government. (2019, August 27). *High impact teaching strategies in action: Differentiated teaching.* https://www.education.vic.gov.au/school/teachers/classrooms/Pages/approacheshitsdifferentiation.aspx

19. Tomlinson, C. A. (2017). *How to differentiate instruction in academically diverse classrooms* (3rd ed.). ASCD.

20. Tomlinson, C. A. (n.d.). *What is differentiated instruction?* https://www.readingrockets.org/article/what-differentiated-instruction

21. Willis & Mann (1999).

22. Delisle, J. R. (2015). Differentiation doesn't work. *Education Weekly, 34*(15), 36. http://ew.edweek.org/nxtbooks/epe/ew_01072015

23. Gng. (2016). *Education: One size no longer has to fit all.* https://digital.hbs.edu/platform-rctom/submission/education-one-size-no-longer-has-to-fit-all/

24. Tomlinson (n.d.).

25. Ohanian, S. (1999). *One size fits few: The folly of educational standards.* Heinemann.

26. Gng. (2016). *Education: One size no longer fits all.* https://digital.hbs.edu/platform-rctom/submission/education-one-size-no-longer-has-to-fit-all/

27. Medina, J. (2009, July 22) Laptop? Check. Student playlist? Check. Classroom of the future? Check. *New York Times.* http://www.nytimes.com/2009/07/22/education/22school.html

28. Rosenberg, T. (2015, March 13). Reaching math students one by one. *Opinionator* (*New York Times* blog). http://opinionator.blogs.nytimes.com/2015/03/13/reaching-math-students-one-by-one/?_r=0

29. Hall, T. (2002). *Differentiated instruction.* CAST. www.cast.org/publications/ncac/ncac_diffinstruc.html; cited in Huebner, T. A. (2010). What Research Says About . . . / Differentiated Learning. *Educational Leadership, 67*(5). http://www.ascd.

org/publications/educational-leadership/feb10/vol67/num05/Differentiated-Learning.aspx

30. Lockhart, S. (2019). *High impact teaching strategies in action: Differentiated teaching.* https://www.education.vic.gov.au/school/teachers/classrooms/Pages/approacheshitsdifferentiation.aspx

31. Tomlinson, C. A. (2015, January 28). Differentiation does, in fact, work. *Education Weekly.* http://www.edweek.org/ew/articles/2015/01/28/differentiation-does-in-fact-work.html (emphasis added).

32. Masters, G. (2015). *Addressing the learning needs of all students.* https://www.acer.org/au/discover/article/addressing-the-learning-needs-of-all-students

33. Tucker, G. C. (n.d.). *Differentiated instruction: What you need to know.* https://www.understood.org/en/learning-thinking-differences/treatments-approaches/educational-strategies/differentiated-instruction-what-you-need-to-know

34. Osewalt, G. (n.d.). *5 common techniques for helping struggling students.* https://www.understood.org/en/school-learning/partnering-with-childs-school/instructional-strategies/5-common-techniques-for-helping-struggling-students

35. Tomlinson, C. A. (1999). *The differentiated classroom: Responding to the needs of all learners.* ASCD.

36. Welda Consults in response to Schmoker, M. (2010, September 29). When Pedagogic Fads Trump Priorities. *Education Weekly.* https://www.edweek.org/ew/articles/2010/09/29/05schmoker.h30.html

37. Cited in Fachler (2021).

38. Cited in Fachler (2021).

39. Cole, K. (2019). *Differentiated instruction: Definition, examples and strategies.* https://www.schoology.com/blog/differentiated-instruction-definition-examples-and-strategies

40. Berman, S. (2008). *Performance based learning: Aligning experiential tasks and assessment to increase learning.* Corwin Press.

41. Mursky, C. (2011). *Flexible grouping.* https://dpi.wi.gov/sites/default/files/imce/cal/pdf/flexible-grouping.pdf

42. Saaris, N. (2019). *How can students work together in a mixed-ability classroom?* https://www.activelylearn.com/post/collaboration-mixed-ability-classroom

43. IRIS Center. (n.d.). *What is differentiated instruction? Page 2: General principles.* https://iris.peabody.vanderbilt.edu/module/di/cresource/q1/p02

44. Cox. J. (2020). *6 Teaching strategies to differentiate instruction.* https://www.thoughtco.com/specific-teaching-strategies-to-differentiate-instruction-4102041

45. Miller, R. (2018). *How to use flexible grouping for differentiated instruction.* https://www.goguardian.com/blog/how-to-use-flexible-grouping-for-differentiated-instruction

46. Cited in Fachler (2021).

47. Hatfield (n.d.).

48. Cox (2020).

49. Miller (2018); Johnson, B. (2011). Student learning groups: Homogeneous or heterogeneous? *Edutopia* [Blog]. https://www.edutopia.org/blog/student-grouping-homogeneous-heterogeneous-ben-johnson; IRIS Center (n.d.).

50. Tomlinson, C. A. (2010). *Different strokes for little folks: Carol Ann Tomlinson on differentiated instruction.* https://www.educationworld.com/a_issues/chat/chat107.shtml

51. Education World. (n.d.). *Differentiated instruction.* http://www.educationworld.com/a_curr/strategy/strategy042.shtml#sthash.6E6Mm5Kv.dpuf

52. Relay/GSE. (2019, November 4). *To differentiate or to track.* https://www.relay.edu/news/2019/11/04/differentiate-or-track

53. Cotton, K. (1993). *Nongraded primary education.* https://educationnorthwest.org/sites/default/files/NongradedPrimaryEducation.pdf

54. Relay/GSE (2019).

55. Njagi, M. W. (2014, November). Teachers' perspective towards differentiated instruction approach in teaching and learning of mathematics in Kenya. *International Journal of Humanities and Social Science, 4*(13). http://www.ijhssnet.com/journals/Vol_4_No_13_November_2014/28.pdf

56. Farkas, S., & Duffett, A. (2008). *High-achieving students in the era of NCLB: Part 2.* https://edex.s3-us-west-2.amazonaws.com/publication/pdfs/20080618_high_achievers_7.pdf

57. Delisle (2015).

58. Farkas & Duffett (2008), p. 65.

59. Reis, S. M., Westberg, K. L., Kulikowich, J., Caillard, F., Hébert, T., Plucker, J., Purcell, J. H., Rogers, J. B., & Smist, J. M. (1993). *Why not let high ability students start school in January? The curriculum compacting study.* National Research Center on the Gifted and Talented, University of Connecticut.

60. Quoted in Delisle (2015).

61. Schmoker (2010).

62. Delisle (2015).

63. Delisle (2015).

64. Boondoggle. (2022, January 29). In *Wikipedia.* https://en.wikipedia.org/w/index.php?title=Boondoggle&oldid=1068557688

65. Delisle (2015), emphasis added.

66. Delisle (2015).

67. Cox, J. (1983). Continuous progress and nongraded schools. *Gifted Education International, 2*(1), 61–65. https://journals.sagepub.com/doi/pdf/10.1177/026142948300200118

Chapter 11

Format

Graded

Some kids can sing—a few really well. Others can't carry a tune and couldn't even if offered a chance to sing back-up in their favorite band. A few can run a less-than-five-minute mile. But most can't and couldn't even if it earned them their choice of any pair of sneakers in the sporting goods store. There are kids who can paint an image well enough to peddle it, but most can't produce anything beyond refrigerator door postings.

What's true for singing, running, and painting is true for solving algebraic equations, writing stories, thinking like a chemist, and all other fields of study. It's only when kids show up for school that common sense is suspended and, in the name of a vague, not-thought-through idea called "a well-rounded education," every kid, no matter abilities, interests, demonstrated skills, life situation, or anything else, is herded through the standard academic hoops.

The final two chapters examine the formats that govern how American teachers instruct within their respective classrooms. This chapter critiques the present format that governs virtually all schools within the United States. Chapter 12 presents an alternative format that is more child-and teacher-friendly. This alternative is significantly more productive for teachers and pupils, particularly for those youngsters who are currently above or below the artificial range of "average," recipients of a teacher's choice to "teach to the middle."

Most present-day teachers (and today's parents) likely do not know an alternative format even exists. As it stands, this highly effective alternative format is found in prolific numbers in schools in many progressive countries outside the United States where children's education remains a top priority, countries that produce the highest levels of literacy. We'd do well to consider it in some form.

Chapter 11

YOUR JOB INTERVIEW

Traditionally, prospective teachers are interviewed by a school's principal (and perhaps selected staff) to evaluate the candidate's teaching promise and qualifications. Because of teacher shortages, you may have some bargaining power with respect to how you run your classes. If you're capable, you're in rare company. Very few people can teach well; fewer have the needed staying power to handle the constant pressure, much of that pressure derived from the antiquated format adopted by our educational system, what we will examine over the next pages.

The interview, therefore, is your audition. At some point during that meeting, you may be asked to share what you will bring to the youngsters that will constructively impact their lives. Now that you're this far into this book, I'm thinking, with your best foot forward, you'll calmly, confidently (with good eye contact) inform the principal and any others in attendance:

> My goal will be to ensure that all my children will be successful learners, that all the kids will be more knowledgeable and confident at the close of the school day than when they first arrived in the morning. If you're wondering how I intend to accomplish that objective,
>
> - I will assess all my pupils' entering skills before presenting my lessons;
> - Today's differential lessons will be developed in part based on how my kids did with yesterday's lessons;
> - I will decide on lessons and exercises for the day only after I've determined what materials best fit each of the children;
> - During a designated early class hour, I will cluster in several small groups youngsters with similar reading and mathematics skills;
> - I will teach individual youngsters throughout the day who need the most intensive instruction;
> - I will advance academically all my pupils, each one progressing as far as his or her current skills allow;
> - I will approach several of my teacher colleagues to discuss team teaching arrangements—by having colleagues at different grade levels working together, we can more easily match curriculum to our youngsters' varied entering skills;
> - I will make my own assessment instruments based on what I've taught the kids and lobby against irrelevant standardized tests that don't assess what I teach or what the kids have learned; and
> - I will not use a "one-size-fits-all" approach to instruction.

If the principal replies, "Hold those thoughts for a moment, please. I'd like several of my senior staff to hear what you have to say." The principal lifts his phone. "Sara, call district and cancel my afternoon meeting with

Superintendent Harris. Tell her I want 15–20 uninterrupted minutes tomorrow, any time. Tell her it's important," he says as he looks toward you. "And Sara, please reach the planning committee; they're in Josh Stewart's room right now. Ask them to drop whatever they're doing and come to my office ASAP. There are things I want them to hear."

If, instead, the principal says, "All that sounds very nice," as he glances impatiently at his watch, "let's revisit it in three or four months," you might look at your smart phone to check the times you've set for the five other interviews you have scheduled this week. The string around your future wedding-ring finger reminds you: "Don't cave."

EDUCATION'S IMPORTANCE

Writing for the *Guardian*, Ian Leslie advised, "Hardly anything matters more than education. With all the worry spent by parents over what school to send their kids." Mr. Leslie suggested that what's "more important is who teaches them when they get there."

He's talking about you and what you will do once in the classroom, precisely the issue that captured University of Melbourne professor John Hattie's full attention. The professor conducted an "assessment of thousands of empirical studies that have been carried out on educational achievement. He concluded that, other than the raw cognitive ability of the child herself, only one variable really counts: What teachers do, know and care about." Dr. Hattie's evidence suggested that "a child at a bad school taught by a good teacher is better off than one with a bad teacher at a good school." He added,

> The benefits of having been in the class of a good teacher cascade down the years; the same is true of the penalty for having had a bad teacher. Such effects do not fall evenly upon the population: the children who gain most from good teachers are those from disadvantaged homes in which parental time, money and books are in short supply. Being in the classroom of a great teacher is the best hope these children have of catching up with their more fortunate peers [classmates, *please*; the dissimilar children collectively are far from peers].

FYI: Being in the classroom of a great teacher is the best hope for *all* kids, the advanced, those who struggle, and all the youngsters in between.

FORMATS

"Formats" represent the way something is arranged. Formats come with rules that explicitly communicate the manner in which something is to be carried out. Virtually all of our traditional twenty-first-century elementary schools employ a format that mirrors the same *lumping* approach found in America in the mid-nineteenth century. Montessori schools remain an exception. Genuine Montessori schools avoid formal grade classifications and the schools "encourage each child to learn at [his or her] own speed." American kids enrolled in traditional K–6 public schools won't experience either of those highly favorable opportunities.

Changing Formats

Formats are changeable though often with considerable difficulty. The president of the United States is elected by the electoral college, "a body of people representing the states of the U.S., who formally cast votes for the election of the president and vice president." To elect the president and vice president by popular vote, what some people prefer, would require a significant change in format.

The master of overhauling formats was Henry Ford. In 1903, Mr. Ford established the Ford Motor Company, and five years later the company rolled out the first Model T. In order to meet demand for the groundbreaking vehicle, Mr. Ford introduced revolutionary new mass-production methods that included large plants, the use of standardized, interchangeable parts, and in 1913, the world's first moving assembly line that produced identical looking cars.

It happens that our current educational system that serves 50 million schoolkids (30 million at the elementary level) has been likened—not too kindly—to Henry Ford's modernization. Teacher Alan Rosenberg stated,

> All of American education has come to resemble Henry Ford's assembly line. Students receive a standardized education. Teachers work as quickly as possible as the product moves by to put in those parts deemed necessary by the administration. Quality-control inspectors watch the workers to make sure they are doing everything as dictated by the owner's manual. In the past decade, the line has been sped up . . . and the raw material at the beginning of the line has decreased in quality. Administration continues to raise output goals yet cuts pay and benefits. The workers, i.e., teachers, have little choice but to comply.

FORMAT INTRODUCTIONS

Most of us know the graded system format from experience—first grade, second grade, third grade, and so on. A few American youngsters have been schooled at an ungraded/nongraded private or independent school where the format and rules vary considerably from those found in graded facilities. For example, kids in these alternative schools who need more help with their lessons receive assistance more quickly, often immediately; kids who need more educational challenging receive suitably demanding assignments more quickly, often immediately; and, rather than required to wait for all their classmates to reach the same level within the curriculum, kids ready for more knowledge are able to move through their curriculum as fast as their skills allow. As a result, not all enrolled kids are fitted rigidly with the same curriculum. FYI: On occasion, determined (quality) public-school teachers, often clandestinely, include a nongraded alternative component to their graded format, finding the blended approach favorable and constructive for many of the kids and for themselves. With few exceptions, the graded and nongrade-formatted schools resemble what's described below.

Graded Schools

"Grade" school, or the more familiar "elementary school," provides an instructional program that's divided into separate and segmented school years or grade levels, kindergarten through sixth grade, for example. Nearly all pupils within a specified grade level, assigned to that grade level by their age, receive the same lessons and work with the same materials all at the same time. Kids labeled "special education," mainstreamed into the general classroom, may receive modified materials.

The question of retention, that is, nonpromotion due to poor achievement, presents a problem for graded schools. Often it is dealt with by passing the youngster on to the next grade even though she lacks the necessary skills to perform adequately with the new, more complex curriculum. In the long run, doing so in the context of the graded system presents the passed-along youngster with few favors short of staying with friends, some who may have little time for socializing as they work with more intricate and enjoyable assignments. (Keeping the youngster back to repeat the same grade is a worse option, as we will discuss later.) Infrequently, an outstanding achiever might skip a grade, advancing beyond her former classmates. More often than not, however, this outstanding student moves along with her familiar classmates and their scheduled curriculum that she has already mastered.

Teachers under the graded format work mostly in isolation; interaction with colleagues is extremely limited. Beyond a day here and there, teachers are provided little worktime for planning, and they are mandated to use a narrow and prescribed curriculum with pupils despite the youngsters' diverse abilities and interests. Accountable to administrators and parents, these teachers face the pressure that comes with standardized testing, undisciplined youngsters, adverse public scrutiny, and often a lack of parental [and administrative] support. Consequently, "burn out" is a major factor.

Ungraded Schools

A nongraded, also called "ungraded," school does not use grade-level designations for students or classes other than perhaps for administrative purposes, that is, homeroom announcements and roll-taking. Curriculum is assigned not by age but by a student's assessed readiness.

> An ungraded school does not formally organize students according to age-based grade levels. Students' achievements are assessed by teachers, and each student is individually assigned to one of several fluid groups, according to what the student needs to learn next.

Progress is reported in terms of individual tasks completed and the manner and quality of the individual youngster's learning, not by subjective letter grades or numerical rating systems derived from comparing classmates with one another. A team of teachers may work with a team of students who are regrouped frequently based on the student's needs, interests, and advancing skills. As suggested, a quality teacher in a self-contained graded classroom may alter his or her instructional approach to reflect the components of a nongraded format, that is, assigning curriculum on the basis of skills not age. Nongraded teachers rarely if ever voluntarily borrow the rigidity of a graded system for their pupils.

Within a nongraded format, students do not move through a predetermined sequence of curriculum levels that may not match their skills. Students' achievements are assessed frequently during the school year by teachers' own instruments, not by a single standardized test at the end of the school year, what is common in a graded format. The continuous progress of pupils is reflected in students' growth of knowledge, skills, and understanding. Again, each student is individually assisted or assigned to one of several flexible groups, where, again, groups are configured on the basis of the youngsters' current skills.

Pupils advance along a continuum of simple though more complex material at their own pace, where the teacher's focus is on each student's continuous academic progress, not just being promoted to the next grade at the end of a school year. (More on "continuous progress" as we proceed.) Because reading, math, and writing are most often taught in groups of pupils possessing similar readiness skills, teachers acquire a heightened awareness of individual student's particular strengths and weaknesses what prepares them to modify the curriculum to fit the youngster's abilities. It's typical that many pupils work on different exercises and materials throughout the school day. All youngsters advance beyond their current readiness at their own speed. Each student's self-improvement (*growth* beyond their assessed readiness baseline) is the overall goal rather than being first or best or highest as measured by a standardized instrument.

Today's Configuration: Pupil Differences
Inside Today's Classrooms

In any graded classroom, from kindergarten to the senior year in high school, students enrolled will differ from one another on virtually all measures and characteristics, including most essentially acquired skills and native intellect. Unlike public schools, some private and for-profit Charter schools have stiff entrance requirements for their students. In such a case, the variability among enrolled pupils is considerably less than that found in the majority of public schools.

Today, all public schools (and some charter schools) are mandated to serve all youngsters who enter through the schoolhouse door. As a result, most every current public-school teacher will find in his or her classroom what James Delisle described in the last chapter: "a smattering of gifted kids, a few English-language learners, and a bunch of academically average students." Teachers will likewise have within the same classroom academically challenged youngsters as well as youngsters who differ in culture, attitude, motivation, history, health, and parental upbringing.

Either by direct observation, responses to assigned exercises, or an administered CRT, the observant teacher in a grade-formatted classroom will know within days (if not the hour) that he or she will need to modify materials and lessons to fit the diverse kids if the teacher hopes to help *all* the youngsters experience anything close to school success. While the quality teacher within a grade-formatted classroom might like to provide the youngsters' materials that fit their educational needs, the classroom's strictly regulating clock and calendar that governs what the teacher does leaves virtually no time for that quality teacher to be so educationally progressive.

An exception may exist—a rare teacher within a grade-formatted classroom who makes the decision to ignore the restrictive clock and calendar. If he or she chooses to accommodates those students who need assistance, assigning a different book perhaps, a different set of math problems, a modified writing assignment, or giving them more time to complete what some youngsters complete in less time allowing them to take on new work, that teacher for that moment in time will have altered the graded classroom to fit more closely with a nongraded/ungraded format. Privately, that accomplished, forward-thinking teacher might delete from his or her vocabulary, "I teach second grade." Replacing it with, "I teach the kids in my second-grade classroom helping all of them advance through the curriculum."

Related, this from Sandra Stone, former director of the National Multiage Institute based at Northern Arizona University in Flagstaff: "The emphasis [must be] on the child rather than on the curriculum." The idea is "very much a child-centered approach that assesses children's understanding and chooses curriculum pieces to fit their needs." If the teacher see herself merely as a third-grade teacher, she operates within this limited scope: "This is *what* I teach." If the teacher sees herself as the mentor of multifaceted, diverse, perhaps multiage-kids with varied abilities and varied experiences, she's guided by: "These are the *children* I teach." The attitudinal difference from the start can be either restrictive or innovative, one group of children seen without being seen, the other group of children with the chance to reach new educational heights. Such elasticity is rarely, if ever, the teacher's option—the format dictates the rules within which the teacher must operate. The graded systems' rules are unbending. A traditional second-grade teacher teaches second grade material to all of his or her same-age schoolkids whether or not the materials best fit the youngster's academic readiness. This rigidity, which is seldom eased by either a child's enhanced academic readiness or noticeable deficiencies, is likely to continue throughout—and extend beyond—elementary school. Teachers are rarely offered the time to accommodate the youngster. If it happens, it's the extraordinary teacher's own doing. Our educational system's narrow-mindedness has been noticed.

THE CURRENT TENUOUS STATE OF AMERICAN EDUCATION: CRITIQUES

Astrophysicist Ethan Siegel wrote,

> [Teachers] on any given day, have a slew of unique problems to tackle. These include how to reach, motivate, and excite the people whose education and performance [they're]responsible for. Gifted students, average students, special needs students, and students with severe disabilities are all often found in the same [grade-formatted] class, requiring a deft touch to keep everyone engaged.

If the goal was to achieve the greatest learning outcome possible for each student, [teachers would] need the freedom to decide what to teach, how to teach it, how to evaluate and assess students, and how to structure [their] classroom and curriculum. [They'd] need the freedom to make individualized plans or separate plans for students who were achieving at different levels.

In public education, if teachers do [what's needed], they are penalized. Passion is disincentivized; whatever aspects [they're] passionate about take a back seat to what will appear on the standardized test. . . . A vision for what successful students look like is narrowed down to one metric alone: test performance.

If this were common practice in any other industry, we'd be outraged. Yet in education, we have this unrealistic dream that a scripted, one-sized-fits-all strategy will somehow lead to success for all; that we can somehow, through just the right set of instructions, transform a mediocre teacher into a great one. By taking away the freedom to innovate, we aren't improving the outcomes of the worst teachers or even average teachers; we're simply telling the good ones that their skills and talents aren't needed here. Until we abandon the failed education model we've adopted . . . public education will continue to be broken.

Leonard Billet, professor of political science, stated,

At the elementary and secondary level, the quality of schooling varies tremendously: outstanding in some wealthy suburbs of major metropolises, excellent or reasonably satisfactory in many small towns and rural areas, incredibly bad in the inner cities of major metropolises. The education, or rather the uneducation, of black children from low income families is undoubtedly the greatest disaster area in public education and its most devastating failure. This is doubly tragic for it has always been the official ethic of public schooling that it was the poor and the oppressed who were its greatest beneficiaries.

Milton Friedman, 1976 Nobel Memorial Prize winner, lamented,

The tragedy, and irony, is that a system dedicated to enabling all children to acquire a common language and the values of U.S. citizenship, to giving all children equal educational opportunity, should in practice exacerbate the stratification of society and provide highly unequal educational opportunity.

Recently, historian David M. Perry explained,

Across society, the pandemic has intensified preexisting inequalities and, perhaps, made them more visible to folks who weren't paying attention previously. The problems in our schools exacerbated by a year of distance, lockdowns, fear and unequal access aren't new. But as we transition out of the Trump presidency—and then, eventually, the pandemic—every school, every official, every state education department and especially the Biden administration has an opportunity to ease the burdens of a lost year and to try to do things better in the future. It's an opportunity we can't afford to squander.

In a different neighborhood, a bright spot within our schools does exist, according to professor Jack Schneider, who reminded us that the current "educational system does a fine job with youngsters we embrace, youngsters for whom [the system] accepts responsibility and provides support." (That uplifting view assumes, of course, that we actively *do* embrace and support those youngsters and their special talents—what the grade-formatted system often neglects, e.g., the Pasadena youngsters mentioned in the first chapter and Daniel Lattier's "bright" Baltimore youngsters mentioned in chapter 7.) Dr. Schneider added a less sanguine reality, "And [this educational system] works in a different way for those [students] we have collectively refused. When a school fails, it is because we have failed." Fitting for the following: We know that

> high-achieving students of color are an increasing share of the overall student population, but many find themselves left out of the academic fast lane. Instructor bias, inept teacher prep programs, a subjective screening system, and a lack of funding often conspire to keep young minority scholars out of the academic fast lane.

Add to those impediments the graded format within which these exceptional youngsters, and struggling kids as well, are easily moved to the side. Not so the alternative system.

The Relative Virtuosos

Supporting *selectively* (privileged) advanced youngsters is a relatively easy task for quality teachers when we acknowledge the many gifts these academically ready kids bring with them when the school bell summons. In their own way, they are relative virtuosos even before they enter the school building.

- They're self-starters, flush with intrinsic motivation.
- They're eager, independent learners.
- Their skills (in many curriculum areas) are advanced.
- They bring with them a refined language rich with the ability to communicate, ask questions, offer alternatives, challenge doctrines, argue in favor of right over wrong, and problem solve what stands in the way of their progress.
- They're invested in their own education, believing learning is important.
- They have a familial support system that's dedicated and ever present.

- They're energized and incentivized to improve themselves and quite often those around them.
- With doors left wide open, these exceptional youngsters of multiple shades enjoy mostly a history of school success.

Other Youngsters

Not so with many kids toward whom the educational system has turned its back *and* closed its doors. Many of these youngsters have known little if any concrete school success. Many lack any degree of school-related confidence. Many face a troubling curriculum, its content and pace beyond their current abilities. Many are without the simplest of basic skills—language. Often with less literate parents, many of these youngsters are read to less frequently and exposed to less complete language at home, their parents struggling to satisfy the kids' basic physical needs. Consequently, the youngsters bring fewer words to school, essential tools necessary for learning and adapting to school in general.

(FYI: Current researchers duplicating psychologists Todd Risely and Betty Hart's decades-earlier efforts suggested the word differential between high-income and low-income groups was about four million by the time the children turned four with school just around the corner. That's four million fewer words at the kids' disposal. Note this please. A four-or five-year-old with four million fewer experienced words in his suitcase as he enters school will face a rough educational road, especially if his safe mode is to remain silent as the educational world whizzes by without him. Psychologists and speech and language pathologists remind us that possessing good language skills builds confidence and provides youngsters multiple ways to adequately express themselves. As important, rich language skills help a youngster better understand how others—teachers, principals, *and* classmates—use words to express their ideas, reactions, and feelings, all important for young, uncertain children entering school.)

Where Does the Poorly Prepared Child Go for Help?

In the absence of home support where important skills such as a good working language are normally learned, where then must the ill-equipped child go to become more academically and socially proficient? There's only one realistic resource that can make a huge difference: Our schools. With many contact hours a day already scheduled, with multiple professionals under one roof, with a decently stocked classroom that provides what's missing at home, the classroom and the willing, forward-thinking teacher's skills are the best means to improve the children's challenging circumstances.

With This Caveat

Our schools, yes, but *not* as our classrooms are formatted today, not even when guided by the most dedicated, conscientious educator. In today's educational system, as insensitive to teachers as it is to most pupils, susceptible youngsters are often adrift within minutes of a teacher's first spoken instructions. The system left standing in its current form promises little hope for generations of passed over kids.

THE ASPEN INSTITUTE ON EDUCATION

On May 7, 2020, the Aspen Council released the following mandate:

> The coronavirus pandemic has upended the school year for 50 million American students, and revealed the inequities that plague our [educational] system. Going back to the *status quo* [without] finally dealing with our weaknesses would leave many students and communities without what they need educationally. The nation [must] renew the promise of public education as an engine of opportunity.

THE GRADE-FORMATTED SYSTEM: THE STATUS QUO

The advantages of the graded [formatted] system have been thus enumerated:

1. They economize the labor of instruction;
2. They reduce the cost of instruction, since a smaller number of teachers are required for effective work in a classified or graded school;
3. They make the instruction more effective, inasmuch as the teacher can more readily hear the lessons of an entire class than of the pupils separately, and thus there will be better opportunity for actual teaching, explanation, drill, etc.;
4. They facilitate good government and discipline, because all pupils are kept constantly under the direct control and instruction of the teacher, and, besides, are kept constantly busy;
5. They afford a better means of inciting pupils to industry, by promoting their ambition to excel, inasmuch as there is a constant competition among the pupils of a class, which cannot exist when the pupils are instructed separately;
6. On the other hand, many objections have been urged against the system of graded schools, chief among which is, that the interests of the

individual pupil are often sacrificed to those of the many, the individual being merged in the mass.

The above points were written in 1877.

The Graded System: Beginnings and Beyond

"The graded school system was driven by a need for managing large numbers of students rather than for meeting individual students' needs. [Our current] graded school has survived as the dominant organizational structure since its emergence 150 years ago." (The importance of the aforementioned sixth point where the "individual was sacrificed to the many" was totally overlooked in the hurried shuffle to move all the schoolchildren as a body of one through the system's fixed curriculum. The individual youngster was an unwanted burden to those nineteenth-century authorities who assumed positions of control. Today's graded format share vestiges of that perspective. We most often teach large groups of kids as one.)

Shifting Priorities

As noted earlier, in the early part of the nineteenth century (from 1806 to the 1830s), American schools were flexible, adaptive, and child-centered. The relative tranquil and productive atmosphere where learning was enjoyable and worthy underwent a major transformation when the country began to find its entrepreneurial footings.

Large-scale industrial development altered America's landscape. Growth, jobs, and wages ushered a wave of people (local and foreign) into the country's urban centers. Many of the arriving immigrants were strong, eager to work, and uneducated. Many spoke pidgin or no English. (Pidgin English includes mixing words of more than one language with very simple grammar and vocabulary.) Many brought with them their raggedy, wet-nosed children where schools served for the parents as much a custodial role as a place for their children's learning.

En Masse

In unprecedented numbers, the workers' children descended on the ill-prepared available schools and their minimally trained educators. The youngsters were as diverse as the locations from where their parents hailed. Their languages differed as did their cultures, traditions, and foods. Their differential reading abilities and sense of numbers were as varied as points on a compass. Some of the youngsters were church mice; others during the first school days were hellions who had no sense of compliance or respect for others, including teachers. The expectations their parents held for their children ran the gamut from great hope to irrelevance, and every gradation in between.

A Solution Needed

From an administrative point of view, the tsunami of children overwhelmed. Galloping numbers of kids created an immediate need for an easily installed orderly form of education. The answer to the chaos slowly took shape. Schools would provide rows of same depth holes within which perceived identical pegs could be fitted; one peg considered indistinguishable from another. Battered teachers heaved a sigh of relief. They could stand at the room's front and lift their baton as might the leader of a band playing a one note tune, all the while keeping the youthful ensemble fixed precisely in place.

> Virtually the only organizational arrangement was the graded classroom serving one age group of children presumed to be at roughly the same stage of academic development and taught by one teacher in a self-contained classroom. School architecture honored and entrenched this arrangement by providing rows of box-like classrooms each effectively separated from the others.

Without solid theory, public education took root with an adopted "philosophy that its instructional programs would be divided into equal segments to be mastered by children of the same age." The uninspired metronomic system treated all children of the same age as if *by age* they were identical in body and mind and ability. The colorless approach, void of imagination, would have won at least one noted admirer, the same wealthy industrialist who once said of his famous Model T Ford, "You can have any color of vehicle you want so long as it's black."

Regimentation

> A journalist observer of the schools in the 1890s wrote: "The unkindly spirit of the teacher is strikingly apparent; the pupils, being completely subjugated to her will, are silent and motionless, the spiritual atmosphere of the classroom is damp and chilly. The factory-like system in the nineteenth century schoolroom was not accidental."

Curriculum by Age: An Ill-Considered Convenience

With limited professional literature on early child development, five-year-olds spent a school year together working on what a self-described authority said five-years-olds *should* work on. That's *all* five-year-olds. Same work, same materials, same pace. Six-year-olds spent the school year together working on what the same self-described authority said six-year-olds *should* work on. That's *all* six-year-olds. Same work, same materials, same pace. The sequence continued until the children finished what they could, dropped out of school, or the teacher ran out of something to present. Disruptive pupil rumblings designed to modify the system were short-lived; the strict teacher saw to that. No educators inside school raised any questions, objections, or concerns that addressed the poorly considered plan that hardened in place like rapid set concrete. The educational ship had sailed with no sense of where it headed.

Administrative Needs

The immutable plan fit the needs of the mid-nineteenth-century stiff-collared educational administrators. Their newly fashioned educational system dictated that children would be provided discrete servings of skills fenced in by grade levels and age. No thought was given to children who might not fit into the narrow educational band either because they were bored by the stale previously learned curriculum or because they were trounced by the puzzling material and the dizzying speed with which it was presented.

Teachers were equally partitioned and made responsible for specific portions of what children would be taught, the material, again, dictated by age and consequent grade levels. This would give rise to educators who, despite the marked differences in their pupils' skills, referred to themselves as teachers of a specific grade—for example, "second grade teacher"—a practice as we know that continues without argument or careful analysis well into our current twenty-first century. The early teachers had no need to consider any individual child, beyond making sure that the nineteenth-century child did what every other nineteenth-century child did whether or not it fit a youngster's interest or readiness. Orderliness and regimentation, like the slow, regulated beat of the aforementioned metronome, prevailed. The disciplined regimented pulse reinforced the complacent administrators' mistaken belief that all was well.

An Effort to Reformat Schools

All wasn't well.

> The disadvantages of the graded system's rigidity were recognized in the 19th century. Efforts to create different schooling models and achieve greater flexibility continued well into the twentieth century, though those efforts were

handicapped by the publishing industry. The McGuffey readers that first came out in the mid-19th century provided schools with materials that were graded through six levels of difficulty [first grade, second grade, third grade, etc.]. So popular, other individuals began writing books that provided materials—arithmetic, social studies, science, all strictly ordered by grade level, effectively ignoring youngsters' skill variability within the grade level.

Teachers with a trumped-up sense of confidence told the seated children to open their McGuffey books to a certain page believing all the youngsters would be equally served. They were the same age, after all; it must be the right approach. The mistaken rationale endures today.

Later,

John Dewey's laboratory school at the University of Chicago (1893–1903) questioned reliance on the capability of any one teacher to understand and present the entire curriculum of a given grade. The expressed doubt stimulated new discourse about the self-contained aspect of gradedness. Among the most entrenched features of the graded elementary school was the provision, unique at the time, of a separate room for each teacher. Given the prevailing patterns of individual teachers' supervision and of disciplinary control of pupils, there was little if any opportunity, or temptation, for teachers in graded schools to join forces or to permit the mingling of pupils from different classrooms. Self-containment for them became a way of life.

That was a major topic in education circles in the first days of the twentieth century. Nearly a hundred years later, the same issue prevails.

"Self-Containment" and Resulting Isolation

Professor Robert H. Anderson wrote,

This brings us to what probably has been the single greatest obstacle to successful and enduring [educational] reform: the non-existence of a true profession of teaching. No other so-called profession tolerates such inadequate preservice [college/university] preparation, and none is as addicted to the practice of working in isolation. . . . Few educated adults in the national work force function under such constricting working conditions as do teachers even in wealthy communities. All too few, and too limited, are the opportunities provided to teachers for updating and expanding their skills. Add to these the range of unfamiliar and disturbing problems that the typical American teacher faces in today's schools. *Survival* is itself a major achievement and venturing into any challenging new projects, such as [teacher] teaming [much less as a modified instructional format] is often seen as unmanageable.

"Survival Mode": A Teacher's Guide (in a Grade-Formatted School)

"They" say that the first year of teaching is all about survival. It is about making it through the day, the class, the hour without pulling your hair out, yelling, crying, or locking yourself in the bathroom. Many "theorists" call it "survival mode."

It is a mode that we are supposed to avoid with preparation and planning, but hardly any of us do [avoid it]. Survival mode is a way of working that almost every first year teacher goes through, but it is only temporary. My hair actually started falling out my first year teaching. Full-blown alopecia, which I'd never experienced before in my life. [Know that] you are not alone.

So you've been teaching for two months now. You lost your voice in week one. It came back in week two. Your spouse is getting frustrated because you never want to talk about your day. They [the spouse] don't understand that you talk all day and can't bear to open your mouth again, not to mention that it now hurts to talk.

You got a cold in week three and the flu in week six. The weekend after your first full week of teaching, you felt like you were in a drug-induced fog. You wanted to sleep until noon, but there were too many things to do! You had to take advantage of all the planning time. You're trying to get creative with your lessons, incorporate music, really make the content significant to the students' lives, but you're dying.

You've either gained or lost five pounds in the past two weeks. Tomorrow is Monday. You only have lessons prepared through tomorrow. Can you possibly make it through another week?

You will, and it will get easier. Each day gets a little easier and each year gets a little better, but it never, ever gets effortless. If it starts to feel easy, you probably aren't doing a good job anymore.

COLLABORATION AND TEAM TEACHING

It's well known that "when teachers collaborate and see themselves as a team rather than solo practitioners, classroom learning thrives." Discussing this topic, Katherine Boles and Vivian Troen, co-authors of The Power of Teacher Teams, stated,

> KB: It is essential for teachers to work collaboratively in teams, yet we must recognize that for more than 150 years, teachers have engaged in solo practice and have been prevented by the resultant school culture from collaborating with other teachers to perfect their practice. . . . It is important to understand and acknowledge that changing the norm of autonomy to the norm of fully collaborative collegiality is a major obstacle on the path toward helping teachers work effectively in teams. Another obstacle is that school culture supports the

[mistaken] notion that all teachers are equal in proficiency, which makes the effort to promote leadership among teachers (an essential element of teacher teaming) all the more difficult.

VT: Another obstacle to the success of teacher teams is the lack of team training. Unfortunately, unlike teams in the corporate world, teachers are not generally given team training in any meaningful way. The result is the perpetuation of the long-established isolated status quo. Putting a group of teachers together and telling them "Okay, you guys are a team, now work together" is like saying, "Poof, you're a team!" There is no magic yet leaving uncoached and unguided teachers to work things out by themselves is a recipe for failure.

KB: The many advantages gained by colleagues working in teams have been well documented in a broad range of institutions—from medical to corporate to legal to the military. These include: Increased productivity; Improved communication skills; The synergy of skills' diversity; Improved problem solving; Smarter use of combined resources.

VT: Teachers who work in teams gain exactly the same advantages. In addition, teachers who work in teams can collaboratively examine and analyze student work; address issues of class management; learn new curriculum; observe one another's practice; provide additional support for new teachers; provide roles for veteran teachers as mentors.

KB: The role of the principal is key. It's the principal's job, as instructional leader, to be a champion for the team's success. It's the principal who leads by articulating a vision that emphasizes collaboration and then by laying the foundation for success by providing the time, resources, and support structures.

To those principals, Tim Muir (the article's author) suggested,

Set aside time at least once a month for content-area teams to talk with each other about what is working and not working in their classrooms. As you build a professional learning culture, it might be helpful to provide a focus for teachers' time together. You could have them bring a certain assessment to the table to evaluate data. Ask them to share stories from a specific lesson they gave. They can then talk about what went well and what didn't.

THE GRADED SYSTEM'S ESSENTIAL WEAKNESS: IGNORING CHILDREN'S DIFFERENCES

Clear to even the most inattentive observer is that "children [vary] in intellectual, social, and emotional development just as they differ physically."

No educational authorities involved with the 1860 graded system chose to consider the uniqueness of their newly in place youngsters. It wasn't their priority. Nor the priority of many educators who followed.

Horace Mann

Mann was a Massachusetts educational crusader who led the change from a one-room schoolhouse that taught different-age children (with different readiness skills) under one roof to what we have today: a multilevel graded format that distributes children into separate grades *by age* all placed in different locations throughout a school building. During the mid-nineteenth century, Mann's structured "age grading" system that strictly controlled the children's movements and curriculum proved to be popular [with administrators] and soon became the model for other public-school systems around the country. Prominent in Mann's manner of schooling, all the kids of the same age were provided the same materials and lessons, the approach based on the belief that same age kids were ready for the same instruction. The strictness of the school smoothed out whatever edges the kids brought into the school building. Under the firm ruler, it seemed adequate to feed them the same spoonful of porridge.

Today's American Kids

Mann and other proponents of the regulated system could never have imagined our twenty-first century youngsters, no more than we can foretell the needs of future schoolchildren two centuries from today. As poorly suited as was Mann's graded system for *his* generation of kids—the U.S. population at the time about 30 million, he didn't consider what gathered on the distant horizon—a U.S. population that would expand from 280 million at the turn of the twentieth century to some 441 million in 2065. Of that increase, 103 million are projected to be immigrants.

Writing at the very end of the twentieth century, William Booth, a *Washington Post* staff reporter, wrote,

> The newly arrived [in our country] today can be roughly divided into two camps: those with college degrees and highly specialized skills, and those with almost no education or job training. Some 12 percent of immigrants have graduate degrees, compared to 8 percent of native Americans. But more than one-third of the immigrants have no high school diploma, double the rate for those born in the United States.

English rarely represents their (or their offspring's) functional language, what will impact significantly their children's schooling, most particularly their English reading skills. Such glaring deficiencies need immediate, extensive, and individualized teacher-assistance, what the graded system is ill-equipped to provide.

How well does Horace Mann's uncompromising graded system accommodate naturally diverse young children, most who will head to public school? Kindly put, not very well.

TODAY'S GRADED FORMAT

What We Know

In varying nuances, our kids differ in virtually all respects; our current labile times assure such variability. With 25 or more kids in attendance, gauging these differences, planning for them, and implementing a lesson strategy for the entire group of diverse kids is neither practical nor possible. Compounding the issue, these differences are never static. Events experienced by each youngster can affect a child's interests, abilities, and needs. Just when a teacher thinks she has her ducks in a row, the ducks duck out and come back as turtles or hares or flat-footed, slack-jawed hippopotami.

Targeting the Middle

Operating within the graded format, today's teachers have dealt with the impossible challenge by teaching to the middle distribution of their class. Predictably, this practice did a disservice to those students with higher and lower skillsets and native abilities that were far from ordinary. Administrator Derrick Meador shared, "Many classrooms now regularly exceed 30 students, and it is not uncommon for there to be more than 40 students in a single class. Teaching in an overcrowded classroom can be frustrating, overwhelming and stressful." Meador, the superintendent of Jennings Public Schools in Oklahoma, continued:

> An overcrowded classroom presents challenges that can feel nearly impossible to overcome, even to the most effective teachers. Students perform better when the teacher is able to give one-on-one or small-group instruction on a regular basis. As classroom size increases, this becomes increasingly difficult to do. Struggling students fall further behind. Teachers have no control over how many students are in their classes. [In the graded classroom], teachers should understand that can't spend time with each student every day; they will not get to know each student on a personal level.

Ever the optimist, though his glasses are a tad foggy, Mr. Meador suggested that "most teachers now find a way to differentiate and accommodate every student according to their own individual needs," a claim certain to reflect the honorable man's wishful thinking rather than the school day's reality. Superintendent Meador did concede that this differentiating and accommodating "comes at a price: It is a difficult and time-consuming task. Teachers must meet every student where they are," he said thoughtfully. He offered to any fellow administrators who listened, "They, the teachers, must have time to do so," he said. Then, as if vanquished, a subdued Superintendent Meador reluctantly acknowledged, "The time [provided] is never sufficient," a fact that portends poorly for kids and teachers and parents who want their kids to learn more every day.

The Graded System's First Presence: Kindergarten

Across the country, kindergarteners are pressured to meet academic standards that both teachers and experts say is beyond many kids. Defined by high stakes testing and rigorous state standards, children in kindergarten are held to such high standards that one academic paper called it "the new first grade." Journalist Gail O'Connor stated, "There's so much pressure on parents. We all hear the same scary news about kindergarten being 'the new first grade.'"

Jacque Gorelick explained,

> When I started teaching 15 years ago, kindergartners skipped into classrooms and dipped large brushes into paint, creating rainbows and fields of flowers on easels. They counted seeds in lemons and weighed watermelons grown in nearby gardens to work out math equations. They strung just-learned letters into "words" using phonetic spelling. They began to read, write, count and add, but if they didn't come preloaded with these skills—if they were average—they still belonged.
>
> These days, the average child in our schools is on precarious footing. Leaders in education [on the one hand] tout the benefit of a growth mind-set and making mistakes. [The call is to] *embrace imperfection.* Schools host screenings of documentaries about managing angst and anxiety. At the same time, [they] crank up the intensity in our kids' classrooms, sending parents and students a mixed message. Which is it: balance and self-care; or rise to the rigor? Kindergarten is the new first grade, and middle school is engineered as a fast track to the Ivy Leagues. New curriculum sifts the exceptional from the average, often allowing the latter to struggle—all for the sake of high-test scores, college acceptance rates and district accolades.

Ms. Gorelick added,

Education has become a high-stakes Rube Goldberg machine, propelling our kids from one academic pressure to the next with no end in sight. What has existed until now as an implied tenet, is becoming a tangible reality: Be exceptional, or be a failure; there is no middle ground.

Graded Format in Earnest

The graded system begins in earnest during today's kindergarten much to the chagrin of many early childhood specialists. Many of these specialists believe that kindergarten should be a joyous year-long learning experience for a very young child where through rich and meaningful experiences the encouraged child wants to learn more.

Others take a more determined stance that kindergarten is a time for children to buckle down and prepare themselves for first grade. This to a point where a child must show himself ready intellectually and skill-wise for the ensuing grade, the promotion to the grade precariously hanging in the balance. This attitude provoked *The Atlantic*'s Erika Christakis to write,

> Until recently, school-readiness skills weren't high on anyone's agenda, nor was the idea that the youngest learners might be disqualified from moving on to a subsequent stage. But now that kindergarten serves as a gatekeeper, not a welcome mat to elementary school, concerns about school preparedness kick in earlier and earlier. A child who's supposed to read by the end of kindergarten had better be getting ready in preschool. The same educational policies that are pushing academic goals down to ever earlier levels seem to be contributing to the fact that young children are gaining fewer skills, not more.

Heavy Academic Content

Critics argue that focusing heavily on academic content in kindergarten—and preschool—is not the best for most young children and can crowd out other important types of learning experiences that help develop social skills or foster physical and mental health. Erika Christakis wrote,

> Step into an American *preschool* classroom today and you are likely to be bombarded with what we educators call a print-rich environment, every surface festooned with alphabet charts, bar graphs, word walls, instructional posters, classroom rules, calendars, schedules, and motivational platitudes—few of which a 4-year-old can "decode," the contemporary word for what used to be known as reading. The stress parents feel is palpable. . . . Parents worry that if they pick the "wrong" preschool or ease up on the phonics drills at home, [the] child might not go to college. She might not be employable. She might not even be allowed to start first grade!

The Buckle-Down Crowd's Gigantic Blunder: A Lesson to Be Learned

When President Franklin Delano Roosevelt said famously during his 1933 inaugural address, "You have nothing to fear but fear itself," he obviously was thinking of a twenty-first-century terrified mom with a kindergarten child's future hanging precariously. If Mom and her child resided in Minneapolis in the spring of 1984, she had every reason to be deeply worried. The school superintendent of Minneapolis at the time "ordered a competency test for the [kindergarten] youngsters before they could be promoted to first grade. About 15 percent of the 3,000 pupils,—460—flunked [the test] and were candidates to be held back."

The Minneapolis school superintendent earned no ribbon for the manner in which he approached his youngest students. Not because he wanted them to possess some paper-and-pencil first-grade skills—recognition of the alphabet, colors, the counting of numbers to 31, and the addition of coins to total 10 cents, all well and good—but because of what he dangled over the children's *and* their parents' heads if the kids did not adequately meet *his* standards. He decided that flunking a four–five-year-old as a consequence for failure to pass such a test was apparently a sufficient motivator to turn the kids around. For some kids, perhaps, with adverse emotional consequences in an unknown number of cases. Not for others, however, already jaded by their school experience, what at their young age they already wished to avoid in its entirety. Punishment (or its threat) will not turn them around. Another approach might have. (The superintendent obviously knew nothing about the effects behavioral contingencies have on kids.)

Entry-Level Stuff

The Minneapolis superintendent could have easily created an alternative to his poorly considered approach, one that represents a major problem with our schools today—that is, what's at fault. Think about this please. The man could have issued a directive to his staff of teachers to administer his "baseline" assessment instrument *every* couple weeks *during* the school year to allow his teachers to see how well *their teaching strategies* were helping the children learn their letters, numbers, colors, and the addition of coins to total 10 cents. For those youngsters who had yet to acquire all of what the superintendent had in mind, *perhaps* the teachers knew enough to *change their* instructional methods. *It was those methods that failed, not the kids.* And, the skills the youngsters did acquire, even if not all of them, could be carried with them when they moved on to first grade where the graded teacher might have found a minute or two to surreptitiously do a little accommodating.

Perspective Drives Educational Philosophy

Kris Perry, the executive director of the First Five Years Fund, an early childhood education advocacy group, took exception to this. She maintained, "You can have rigorous kindergarten and first grade as long as children are getting the social and emotional support they need. What's needed," Ms. Perry suggested, "is high-quality early childhood education prior to kindergarten especially [for] low-income and minority students. They need to be more prepared." Better-prepared preschoolers? Oh my. I'm compelled to argue that *preschoolers* and *kindergarten* and *rigorous* don't go well together, sort of like inviting neighborhood kids over, the invitation reading—for "happy birthday cake" *and* available "Kaopectate." Probably a lot of "no-shows."

Responsibility

Ms. Kirk states that the children must be more prepared for their schooling. That narrow perspective may work in a household where parents accept responsibility for their child's education, that is, parents who spend considerable quality time with their youngsters' schooling. But in our current educational world, Ms. Perry's position is fated to maintain the gap between the self-starters and their parental supporters, and those counter-kids who need first and foremost to know the feeling of school success, rigor far aside.

The *Washington Post*'s Valerie Strauss argued,

> Preschool and kindergarten have become increasingly academic for years, often to the exclusion of structured play-based learning that has long been seen by experts as being the best way for young children to be educated. Things have gotten to such a point that children who leave kindergarten without having learned to read are often considered failures.

Interviewing Phyliss Doer, a veteran kindergarten teacher, Strauss was told that "many children are doomed right out of the gate."

A Different Attitude

Today, it's the educational system that must be equipped and prepared for the children, pre-school, kindergarten, and beyond. Prepared attitudinally and equipped materially for the children's significant diversity and the wide-ranging skillsets those same-age youngsters present once in the classroom. Many youngsters enter the classroom without much parental support. Anything less than a sharp shift in our thinking will leave us exactly where we are—with failing schools and failing kids.

If the school and its staff are not ready for the wide-ranging incoming kids, the grade-formatted system *will* assuredly set those kids further back. In school, building on what kids can do is imperative. If a child enters kindergarten a full-fledged reader, provide her a book commensurate with her skills. But don't force the same book on the friend she's chummy with who's still working on her alphabet. Good kindergarten teachers know how to advance both.

The Graded System's Calendar-Driven Curriculum

Teachers have always used the school year's calendar to make their [curriculum] plans. Calendar-driven curriculum that stays on schedule in a graded-formatted classroom *guarantees* a disconnect between a teacher's lessons and an unknown number of children's preparedness to grasp what's presented. It's the formula for multiple curriculum mismatches. A youngster's in-class struggles with his assignments does not tell the teacher what lessons to prepare for tomorrow's class. The calendar does. Recall from the earlier cited Wilson® reading system: "The next lesson is written based entirely upon the student's understanding of concepts and skills taught in the current lesson." That's child-driven teaching, not calendar-driven.

Children's subject mastery within the graded system's rigidity requires precisely what teachers aren't provided: time to be creative, to be flexible, to repeat, to expand, to devise best fits between the children and their curriculum, to monitor progress, and perhaps to change instructional directions even in mid-stream. None of that will happen with any regularity (if ever) in a grade-formatted school where the calendar—not the children's achievement—governs the curriculum's pace and content.

Professor John Goodlad, on a personal note, stated,

> I am somewhat embarrassed to admit that it has taken me most of my life to come to the conclusion that many things not making much sense persist because they serve too many people too well. The graded system serves well record keepers, textbook publishers, administrators oriented to management, and [some] parents and teachers, and others. The fact that it does not serve children and youth well is too often a secondary consideration.
>
> The changing demographics, more than philosophical arguments, will force us into a search for school practices designed to accommodate these individual differences without loss of educational quality in schools. More than ever before, the search must be for ways to assure both quality and equity. In the best of all [educational] worlds, elementary-age children would be educated within a team-taught, multiage, nongraded format [where] the unique needs, interest, abilities, and learning rates, styles and patterns of each child will determine his

or her individual curriculum. It is my hope and expectation that nongrading will be found to serve very well this important educational cause.

NOTES

1. Marion Brady in Strauss, V. (2014, February 24). One way to help solve America's major curriculum problem. *Washington Post.* https://www.washingtonpost.com/news/answer-sheet/wp/2014/02/24/one-way-to-help-solve-americas-major-curriculum-problem/?utm_term=.cdf1a4873a4c

2. See Buttner, A. (2021). *The teacher shortage, 2021 edition.* https://www.frontlineeducation.com/blog/teacher-shortage-2021

3. Leslie, I. (2015, March 11). The revolution that could change the way your child is taught. *The Guardian.* https://www.theguardian.com/education/2015/mar/11/revolution-changing-way-your-child-taught

4. Leslie (2015).

5. Kennedy, R. (2019). *5 clues that it might not really be a Montessori school.* https://www.privateschoolreview.com/blog/5-clues-that-it-might-not-really-be-montessori-school

6. *Electoral college fast facts.* (n.d.). https://history.house.gov/Institution/Electoral-College/Electoral-College/

7. Rosenberg, A. (2011, September 26). Assembly line education. *Washington Post.* https://www.washingtonpost.com/opinions/an-assembly-line-education/2011/09/26/gIQA8RJR5K_story.html

8. Omt5044 [username]. (2019, February 21). *Effects of standardized testing on educators.* https://sites.psu.edu/total9edu/2019/02/21/effects-of-standardized-testing-on-educators

9. Edsys. (2019, March 29). *Top 21 classroom challenges, according to teachers.* https://www.edsys.in/classroom-challenges-according-to-teachers

10. Ungraded school. (2021, July 21). In *Wikipedia.* https://en.wikipedia.org/w/index.php?title=Ungraded_school&oldid=1034748769

11. Pavon, B. N. (1992). The benefits of nongraded schools. *Educational Leadership, 50,* no. 2. http://www.ascd.org/publications/educational-leadership/oct92/vol50/num02/The-Benefits-of-Nongraded-Schools.aspx

12. Delisle, J. R. (2015). Differentiation doesn't work. *Education Weekly, 34*(15), 36. http://ew.edweek.org/nxtbooks/epe/ew_01072015

13. Underwood, J., & Jones, M. (2017). *Multi-age learning: How it's different and why that matters.* https://highmeadows.org/multi-age-learning-different-matters

14. Seigel, E. (2107, December 6). How America is breaking public education. *Forbes.* https://www.forbes.com/sites/startswithabang/2017/12/06/how-america-is-breaking-public-education/?sh=e70f1997f18b

15. Billet, L. (1978). *The free market approach to educational reform.* Rand Paper p-6141. The Rand Corporation, pp. 27–28.

16. Friedman, M., & Friedman, R. (1979). *Free to choose.* Avon Books.

17. Perry, D. M. (2021). (2021, January 12). *Opinion: America's educational system is in need of dramatic reform.* https://lite.cnn.com/en/article/h_45d19af022b5c8bce12fdcb01e273417

18. Schneider in Strauss, V. (2018, October 15). How are American schools really doing? *Washington Post.* https://www.washingtonpost.com/education/2018/10/15/how-are-americas-public-schools-really-doing

19. Strauss (2018).

20. Rosales, J. (2016). *Closing the opportunity gap for talented students of color.* https://www.nea.org/advocating-for-change/new-from-nea/closing-opportunity-gap-talented-students-color

21. Kamenetz, A. (2018, June 1). Let's stop talking about the "30 million-word gap." NPR. https://www.npr.org/sections/ed/2018/06/01/615188051/lets-stop-talking-about-the-30-million-word-gap

22. Aspen Institute. (2020, May). *Aspen Institute issues recommendations for states to support social, emotional, and academic development in the pandemic era* [Press release]. https://www.aspeninstitute.org/news/press-release/state-actions-covid-19 (emphasis added).

23. Kiddle, H., & Schem, A. J. (Eds.). (2017/1877). *The Cyclopedia of Education: A Dictionary of Information for the Use of Teachers, School officers, parents, and others.* Forgotten Books, pp. 375–77.

24. Miller, B. A. (1989). The milligrade classroom: A resource handbook for small, rural schools. Northwest Regional Educational Laboratory, 1989, p. ix. Cited in Cotton, K. (1993, April). *Nongraded primary education.* Northwest Regional Educational Laboratory. http://educationnorthwest.org/sites/default/files/NongradedPrimaryEducation.pdf

25. Anderson, R. H. (1973). *Organizing and staffing the school.* https://www.tcrecord.org/AuthorDisplay.asp?aid=24087

26. Lewis Jr., J. (1969). *A contemporary approach to nongraded education.* Parker Publishing.

27. Zinn, H. (1999). *A people's history of the United States.* HarperCollins, p. 263.

28. Goodlad, J. I., & Anderson, R. H. (1987). *The non-graded elementary school.* Teachers College Press.

29. Goodlad & Anderson (1987).

30. Anderson (1992), emphasis added.

31. A Teacher's Guide. (2019, June 21). *Survival mode.* http://www.wannabeteacher.com/survival

32. Muir, T. (2018). *How to align curriculum and still empower teachers to teach their own way.* https://www.weareteachers.com/avoid-curricular-chaos/

33. Fay, B. (2015). *Go team?* https://www.gse.harvard.edu/news/uk/15/03/go-team

34. Muir (2018).

35. Gaustad, J. (1994). Nongraded education: Overcoming obstacles to implementing the multiage classroom. Oregon School Study Council. https://files.eric.ed.gov/fulltext/ED379744.pdf

36. PBS. (n.d.). Only *a teacher.* Retrieved February 4, 2022, from https://www.pbs.org/onlyateacher/horace.html

37. Marche, S. (2015). Immigration has been and will always be, the American way. *Esquire.* https://www.esquire.com/news-politics/news/a38349/pew-research-center-immigration

38. Booth, W. (1998). One nation, indivisible. Is it history? *Washington Post.* https://www.washingtonpost.com/wp-srv/national/longterm/meltingpot/melt0222.htm

39. Meador, D (2019). *Solutions for teaching in an overcrowded classroom.* https://www.thoughtco.com/teaching-in-an-overcrowded-classroom-3194352

40. Meador (2019).

41. Alvarez, B. (2015). *The reading rush: What educators say about kindergarten reading expectations.* https://www.nea.org/advocating-for-change/new-from-nea/reading-rush-what-educators-say-about-kindergarten-reading

42. Martin, J. (2020, February 4). *Play is disappearing from kindergarten. It's hurting kids.* https://www.edsurge.com/news/2020-02-04-play-is-disappearing-from-kindergarten-it-s-hurting-kids

43. O'Connor, G. (2016, January 14). Why I hate kindergarten redshirting. *Parents Magazine.* https://www.parents.com/parents-magazine/parents-perspective/why-i-hate-kindergarten-redshirting. See also Camera, L. (2016, January 7). Welcome to first grade kindergarten. *U.S. News.* https://www.usnews.com/news/articles/2016/01/07/kindergarten-today-looks-like-first-grade-a-decade-ago; Strauss, V. (2016, January 19). Kindergarten the new first grade? It's actually worse than that. *Washington Post.* https://www.washingtonpost.com/news/answer-sheet/wp/2016/01/19/kindergarten-the-new-first-grade-its-actually-worse-than-that/?utm_term=.7fc83b0b006d

44. Schwartz, K. (2015). *Growth mindset: How to normalize mistake making and struggle in class.* https://www.kqed.org/mindshift/41700/growth-mindset-how-to-normalize-mistake-making-and-struggle-in-class

45. Gorelick, J. (2019, January 8). There is no room for "average" students these days. Here's why that worries me. *Washington Post.* https://www.washingtonpost.com/lifestyle/2019/01/08/there-is-no-room-average-students-these-days-heres-why-that-worries-me

46. Gorelick (2019).

47. Marzollo, J. (n.d.). *The new kindergarten.* http://www.jeanmarzollo.com/KINDERGARTEN/chapter_one.html

48. Christakis, E. (2016, January). The new preschool is crushing kids: Today's young children are working more, but they're learning less. *The Atlantic.* https://www.theatlantic.com/magazine/archive/2016/01/the-new-preschool-is-crushing-kids/49139

49. Christakis (2016).

50. See History Matters. (n.d.). "Only thing we have to fear is fear itself": FDR's first inaugural address. Retrieved February 4, 2022, from http://historymatters.gmu.edu/d/5057

51. Anonymous. (1986, January 5). Follow up on the news; on flunking kindergarten. *New York Times.* https://www.nytimes.com/1986/01/05/nyregion/follow-up-on-the-news-on-flunking-kindergarteng.html

52. Camera (2016).

53. Strauss, V. (2019, May 8). Kindergarten teacher: "Why our youngest learners are doomed right out of the gate"—and a road map to fix it. *Washington Post.* https://www.washingtonpost.com/education/2019/05/08/kindergarten-teacher-why-our-youngest-learners-are-doomed-right-out-gate-road-map-fix-it

54. Strauss (2019).

55. Jacobs, H. H. (1997). The need for calendar-based curriculum mapping. In *Mapping the big picture: Integrating curriculum and assessment K–12* (Chapter 1). ASCD. http://www.ascd.org/publications/books/197135/chapters/The_Need_for_Calendar-Based_Curriculum_Mapping.aspx

56. Goodlad & Anderson (1987).

Chapter 12

Format

Ungraded

Dr. Katherine Schweitzer, former principal and current teaching and learning director at Oregon Trail School District, wrote,

> The elementary classroom is at a precarious point. With implementation of Common Core State Standards in many states, much higher learning targets and expectations and budget woes, teachers struggle with how to make expected progress with students. The expectations are much higher, yet the problems remain the same: too many students with drastically different ability levels, not enough time, and not enough resources. With a system that struggled to meet the previous expectations, the question becomes: how will these new expectations be met with that same system in place? At some point, "thinking outside of the box" and looking for schools and methods that succeed with a different approach needs to be considered.
>
> Even more concerning becomes the matter of interventions. Many teachers will express that teaching to a student's age is as arbitrary as teaching to their shoe size. Public education, with best of intent, has urgently tried to saturate the grade-level classroom with interventions to address the different needs of the students. However, the foundation of "teaching to the middle" still remains the same, and the rapidly disappearing supports and interventions are simply not enough to make this model effective. The basis of public education has been to cover the mandated curriculum and standards, and many students are simply left behind due to lagging skills (especially those that have low skills but do not qualify for services.)
>
> So what is the answer? How do we create more time? How do we create interventions in the classroom that serves a huge range of student abilities? If our current model is ineffective, then perhaps it is time to consider a structural change.[1]

Education professor Richard I. Miller stated,

The nongraded school is one without grade failure and/or retention; it has individualized instruction with the purpose of permitting youngsters to progress as they—individually—show competence to do; and it permits sufficient flexibility in the instructional program to make instructional adjustments both in terms of intrapersonal variability (differences within an individual) and in terms of interpersonal variability (differences among individuals).[2]

Larry Cuban, professor emeritus in Stanford University's School of Education, explained,

Throughout the [early] 19th century, non-graded schools were everywhere. At that time, such places were called the one-room school. Children and youth from age 6 to 14 or so gathered in the schoolhouse every morning and over the course of the day, the teacher taught different subjects to individuals and small groups that kept changing as the content changed. By the late-19th century, however, the innovation of the age-graded school of eight classrooms with a teacher in each one room transmitting a portion of the curriculum to children grouped by age–six year olds in the first grade, eight year olds in the third grade took hold initially in urban districts and then in the emerging suburbs. By the middle of the 20th century, urban, suburban, and rural schools were age-graded, and the one-room schoolhouse had nearly disappeared.

Beginning in the 1950s, scholars and practitioners seeing the shortcomings of the age-graded school and wanting individual children to master content of different subject at their own pace and in mixed-age groups started a small number of elementary non-graded schools, Throughout the next decade and a half, such schools flourished. . . .

As an organization, the age-graded [formatted] school allocates children and youth by their ages to school "grades," [e.g., 1st/2nd grades]; it sends teachers into separate classrooms and prescribes a curriculum carved up into 36-week chunks for each grade. Teachers cover each chunk assuming that all children will move uniformly through the 36-weeks to be annually promoted (or retained).

Obviously, students do not learn at the same pace. If some fail to learn fractions in the allotted time, then algebra becomes a serious problem later in their school career. And just as obviously, all teachers do not cover the assigned content and skills within the time allowed. So students then become unprepared for the next grade or sequence of academic subjects. . . . [Looking for an explanation, the educators decided that] these students [were] "misfits." Educators called them: *pupils of low I.Q., laggards, slow learners, mental deviates*. The message of the labels was clear: They were students who simply did not have smarts.[3]

Perhaps the "lack of smarts" fit those who labeled the kids.

AMERICA'S DIVERSE STUDENT POPULATION

John Goodlad and Robert Anderson recounted, "The [1983 Nation at Risk] report said very little about accommodating successfully a diverse student population exceeding anything we had known so far."[4] Nearly four decades later, with student diversity greater *now* than when the report was issued, the call for change has become more urgent. Borrowing the professors' words,

> The search must be for ways to assure both quality and equity . . . where each student is an entity unto himself and is judged not [in comparison to] other students, but by the results of his own endeavors measured against his own abilities, interests, and potential.[5]

The search leads us to the paradigm known as the "nongraded" school. All or selected components of that structure will meaningfully improve our educational system.

THE NONGRADED SCHOOL

The nongraded format acknowledges that all children bring with them to school innate and acquired differences that must be considered and accommodated, differences that age, culture, parentage, and/or race cannot foretell. As such, each youngster is provided tailored curricula and instruction that best fit their determined academic strengths and weaknesses, each child can proceed as fast as their skills allow, and no child is required to proceed through the curriculum in lockstep with classmates.

Adaptive Educators

> Some quality teachers who recognize the inevitable conflict between age/grade-determined curriculum and the realities of our diverse pupil population work around the artificially created academic barriers created by the graded format. By their actions, these teachers turn the classroom into a nongraded classroom where curriculum is modified to meet the needs of the pupils—those who need more time with a subject, and those who would benefit from more challenge.[6]

If a school is staffed entirely by such forward-thinking teachers . . .

- Where age and grade-level no longer dictate curriculum;

- Where each child's curriculum is individualized and based on the child's readiness that is assessed *before* instruction;
- Where each child's learning is briefly assessed *after* instruction, allowing for future instructional modification (e.g., exit cards, three-minute CRTs);
- Where teachers and their instruction are set to accommodate pupils' ever-changing readiness skills;
- Where gathered multi-age youngsters based on similar readiness skills are clustered in ever-changing, flexible skill-groupings and instructed by an individual teacher or teams of teachers with specialized educational talents;
- Where differentiated instruction is the rule, not the exception;
- Where pupils work on assignments and projects that suit their skill-readiness level rather than working on what all other same-age students are assigned;
- Where pupils are challenged to better themselves academically rather than better their classmates;
- Where, with self-constructed line graphs, pupils learn to track their own progress over time with reading, spelling, mathematics, and other subject areas assigned by their teachers;
- Where pupils are encouraged to learn as much as they can as fast as they can;
- Where teachers are available to *any* pupil who needs more help or more challenge with curriculum;
- Where critical thinking, problem-solving, analyzing, and collaboration are infused in all basic studies;
- Where continuous progress replaces grade retention;
- Where assessment is formative, ongoing, criterion-based, individualized, diagnostic, and nonstandardized;
- Where year-end assessments based on material covered by classroom teachers are drawn from teacher-made CRTs;
- Where standardized year-end assessments are optional;
- Where progress is reported in terms of tasks completed, not by arbitrary letter grades or rating scales[7];
- Where earned free time is set aside for pupils to work on projects based on their special interests and passions, providing teachers time with other youngsters; and
- Where no school calendars and no classroom clocks impede teachers' instruction

. . . then the school is guided by a nongraded/ungraded format.

FYI:

Continuous progress, an integral part of the nongraded concept [makes retention unnecessary]. [It], can be visualized as a gradually inclined ramp that accommodates a pupil's sustained upward growth. This in contrast to graded education which resembles a stepladder where each rung (each grade level) is the same distance as the subsequent and preceding rung. In the past, single-curriculum presentations were typically presented to an entire class at a comfortable paced that was set for the average learner. Unintentionally, the grade-formatted instructional sequence had the effect of holding back fast learners while frustrating and confusing learners who struggled to keep up. At year's end of a graded school, students either moved up a whole "step" to the next grade or remained on the same "step" for an additional year often with the *same* teacher who uses the *same* strategies. [This despite the fact the youngster likely mastered a portion of the curriculum that he now must endure again.] This is not the case with a continuous progress format. The goal of such continuous progress is to enable students to cover ground at their own pace, regardless of their age, neither spending extra time on material they have already learned, nor being rushed on to new material before they have mastered the prerequisites.[8]

Active Intervention Rather Than Retention

Lawyer Pam Wright spoke about a school's decision to retain a youngster who exhibited (early on) red flags, especially in language areas—reading, spelling, writing. Ms. Wright said,

> The school believes his problems are due to "immaturity." Oddly, this immaturity doesn't affect his ability to learn subjects like math or science. The school's solution to this problem is to retain the child while they continue to do the same thing with him, waiting for a different outcome. This is often called the "Wait to Fail" approach. Although retaining kids in hopes that "maturity" will cause them to learn to read, write and spell has been discredited for decades, this news doesn't seem to have reached many people who work in schools.[9]

Such would not happen in a nongraded school.

NONGRADED FORMAT IN OPERATION: A FIRST LOOK

Central to the nongraded concept, students are grouped according to their level of performance, not their ages. Sometimes this grouping is done for just one subject; sometimes it is done for many subjects again according to their performance. A nongraded reading class, for example, might contain five-, six-, seven-, and eight-year-olds, all reading at what would ordinarily be considered perhaps "second grade." Though their ages vary, their readiness skills for reading are similar. Having them work together with a quality teacher will result in all of the students becoming better readers, their ages irrelevant.

Students are allowed to proceed through the grades at their own rates. Some may take longer than usual to complete the elementary grades, while others may complete elementary school in less time than usual. Because a school has classes at many levels, a child who leaps ahead or falls behind can easily be moved to a more appropriate setting for portions of a school day that better match his or her current entering skills. Advanced kindergartener (now Dr.) Daniel Lattier, who you met in chapter 4, would not be made to sit in a bean bag while his teacher taught other youngsters. He'd be walked to a different location within the school that would continue to educationally challenge the bright youngster.

As suggested, a retained child in the graded system is made to repeat a *whole year* of content—some of what he or she conquered without struggle. Spending a second year going over the same curriculum (with the same teacher) seems a poor option, especially for a low achiever who, under those conditions, has little reason to better himself. He, too, would find himself in the presence of a new teacher (or group of teachers) prepared to move him beyond his current readiness skills. Thus, nongraded schools provide an alternative approach to retention, social promotion, and the question of an advancing youngster "skipping" a grade.

Stretching the Curriculum, Not the Child

Professor John Goodlad wrote,

> Greek mythology tells us of the cruel robber, Procrustes (whose name means "He who stretches"). When travelers sought his house for shelter, they were tied onto an iron bedstead. If the traveler was shorter than the bed, Procrustes stretched him out until he was the same length as the bed. If he was longer, his limbs were chopped off to make him fit. Procrustes shaped both short and tall until they [adjusted to the only bed that was available].[10]

The metaphorical bed is a graded school's fixed curriculum. Professor James Lewis Jr. stated,

> Individualized [personalized] instruction which permits each child to progress at his own level of interest and ability lies at the core of the nongraded concept. Rather than stretch and fit the child into the grove of instruction, [the nongraded concept] proposes to stretch and fit the instruction to the individual child.[11]

What We've Known for Countless Years

Educator Joan Gaustad explained,

> Children vary in intellectual, social, and emotional development just as they differ physically. They may progress in spurts, hit plateaus, and even regress at times in any of these areas, rather than progressing at a steady, predicable rate. Not only do children develop differently from same-age peers [classmates], but individuals may develop at different rates in different areas of functioning, all of which requires open-ended learning opportunities that are accessible to children at different levels of ability and readiness.[12]

Graded schools are prewired to ignore these readiness differences, what produces issues we see all too often in today's U.S. schools. Phu N. Ly, a second-grade teacher, wrote,

> By October, I discovered that my students' developmental levels ranged from pre-primer reading, writing, and math levels to that of third grade. I constantly ask myself, "How can I keep 'Gabriel,' a very bright student who always manages to finish his work before the rest of his classmates, occupied for the last ten minutes while the rest of the class is still working and I'm still teaching a reading group? How can I continue to challenge and stimulate students who are at third grade reading and math levels while allowing students who are at pre-primer to second grade levels to keep their pace?"[13]

The answer: The teacher can't, despite her principled intentions.

THE TWENTY-FIRST CENTURY: TODAY'S SCHOOLKIDS

If we wish to improve our disappointing educational outcomes and eliminate to whatever degree possible the emotional side of an unsuccessful educational experience, the graded format as used in today's schools should be thoroughly modified or shelved. In 1959, John Goodlad told the educators of his day,

> Social and economic change are steadily making graded education less suitable. On the brink of the twenty-first century, the time is ripe for the nineteenth-century graded model of education to give way to a new instructional model, one that accepts and embraces the uniqueness of every child.[14]

Professor James Lewis Jr. said,

The only direction left in which to move must be toward a change in the present traditional [graded] structure so that the diverse, individual needs of [all] students can be adequately served by the public schools. The nongraded educational philosophy permits a child to learn at his own rate of speed according to his capabilities and without fearing the ogre of failure or the humiliation of not being able to achieve equally with another student. The nongraded concept maintains that children are not alike, and each child should be educated differently. Gone are terms such as "average," "slow," or "fast," in designating children or groups of children. Gone are weekly or monthly lesson plans arranged by teachers in advance of meeting the students in their classes. Gone are the stereotyped lectures and lesson plans used over and over from one year of teaching to the next.[15]

Inside a Nongraded School

In today's schools with two same-aged children seated next to one another in any classroom, chances are one of the two children will have acquired more useful mathematical experiences and a greater mathematical skill set than the other. The same two children, however, with different subject matter, reading, for example, may well reverse their order, the lesser of the two's skills now the more advanced. Life's attributes and experiences guarantees that clear possibility. In a nongraded school served by teachers who differentiate curriculum based on readiness skills, the two children's variations present no cause for parental [or school administrator] concern. The nongraded teachers are ready; they know what to do. "The job of elementary education is not to promote senseless races between the two. The real job [for the teacher] is to keep both children tuned and operating at top-level efficiency and then to clear the roadblocks so that each may proceed at his or her unique pace."[16]

In graded systems where time and calendar dates are issues, the above prospects won't be realized. Holding the same expectations for both children, the system would provide both youngsters with the same curriculum void of any attempt at differentiating instruction. Measured by the same quiz, their scores compared, the children compared, one child in one domain will be a relative success, the other a relative failure.[17]

Again, such would not happen in a nongraded format. Within the nongraded system, each youngster would be measured against his or her own individual entering skills. Achievement growth beyond those entering skills would constitute success for both children. Staffs' perceptions about both children would be more likely positive, the kids' improvement, even when not equivalent, encouraging. Youngsters' perceptions about themselves would be positive as each counts his or her own gains. Teachers, too, can enjoy a sense of their own accomplishments, leaving us a good chance at a welcomed win-win.

Maximum Opportunities

> Nongradedness is defined in terms of respect for, and optimism about, individual differences. It calls for the provision of a pleasurable, challenging, and rewarding learning atmosphere where there are maximum opportunities for productive interaction between the learners and the involved educators. Within a nongraded setting the curriculum is both integrated and flexible. Similarly, the timetable for the academic progress of each unique child is flexible. The assessment of students is individualized, and evaluation is continuous, comprehensive, *and* diagnostic.

Barbara Nelson Pavan wrote,

> Students are active participants in their learning and in the collection of documentation to be used for assessment and evaluation. The continuous progress of pupils is reflected in students' growth of knowledge, skills, and understanding, not movement through a predetermined sequence of curriculum levels where improperly matched lessons and exercises [curriculum mismatches] are likely.[18]

(As a reminder, diagnostic assessment is a form of preassessment that allows a teacher to determine students' individual academic strengths, weaknesses, knowledge, and skills *prior* to instruction. It is primarily used to analyze student curriculum difficulties and to guide (a teacher's) lesson and curriculum planning.[19])

Comparative Formats

Restructuring the current nineteenth-century educational model will need dedicated educators who can see the issues that distinguish the graded system from the nongraded system. It, too, will need parents to understand the difference between what they are used to—the graded system—and what may sound very different: the nongraded school. Best if parents can move beyond the formats' names and consider their own child bettering himself every day, smarter, more able, more excited about learning, more looking forward to returning to school. The advanced child will advance further. The low-achieving child will feel what it's like to achieve and begin to achieve rapidly.

Because our student population has changed so dramatically from what it was centuries past, we need to consider a paradigm more suited to today's diverse children, one that is more agreeable to exceptional educators who guide the youngsters' learning. Making a change from old to new requires administrators, educators, and parents to know (and be able to articulate) the major differences between them.

See table 12.1 for a comparison of the aspects of nongraded and graded schools. In graded formatted classrooms, time and the passing of time are the constants in schooling. In nongraded schooling, *learning* has become the constant.[20] As Dr. Katherine Schweitzer described, in a multiage flexible nongraded setting,

> there are some whole group activities to build community, teacher-led groups for skills and assessment, student-led groups for supported practice, and dyads for mentoring and tutoring. There are very few instances where the entire group goes from one activity to another, which is a tremendous source of wasted time in the traditional [graded] classroom.[21]

Teachers as Individuals and as Team Members

Often, a team of teachers will work with a team of pupils who are grouped by readiness skills and regrouped frequently as their achievement/readiness skills advance. It's not uncommon to have multiage groupings where kids two years (or more) apart work together. Other times, multiage groups, again with similar readiness skills, pursue complex problem-solving activities in interdisciplinary thematic units.[23]

Kenneth Schatmeyer, a professor of teacher education at Wright State University, described "the beauty of the multiage approach." He told Priscilla Pardini,

> When you do away with grade levels, it forces teachers to look at the individual needs of each child. There's no research that shows that the graded [format] helps children at all. In fact, if anything, it's completely the antithesis of developmentally appropriate practice.[24]

NONGRADED CLASSROOMS: NO SILVER BULLET

Teachers as the mainstay of any education effort must possess what few noneducators appreciate, what the vast majority of us lack.

> In-depth knowledge of child development, thorough knowledge of different theories of learning, a large repertoire of instructional strategies, and the skills to design and modify (often on the spot) curriculum. Above all and without slipping an inch, [teachers] must be able to adapt instruction to the needs of individual learners and groups of children in their particular nongraded classroom.[25]

Table 12.1. The Difference between Nongraded and Graded Schools

Nongraded Schools	Graded Schools
Diverse skills are embraced. Instruction and materials are individualized.	Diverse skills are overlooked. All children receive the same instruction and same materials.
Should do is replaced by *what is*. *What is* represents the child's current strengths and current entering skills. All instructional programs are built on the child's current strengths; all children are provided the opportunity to advance beyond their current entering skills.	Children are instructed based on what they're expected to know in their current grade according to some local, state, or national standard. *Should know* represents a degree of achievement derived from performance of the majority of same-age children—the gauge used to instruct all the children. Talented youngsters and struggling youngsters are provided instruction designed for the class average.
Curriculum is child driven. Lessons are developed after children are assessed beginning school's first day. Lessons are directly related to a child's assessed skills. The outcome of Monday's lesson influences what the teacher provides on Tuesday.	Curriculum is driven by the calendar. Lessons are planned before kids arrive. Preplanned lesson plans are based on age/grade level assumptions that will not match some youngsters' skills. An individual pupil's performance has no impact on tomorrow's group lesson. The lesson is already written.
Progress is defined as daily improvement beyond each child's assessed entering skills.	*Progress* is often defined in comparison to other pupils' scores on standardized tests or summative tests administered many weeks after relevant lessons.
Nonstandardized criterion assessment occurs weekly if not daily. The assessments are used to build strategies, strengthen teachers' instruction, and solve curriculum errors. Practice quizzes are based on recently taught content. They provide near-immediate feedback to help students improve.[22] (They are our CRTs.)	School-wide standardized assessment occurs once or twice a year. Traditional summative tests every 6 weeks allow kids time to dig deeper academic holes for themselves. Statistically massaged percentile comparisons define achievements while providing neither teacher nor parent with timely, usable information if both wish to intercede on behalf of a bored or struggling child.
Children move through curriculum as fast and as far as they can go without time restraints.	Children move through curriculum according to teachers'/administrators' preplanned schedule and the school district's pre-drawn calendar.
Children work on materials based on skills they have mastered, and curriculum errors they currently make.	Children work on material whether or not they have mastered prerequisite skills or mastered the topic.
Success is defined as growth beyond measured entering (readiness) skills.	*Success* is defined by summative tests and by standardized test scores.

Nongraded Schools	Graded Schools
Ideally, team teachers are assigned to children with similar readiness skills. Children move to other teachers based on their advancing skillsets or areas where they are struggling.	Individual teachers are assigned to diverse group of students. Children—the advanced, the low achievers, and all others in between—remain with the same teacher, who presents the same lessons to all the pupils throughout school year.
Depending on the task, groupings will be either multi-aged, multiskilled youngsters or likely multiage youngsters with similar entering skills.	Groupings are same-age children with widely varying skillsets.

Source: Berwick, C. (2019). *What does research say about testing?* https://www.edutopia.org/article/what-does-research-say-about-testing

There's nothing magical about nongraded classrooms, multiage classrooms, or how we configure children within a classroom. Teachers and parents looking for the proverbial "silver bullet" will be sorely disappointed if grouping children is all that's considered necessary. Someone else in that classroom holds the position of key component, that is, teacher. Madeline Hunter reminded us, "A skilled teacher in any organizational scheme is better than a mediocre teacher in the best nongraded or team-taught school."[26]

Nongraded Overseas

We seem to be the last people in the civilized world to understand that the continuous progress of pupils is reflected in students' growth of knowledge, skills, and understanding, not movement through a predetermined sequence of curriculum levels.[27] For example, "in Australia, New Zealand, Netherlands, Finland, and Canada, with the highest literacy rates in the world, nongraded classrooms are common educational practice."[28]

Not Here at Home

Where once Kentucky and Oregon mandated nongraded primary units as vehicles for school improvement, and other state departments of education and school districts had in place or were considering the implementation of nongraded programs (e.g., Tennessee), nongraded public schools today *are* virtually absent from the American scene. Multiple reasons account for the absence of nongraded public schools.[29]

- No Child Left Behind's requirement that included high-stakes testing virtually eliminated the concept of nongraded, continuous progress. Standardized tests are grade-fixed and grade-inflexible.

- College-level instructors provided no extensive nongraded training programs for teachers and/or administrators. Many of these instructors had little to no knowledge of the nongraded approach.
- Most book publishers who sold schoolbooks designed for specific graded levels lobbied against nongraded schooling. They imagined book sales would decline, their profits more important than the kids' education.
- No general support from school systems for innovation and diversity in program offerings also took down the nongraded movement. Administrators made that decision. Nongraded instruction required too much time. It is easier administratively to fit all children in the same curriculum box—what was certain to yield poor test results, not to mention wrong interpretations of test results and kids' skills. The inferior test results reflect the inferior graded approach that insists on one curriculum for all.

Not to be overlooked, multiple teams of teachers need a variety of curriculum materials to be available within a nongraded approach. School district administrators ignore this need and opt for a set of texts for each grade level, leaving little funds for schools to purchase a variety of materials used with a complex variety of approaches—among them, integrated curriculum and mixed-age grouping of kids with common entering skills.[30] The absence of a nongraded alternative reflects the administrative convenience of the graded system, not its effectiveness. (See table 12.2.)

> A different way to learn is what the kids are calling for. . . . All of them are talking about how one-size-fits-all delivery system—which mandates that everyone learn the same thing at the same time, no matter what their individual needs—has failed them.[31]

Table 12.2. How Diverse Curriculum Needs Are Handled in Graded vs. Nongraded Classrooms

Graded	Nongraded
In a graded formatted classroom, a youngster with curriculum needs above or below the teacher's presented lesson is fixed in place, the youngster's overextended teacher with virtually no time to accommodate the curriculum needs of each diverse youngster. With the teacher's hands tied by the graded format, some children—privileged and underprivileged, advanced and struggling—languish.	In a nongraded formatted school, youngsters with diverse curriculum needs move to multiple, flexible groups with youngsters possessing similar skills to be with multiple teachers who possess skills to help all the youngsters advance, the youngster's designated "grade level" not relevant. What remains relevant is the progress each youngster makes beyond his or her current entering skills.

Mandated Individualizing

By establishing Public Law 94–142 in 1975, the U.S. congress showed it could pass noble laws, thanks almost exclusively to the strenuous efforts of parents and teachers who were fed up with children being treated inadequately by schools. While the emphasis of the law concerned youngsters with disabilities, it did not escape the attention of many in the field of general education that the special education teacher's specific training—a host of acquired technical skills, along with their sensitivity to each youngster's strengths—should be required of the general educator as well.

Professors John Goodland and Robert Anderson wrote,

> It would fall to landmark legislation to force nongradedness into the public schools. The 1975 PL 94–142, (the 94th congress, the 142nd bill) established forcefully that each child, being unique, must be given learning opportunities logically related to a carefully assembled definition and assessment of his or her needs and possibilities. That the law focused upon exceptional children was a long-overdue correction, but the relevance of both the assumptions and the requirements of this law to *all* children should not be lost upon educators. The type of training required of teachers, counselors, administrators, and other involved professionals in "special education" can and should become the standard in "regular" education as well.[32]

Personalized Learning and a Nongraded Format

Consider the following as it pertains to all schoolkids. The approach has the name "personalized learning."[33] It's designed for a nongraded format.

> "Personalized learning" is an educational approach that aims to customize learning for each student's strengths, needs, skills, and interests. . . . To get an idea of what personalized learning is, try to picture a classroom that doesn't have a "one size fits all" approach to education. The teacher doesn't lead all students through the same lessons [because] students learn some skills at different rates. Instead, the teacher guides each student on an individualized journey. The what, when, where and how of learning is tailored to meet each student's strengths, skills, needs, and interests. Kids learn in different ways and at different paces. Personalized learning is a teaching model based on that premise.
>
> Teachers check to see if students are demonstrating the skills they're expected to learn as they progress through their education. Teachers keep an up-to-date record that provides a deep understanding of each student's individual strengths, needs, motivations, progress and goals. These profiles are updated far more often than a standard report card. And these detailed updates help teachers make decisions that favorably impact student learning.

A learner's profile also helps students keep track of their own progress. It gives the teacher, the student, and the parent a way to know if they need to change a learning method or make changes to goals—*before* the student does poorly or fails.

[Teachers] continually assesses students to monitor their progress toward specific goals. This system makes it clear to students what they need to master. The student might work on several competencies at the same time. When they master one, they move on to the next. Each student gets the necessary support or services to help master the skills. The emphasis isn't on taking a test and getting a passing or failing grade. Instead, it's about continuous learning and having many chances to show knowledge.[34]

Caveat

The phrase "It's about continuous learning and having many chances to show knowledge"—embroider that axiom on a pennant, and let that greet all who enter the school building. FYI: "Personalized learning" was designed with special education students in mind, youngsters for whom PL 94–142 was written. Would you think the approach would be valuable for most if not all schoolkids?

BLENDING GRADED AND NONGRADED APPROACHES

Educator Joan Gaustad argued,

> The nongraded school provides for the irregular upward progression that is characteristic of almost every child. Children do not advance evenly, a year of graded accomplishment for a year of living and schooling. They [surge] and stop, regress and advance at varying speeds in both their general and specific development, each child irregularly. The skills of the children enrolled, not the arbitrary designation of grade-level expectancy [e.g., third grade], determine vertical pupil placement and progress.[35]

In 1983, Plano, a suburb north of Dallas, a fairly traditional lower-to upper-middle-class community, developed a nontraditional, continuous-progress approach to education. Although the district maintained the usual first-, second-, and third-grade labels and found them useful for administrative purposes, the grade labels had little to do with the students' instructional level. Students are instructed where they are at each stage of their educational experience, not where someone says they "should be." "Progress extends along a continuum. Students progress at the pace most appropriate for them," explained Kathy Hargrave. "The continuous progress and nongraded models offer a direct approach to matching a student's learning skills with the subject matter taught in a classroom."[36] "The nongraded school encourages this kind of enjoyable learning, this kind of pupil progress."[37]

A NONGRADED SCHOOL: COLORADO

HEADLINES—February 2019

Listed job opening for the upcoming school year. School seeking an elementary teacher for either our multi-age K–1-or 2–3-grade students.[38]

Job Description
- Have a deep understanding and experience in elementary literacy education and intervention.
- Be able to differentiate and individualized learning plans to cater to student needs.
- Utilize data to drive instructional planning.
- Create lesson plans that go beyond the scope of the classroom (experiential learning).

Applicant Requirements
- Our new teacher forges strong mentor relationships with students.
- Our new teacher teaches language arts, mathematics, science, and social studies.
- Our new teacher provides strong early literacy education and interventions.
- Our new teacher is well versed in differentiated instruction and is passionate about meeting each student's needs.

Analysis

Please know that it isn't the particular school or its Colorado location or the school's diminutive size that matters. It's what the teachers and administrators and parents collectively have agreed to do—provide a multiage alternative to the traditional graded system, thereby bringing all the children into a productive and enjoyable educational world that promises each child a better shot at a bright future.

Unique Skills Sought

Of the many positive facets within the above job prerequisites, the importance of one may be missed by many parents and some public-school teachers, a number of both who know only the current graded system that is driven by a calendar date. This centerpiece prerequisite reads: "Utilize data to drive instructional planning."

Utilizing data to drive planning is not new. It's what every formal profession uses to hold itself accountable. Some educators are inclined to speak the words, though they lack an understanding of what *data-driven instruction* represents. Consider the following.

Data Based

James Lewis Jr. wrote,

> What could be more sensible than for a teacher to interview and test her individual students to determine their levels of achievement, ability, and interest *before* preparing a lesson plan which will be relevant to each youngster? Within the nongraded context, day-to-day plans, based on yesterday's class meeting, or yesterday's evaluation of individual progress, signifies a timely and effective education process.[39]

Data represents the child's (daily/weekly) measured achievement, her current acquired skills, what the child can do at or near 100% proficiency. Data represents what the classroom teacher (with time) *observes* and *measures* and *documents* throughout the week, every day, every week. Indispensable information is accumulated.

Instructional planning is driven by the data the child presents to the teacher, her responses to questions the teacher asks, exercises the teacher provides, and observed interactions the child has with classmates as they relate to functional skills. It tells the teacher what the child has learned and what within the curriculum causes the youngster to struggle. The teacher thusly observes the "outcomes" of her current, daily instruction. The teacher will query the youngster to reveal stumbling blocks and will modify often immediately her instructional strategies based on what she observes and assesses. Recall Charlotte Danielson's insistence: "I don't see how you can responsibly say anything other than you have to be flexible and teach students what they have the background to learn. Otherwise, you're setting them up for failure."[40] That's data-driven instructional planning in action.

SCHOOLS: VERTICAL RISE, HORIZONTAL FOOTINGS

"Nongrading is designed to encompass the realities of individual differences. Cooperative and team teaching represents the most promising means of organizing a school *horizontally* with multiple teachers in (multiple) classrooms teaching to varied skills levels."[41] (The multiple classrooms represent different "stations," classrooms throughout the school where kids visit during the school day for specific instruction that fits the child's current skill level. Each "station" is designed to advance the diverse youngsters' different skill sets, most frequently involving reading and mathematical instruction. The arrangement puts an end to curriculum mismatches.)

> The ideal school, then, from an organization standpoint, is one that practices nongrading *vertically* so a child can progress up the skill sequence continuously during the school year as far and as fast as skills permit, and team teaching *horizontally* allowing for multiple classes [stations] to cover multiple facets of subject matter.[42]

Each classroom is designed to meet the different instructional needs and varying entering skills of the diverse schoolkids, what represents the hallmark of nongraded schools.

THE IMPORTANCE OF EARLY SCHOLASTIC ACCOMPLISHMENT

We don't get endless chances to win a child over to learning. In truth, the effort can be snuffed out almost as easily as we douse a candle's small flame. At home, we're way ahead if we can get our child started on a successful note as soon as possible, pre-preschool, if not sooner. Let the youngster casually discover through play or while exploring new experiences that he is a *good* learner, that he *can do* rather than can't do. It's an attitude that serves the youngster well. Success at something is essential for all children. Its absence can be devastating. For a child already stung by frustration at school, already predicting failure, success at a new starting point is critical.

Done right, nongraded, multiage schools are efficient, effective, and child friendly. Whether a child is comfortable as one of the crowd or stands out with unique interests and/or skills, whether a child is leaps ahead or multiple steps behind other youngsters who share education's diverse classrooms, the child's individuality and acquired skill level will be honored and accommodated in a correctly managed nongraded school. In nongraded schools, children are expected to improve on what they know, not fight endlessly with what they don't know. Kathleen Cotton, a researcher in the Northwest Regional Educational laboratory, stated,

While students of any age can be grouped in nongraded clusters, it is nongraded *primary* instruction that is the focus of most current [1960s] interest and activity. This is because research on young children (those eight years old and younger) has revealed that the educational practices most beneficial to these children can best be delivered—and in some cases can *only* be delivered-in nongraded structures.[43]

PROVIDING TEACHERS AN OPTION: A MIDDLE GROUND

If a schoolchild has a quality teacher in a *grade-formatted* classroom, that teacher will be limited to basically one lesson plan designed for all the same-age children who share the same room. Several children may succeed, while many others will be confounded in varying degrees by the teacher's narrowed instruction. Provide that same teacher a *nongraded multiage* format,

- Where that teacher shares lessons and materials and teams with colleagues or has the option to bring nongraded components into her self-contained classroom;
- Where placement within small clusters is flexible and fluid and based on readiness;
- Where that teacher and all colleagues use differentiated instruction to accommodate each youngster's uniqueness;
- Where all the children proceed at their own pace; and
- Where children focus on bettering themselves . . . most (if not all) the youngsters, thanks to the nongraded format, will enjoy continuous progress beyond their original entering skills. That's academic growth.

Advantages

Multiple scholars and practitioners have researched the advantages the nongraded format provides school youngsters and their teachers.

- Since a child may excel in one curricular area and simultaneously have difficulty in another, children are able to work without interruption at different developmental levels, thus avoiding the social or emotional damage typically caused by retention.
- Students often stay with their teacher(s) for more than one year; thus, teachers get to know students well and provide for continuity in their learning.

- Nongraded grouping lends itself to the use of validated practices such as cooperative learning and cross-age tutoring.
- Nongraded arrangements are much more in keeping with the way young children grow and learn.[44]

And for teachers,

- The team teaching and family-like atmosphere typical of nongraded programs leads to increased job satisfaction for teachers.[45]

The enormous advantages gleaned from the nongraded approach challenges us to find some middle ground that allows the methodology to work its way into today's graded classrooms, especially the early years. Educators Lillian Clogau and Murray Fessel, writing a half century ago,

> Pointed out the significance of nongrading as a means of overcoming and meeting the individual needs of the pupils. The philosophy of the nongraded program forces the classroom teacher to note the differences among children in a way the graded structure does not. If we accept the nongraded philosophy, each child is seen as an individual with special needs, problems, hopes and learning rates. If the teacher recognizes and accepts these differences then she begins to make changes in her curriculum, her patterns of interacting with her pupils, her teaching techniques, her evaluations, and her instructional materials in order to accommodate these differences.[46]

A Teacher's Blended Classroom

Once more, please review the earlier presented components representing a nongraded classroom within a nongraded school. Take a moment to consider which of the following *you* could incorporate in your classroom. If you choose only one, if you're able to follow through with that one even with a single youngster, you will have changed the educational system at least for that child. If you gather your colleagues and meet collectively with the principal to discuss all that follows, you will have taken an important step toward modifying the educational system for your school. If you're able to set up a meeting with the schoolchildren's parents where you can discuss much that follows while at the same time fielding their certain questions, you will win over some of those parents who want the educational system changed.

Components and rationale to be shared:

- Age and grade-level will no longer dictate curriculum; this is because both are poor predictors of what curriculum a child needs.

- Each child's curriculum is individualized and based on the child's readiness that is assessed prior to instruction; this is because readiness is more accurate than age or grade level when it comes to assigning curriculum. The beneficial outcome: fewer to no curriculum mismatches impeding the child.
- Each child's learning is briefly assessed after instruction allowing for instructional modification, for example, exit cards, 3-minute CRT; this is because this type of formative assessment provides the accountable teacher the wherewithal to consider his or her goals and his or her instructional methods, what of each might warrant modification to better assist the youngsters.
- Teachers and their instruction are established to accommodate pupils' ever-changing readiness skills; this is because different daily experiences can change a youngster's skills dramatically.
- Gathered multi-age youngsters based on similar readiness skills are clustered in ever-changing flexible skill-groupings and instructed by an individual teacher or teams of teachers with specialized talents, for example, reading, mathematics, science, and so on; this is because children with similar skills make better progress when taught together, and children with disparate skills on topics that warrant different viewpoints—guided by a strong teacher—can learn much from each other.
- Differentiated instruction is the rule rather than the exception; this is because differentiated instruction applied in a nongraded educational system is an essential and proven instructional approach that accommodates the diversity that characterizes our country's school population.
- Pupils work on assignments and projects that suit their skill readiness level rather than working on what all other same-age students are assigned; this is because unlike the graded system that wrongly sees each child as equal in skills and learning rates, nongraded promotes the individual child with his or her unique individual strengths and weaknesses.
- Pupils are challenged to better themselves academically rather than better their classmates; this is because kids neither start at the same mile marker as they proceed toward goals, nor do they progress with equal speed. Each one can experience a sense of success by the growth that is made. Academically, it's better to better oneself.
- With self-constructed line graphs pupils learn to track their own progress over time with reading, spelling, mathematics, and other subject areas assigned by their teachers; this is because seeing the upward projection of the growth curve can provide many a child a sense of accomplishment, for many a strong incentive and reason to keep working hard. "I can do this," the graph shows. A flat line or a decelerated projection

can, with teacher support, spur the child to make improvements. There's considerable science that supports this view.[47]
- Pupils are encouraged to learn as much as they can as fast as they can; this is because the grade-formatted system intentionally erects multiple "stop signs" just when the child wants to go forward, that is, "wait for your classmates to catch up."
- Teachers are available to any pupil who needs more help or more challenge with curriculum; this is because in the nongraded system every child is eligible for assistance; lengthy, time-consuming petitioning for help under adversarial conditions isn't necessary (or beneficial). Consider lawyer Pam Wright's red-flag youngster. He would have been assisted the first moment he began to falter with his language arts.
- Critical thinking, problem-solving, analyzing, and collaboration are infused in all basic studies; this is because each of those skills improves the overall academic (and daily functional) performance of all children and helps youngsters make better life-oriented choices.
- Continuous progress replaces grade retention; this is because no child has ever benefited from being held back and having to face the same curriculum provided in the same manner. The only possible exception is when a parent chooses to wait a year before sending his or her eligible child off to kindergarten, what's called "redshirting"—that is, the child is provided "the gift of time." What parents may not know, "redshirting may do more harm than good." So suggested Diane Whitmore Schanzenbach, a Northwestern University education professor and Stephanie Howard Larson, director of Rose Hall Montessori School.[48]
- Assessment is formative, ongoing, criterion-based, individualized, diagnostic, and non-standardized; this is because all of the different assessment approaches occur many times during the school year, and each and all provide teachers the information they need to modify their lessons and instruction when necessary, what standardized tests are not designed to do.
- Year-end assessments based on material covered by classroom teachers are drawn from teacher-made CRTs; this is because the CRTs assess what the teacher has taught. Standardized tests assess what the distant test publisher thinks the teacher has taught. The difference between the two can be significant.
- Standardized year-end assessments are optional; this is because it's good to have a choice.
- Progress is reported in terms of tasks completed not by arbitrary letter grades or rating scales[49]; this is because grades are subjective and often have very little to do with what a child has done in the classroom. Percentile rankings are massaged statistics that have little functional use

in a classroom or in the child's home. Tasks and projects are quantifiable in their own right, activities that can be observed and measured. They are "permanent products," often what a youngster brings home for a parent's inspection, a piece of paper with problems attempted, words practiced, sentences written, questions answered, alphabet letters written—correctly and incorrectly, or a diorama filled with colorful figures and animals that tell a great story. The active parent wants more than a note or email indicating, "Your child had a good day"; more than learning, "Mary scored as well as the typical student in a national group in the spring of the fourth grade." That parent wants to know specifically what the child was asked to complete, what he practiced, what new task he tried.

- Earned free time is set aside for pupils to work on projects based on their special interests and passions providing teachers time with other youngsters; this is because it's fun and it promotes the child's creative juices.
- No school calendars and no classroom clocks impede teachers' instruction; this is because we want teachers to have the time they need to accomplish what they deem important. No yokes; not cuffs; no roadblocks.

If you're an educational administrator, know that the following questions were raised 50 years ago in preparation to incorporate nongraded principles into the classroom,[50] questions that still need answering if we wish to change some of what we're doing:

- Do we have clear statements of our instructional objectives organized in a realistic sequence and covering the entire span of our program?
- Do we have a sufficient variety of instructional materials on different levels of sophistication so that each teacher can adjust instruction to the range of ability [entering skills] found in each classroom?
- Are we able to move toward greater individualization of instruction so that pupils can actually progress at individual rates?
- Are we willing to use grouping practices that are flexible enough to allow easy movement from group to group within a class, or from class to class within a school?
- Do we have evaluation devices based on our instructional objectives that will provide clear evidence of pupil attainments and facilitate our decisions on grouping and progress?
- Are we finally ready to do something about children's individual differences we have so long "recognized" and have so thoroughly ignored?[51]

RESEARCH AND THE NONGRADED FORMAT

Every effort to incorporate the working components associated with a nongraded/ungraded paradigm into the current graded approach should be made. Several reasons dominate. Historically,

> Looking at the entire array of literature growing out of recent educational research [1950s–1980s], there is simply no research that says graded structure is desirable, or, for that matter, that single-age class groupings and/or self-contained classrooms are to be preferred. . . . A literally graded approach to instruction does not work [not with today's diverse kids]. [Quality] teachers and administrators must constantly subvert it in order to deal with the realities of individual differences. Compromise, invention, adaptation, and disregard for grade level standards are invariably practiced in graded schools, even though many teachers probably do not realize fully how unfaithful to gradedness they find it necessary to be in their daily work with children.[52]

The research division of the National Education Association in 1965 published their perspective on a nongraded approach:

- Children's progress in learning is greater and more continuous.
- Flexibility in grouping has succeeded in fitting the educational program more closely to the needs and maturity of the individual child.
- The slower [and more advanced] children are identified earlier.
- The high pupil-teacher morale.
- There is increased teamwork between teachers, and between parents and teachers.
- Curriculum takes on new meaning.[53]

The 1965 Delgado-Marcano study found the following:

- In the fully nongraded school, [diverse] children were placed in large multi-aged groups, and provisions for individualized and small group instruction were made according to the educational task.
- In the fully nongraded school, major curriculum revisions were initiated in order to satisfy the needs of individual pupils.
- In the fully nongraded school, children were encouraged to learn how to learn on their own through individualized instruction and independent study.
- In the fully nongraded schools the shifting of children within instructional groups or between classrooms was the routine not the exception.

- In the fully nongraded schools team teaching permitted a greater depth in planning for instruction which led to more efficient utilization of the teaching staff as well as to facilitate the continuous progress of the learner.
- In the fully nongraded school the role of the teacher changed from a position of instructor to that of a guide, counselor or helper.[54]

PERSPECTIVES

The National Education Association Instruction, in 1963, wrote,

> The vertical organization of the school [from entrance to graduation] should provide for the continuous, unbroken, upward progression of all learners, with due recognition of the wide variability among learners in every aspect of their development.[55]

B. A. Ritzenhein explained,

> In nongraded organizations, grouping for instructional purposes was more flexible and was not associated with chronological placement of learners. Nongraded grouping practices, based on planning for continuous, sequential growth, tend to encourage increased pupil achievement and improved pupil attitude.[56]

Luther B. Rogers and William F. Breivogel agreed: "Once the concept of 'one teacher, four walls of a classroom, and thirty children' is broken, many possibilities in flexible grouping is possible."[57]

Conclusion

Beyond administrative convenience, the nineteenth-century graded system never provided any educational benefit to the enrolled children. John Goodlad and Robert Anderson (1987) wrote, "In the best of all [educational] worlds, elementary-age children would be educated within a team-taught, multiage, nongraded format" where "the unique needs, interest, abilities, and learning rates, styles and patterns of each child will determine his or her individual curriculum."[58]

NOTES

1. Schweitzer, K. (n.d.). *Considering the community classroom.* https://www.aasa.org/content.aspx?id=29258

2. Miller, R. I. (1967). *The nongraded school: Analysis and study.* Harper & Row, p. 131.

3. Cuban, L. (2019, January 18). *Whatever happened to the nongraded school?* [Blog post]. https://larrycuban.wordpress.com/2019/01/18/whatever-happened-to-the-non-graded-school (emphasis added).

4. Goodlad, J. I., & Anderson, R. H. (1987). *The non-graded elementary school.* Teachers College Press.

5. Lewis Jr., J. (1969). *A contemporary approach to nongraded education.* Parker Publishing, p. 211.

6. Goodlad & Anderson (1987).

7. Pavan, B. N. (1992). The benefits of nongraded schools. *Educational Leadership, 50*(2), 22–25. http://www.ascd.org/publications/educational-leadership/oct92/vol50/num02/The-Benefits-of-Nongraded-Schools.aspx

8. Gaustad, J. (1994). Nongraded education: Overcoming obstacles to implementing the multiage classroom. Oregon School Study Council. https://files.eric.ed.gov/fulltext/ED379744.pdf

9. Wright, P. (2017). *Waiting to fail instead of teaching a child to read.* https://www.wrightslaw.com/info/read.wait.fail.htm

10. Borrowed from Goodlad & Anderson (1987), p. 1.

11. Lewis (1969).

12. Gaustad (1994).

13. Quoted in DePaul, A. (1998). *What to expect your first year teaching.* https://www2.ed.gov/PDFDocs/whatexpect.pdf, p. 3.

14. Goodlad & Anderson (1987).

15. Lewis (1969).

16. Goodlad & Anderson (1987).

17. Stone, S. J. (2012). *The multi-age classroom: What research tells the practitioner.* https://pdfs.semanticscholar.org/0104/629b44ff0ce14eb25b41762e7dd1cd506222.pdf

18. Pavan (1992).

19. Brummitt-Yale, J. (2018). *What is diagnostic assessment?* https://study.com/academy/lesson/what-is-diagnostic-assessment-definition-examples.html; Tookoian, J. (2018). *What is diagnostic assessment?* https://edulastic.com/blog/diagnostic-assessment

20. Hunter, M. (1992). *How to change to a nongraded school.* ASCD. Cited in Stone, S.J. (2004). *Creating the multi-age classroom.* Good Year Books. https://books.google.com/books?id=0gJWvMefGooC&pg=PA266&lpg=PA266&dq=Hunter,+M

21. Schweitzer (n.d.).

22. Berwick, C. (2019). *What does research say about testing?* https://www.edutopia.org/article/what-does-research-say-about-testing

23. Pavan (1992).

24. Pardini, P. (2008). *The slowdown of the multiage classroom.* https://www.aasa.org/SchoolAdministratorArticle.aspx?id=8720

25. Gaustad (1994).

26. Hunter (1992).

27. See also Katz, L. (1995). *The benefits of mixed-age grouping.* ERIC Clearinghouse on Elementary and Early Childhood Education.

28. Kreide, A. (2011). *Literacy achievement in nongraded classrooms* [Unpublished doctoral dissertation]. Loyola Marymount University.

29. Rice, J. C. (2015). *Where have all the nongraded schools and classrooms gone?* https://www.joecrice.com/blog/2015/5/27/q8imbcuterglbtylskklgkvruynlcb

30. Bredkamp, S. (Ed.). (1987). Developmentally appropriate practice in early childhood programs serving children from birth through age 8. National Association for the Education of Young Children.

31. Sarason, S. (1990). *The predictable failure of educational reform: Can we change course before it's too late?* Jossey-Bass.

32. Goodlad & Anderson (1987).

33. Morin, A. (n.d.). *Personalized learning: What you need to know.* https://www.understood.org/articles/en/personalized-learning-what-you-need-to-know

34. Morin (n.d.).

35. Goodlad & Anderson (1987).

36. Goodlad & Anderson (1987).

37. Goodlad & Anderson (1987).

38. *Charter schools are innovative public schools.* (n.d.). https://www.publiccharters.org/

39. Lewis (1969).

40. Pipkin, C. (2013, March 4). *Charlotte Danielson on Teaching and the Common Core.* http://www.schoolimprovement.com/common-core-360/blog/common-core-standards-charlotte-danielson/

41. Goodlad & Anderson (1987).

42. Goodlad & Anderson (1987).

43. Cotton, K. (1993). *Nongraded primary education.* https://educationnorthwest.org/sites/default/files/NongradedPrimaryEducation.pdf

44. Cotton (1993).

45. Cotton (1993).

46. Clogau, L., & Fessel, M. (1967). *The nongraded primary school. A case study.* Parker Publishing.

47. See Discriminative stimulus. (2002). In *Encyclopedia of Psychotherapy.* https://www.sciencedirect.com/topics/psychology/discriminative-stimulus

48. Schanzenbach, D. W., & Larson, S. H. (2017). *Is your child ready for kindergarten? Redshirting may do more harm than good.* https://www.educationnext.org/is-your-child-ready-kindergarten-redshirting-may-do-more-harm-than-good

49. Pavan (1992).

50. Carbone, R. F. (1962, November). A comparison of graded and nongraded elementary schools. *Elementary School Journal, 62.*

51. Miller (1967).

52. Goodlad & Anderson (1987).

53. Survey performed by the Research Division of the National Education Association, 1965.

54. Rogers, L. B., & Breivogel, W. F. (1968). *The nongraded school.* Gainesville: Florida Educational Research and Development Council.

55. National Education Association Projection Instruction. (1963). *Schools for the sixties.* McGraw-Hill, p. 132.

56. Ritzenhein, B. A. (1963). Survey of personnel perceptions of selected factors in nongraded programs in eight Detroit elementary schools [Unpublished doctoral dissertation]. Wayne State University.

57. Rogers & Breivogel (1969).

58. Goodlad & Anderson (1987), p. xvi.

Closing Thoughts

The American educational system has been what it's been for so long that it doesn't know how to be anything different. It's managed by so many managers on so many different levels that it's no longer manageable by anyone on any level. It has the sensitivity of a fistful of knuckles and the subtlety and finesse of a deadweight 220,000-ton freighter adrift without a rudder much less a helmsman. Because it *is*; it goes, aimlessly, retracing the same route at the same pace ever since it came to be in the mid-nineteenth century.

It's infatuated with the word *should*, a first cousin to *ought to*. It cowers in the face of *what is*. It blames others for wrongs, deflects criticism when it's hurled, and pleads ignorance whenever it suits itself—and it suits itself often. But for the glimmer of light found in the fewest of most fortunate places, the public school system established to educate public schoolchildren is a categorical mess. In a country that touts itself as great, this system overlooks schoolchildren who don't fit its fabricated template—a standard that in today's America rejects more than it includes. We can't count on the system to change itself; its legs have been stuck in its own gooey inertia for eons. *Someone* needs to show up before schoolkids find themselves an alternative to the tired, futile "one size fits all."

JUMP SHIP

But here's what you need to know. Anyone on board this stiff-necked pedagogical vessel can clandestinely jump ship—that is, anyone can quietly modify the parochial system to better suit the kids and their mentor. Politely flip the little bird and exclaim, "Not for me! I'm no longer abiding. Lots of wrongs, lots that needs changing." Jump anytime while you wait for those someones to step forth:

- A grade-formatted disenchanted school principal who knows better, who's seen what the current format has produced, who's not afraid to fight the past's single-minded "keep things as they are," who's called together a like-minded group that has covertly met and decided the status quo must give way to innovation for all kids;
- A school board that has analyzed the local curriculum casualties, that has cleared itself from all political influences, that has chosen to do what it's charged to do: look after the schoolkids' education;
- An energized assemblage of American parents, a group in concert from all walks including every layer of social fabric, each ready to support each other, each with stories of school missteps, each determined to guarantee their children the gift of learning, each ready to enlist hundreds more parents who have had the same experiences, all together with voices that will not be drowned out;
- A seasoned, respected teacher's college educational dean who accepts that teacher-prep programs need to shed their nineteenthth-century mentality, to convince responsible public school administrators to do the same, to visit the state house and convince relevant politicians to join in the movement to produce a more effective, forward-thinking, accountable school system that monitors itself and its outcomes, that assures all children *will* be more learned today than they were yesterday.

And you. Yes, you. You've studied hard. You've sought out the best college professors, interviewed them first before registering for class, pressed them to tell you their experience, their agenda, and their course content. You've taken every course that makes you better, stronger, more informed, summer school three years straight, online courses throughout the year. Beginning your third year, when not in class or the library, you ventured to a local K–6 school and found active teachers who adopted you and invited you to participate, professionals who, after learning of your accelerated personally initiated coursework, have allowed you to run small separate (supervised) math groups—one designed for low-achievers, the other high-achieving kids—to read stories to the whole group of first-graders and lead a discussion afterward, to introduce simple, safe, fun science experiments with eager kindergarteners. The experience has bolstered you beyond anything you imagined.

You know yourself. You're a problem-solver. You're conscientious and determined. You will become a teacher to make changes, to make a difference, to ensure all kids know more today than they knew yesterday. That's all kids—the advanced, those who currently struggle, and all the others in between, even the ones who've intentionally stepped on your dainty toes. You'll win those kids over.

You're aware that the current graded format will mince you (and most other teachers) as if you were a coffee bean in a coffee grinder. You're ready to tackle that system, to drum up support for blending nongraded components into your classroom. Once inside the school, having cleared it with your equally determined principal, you intend to find others like you, to get a team together immediately, different grade levels above and below yours to accommodate kids who need what others can better provide. No more solo isolation madness.

And, of course, the basics:

- No assigning curriculum by age or grade level.
- No assigning lessons without knowing the kids' entering skills.
- Formative assessment and differential instruction and error analysis every day.
- CRTs by the bucket-load.
- Homework that builds on skills.
- If a youngster doesn't move up the curriculum ramp, that's your business, your responsibility. It's your strategy. You'll need to change what you're doing, on the spot, no excuses. You're up for that.
- Squeezing everything into a 12–16-hour workday when 30 hours might not be enough. That's your job; there are no jobs more important. There's no job you want more.
- It's the kids' and everyone's future we're talking about.

Bibliography

Beggs III, D., & Burfie, E. G. (1967). *Nongraded schools in action.* Indiana University Press.

Berman, S. (2008). *Performance-based learning: Aligning experiential tasks and assessment to increase learning.* Corwin Press.

Brookhart, S. M. (2010). *Formative assessment strategies for every classroom.* ASCD.

Danielson, C. (2007). *Enhancing professional practice: A framework for teaching* (2nd ed.). ASCD.

Darling-Hammon, L., Falk, B., & Ancess, J. (1995). *Authentic assessment in action: Studies of schools and students at work.* Teachers College Press.

Dintersmith, T. (2018). *What school could be like.* Princeton University Press.

Doubet, K. J., & Hockett, J. A. (2017). *Differentiation in the elementary grades: Strategies to engage and equip all learners.* ASCD.

Fisher, D., & Frey, N. (2014). *Checking for understanding: Formative assessment techniques for your classroom* (2nd ed.). ASCD.

Fisher, M. (2015). *Ditch the daily lesson plan: How do I plan for meaningful student learning?* ASCD Arias.

Frey, N., & Fisher, D. (2011). *The formative assessment action plan: Practical steps to more successful teaching and learning.* ASCD.

Gaustad, J. (1992). *Nongraded primary education.* ERIC Digest, Number 74. ERIC Identifier: ED347637. National Association of Elementary School Principals; U.S. Department of Education, Office of Educational Research and Improvement, Educational Resources Information Center.

Goodlad, J. I., & Anderson, R. H. (1987) *The nongraded elementary school* (rev. ed.). Teachers College Press.

Hunter, M. (1992). *How to change to a nongraded school.* ASCD.

Idol, L., Nevin, A., & Paolucci-Whitcomb, P. (1996). *Models of curriculum-based assessment* (2nd ed.). Pro-Ed.

Koretz, D. (2008). *Measuring up: What educational testing really tells us.* Harvard University Press.

Kreide, A. (2011). *Literacy achievement in nongraded classrooms* [Unpublished doctoral dissertation]. Loyola Marymount University.

Lewis Jr., J. (1969). *A contemporary approach to nongraded education*. Parker Publishing.

Merrow, J. (2017). *Addicted to reform: A 12-step program to rescue public education*. The New Press.

Moss, C. M., & Brookhart., S. M. (2019). *Advancing formative assessment in every classroom: A guide for instructional leaders* (2nd ed.). ASCD.

Payne, C. (2008). *So much reform, so little change*. Harvard Education.

Popham, W. J. (2008). *Transformative assessment*. ASCD.

Rodberg, S. (2020). *What if I'm wrong? And other key questions for decisive school leadership*. ASCD.

Sarason, S. (1990). *The predictable failure of educational reform: Can we change course before it's too late?* Jossey-Bass.

Sarason, S. (2003). *The skeptical visionary* (R. L. Fried, Ed.). Temple University Press.

Schneider, J. (2017). *Beyond test scores: A better way to measure school quality*. Harvard University Press.

Shepard, L. A. (2005, October 10–11). *Formative assessment: Caveat emptor*. The Future of Assessment: Shaping Teaching and Learning (ETS Invitational Conference), New York. https://citeseerx.ist.psu.edu/viewdoc/download?doi=10.1.1.1041.7434&rep=rep1&type=pdf

Tomlinson, C. A. (2017). *How to differentiate instruction*. ASCD.

Tomlinson, C. A., & Allan, S. D. (2000). *Leadership for differentiating schools & classrooms*. ASCD.

Tomlinson, C. A., & Moon, T. R. (2013). *Assessment and student success in a differentiated classroom*. ASCD.

Wagner, T. (2015). *Most likely to succeed*. Scribner.

Index

Abernathy, Gary, 6
ability differences, 37–38, 67–68, 126, 128, 131, 138, 153
academic acceleration, 183; of kindergarten, 173–74, 176; of preschool, 174, 176
achievement gains, from formative assessments, 113
achievement gap, 6, 19
ACT. *See* American College Test
active intervention, 187
Adams, Christy, 40
administrators, 105; of graded system, 167; lumping regarding, 59, 60; nongraded components regarding, 205–6
Advanced Placement Calculus BC course, 11
age-based curriculum, 49, 166–67, 171
Algozzine, Bob, 94
Allan, Susan Demirsky, 125–26
Allman, Carol, 82
American College Test (ACT), 76
American Psychological Association (APA), 54, 115
Anderson, Robert, 9; on ability differences, 128; on diverse students, 185; on graded system, 52; on nongraded system, 207; on Public Law 94–142, 196
Anderson, Robert H., 168
APA. *See* American Psychological Association
Asmar, Melanie, 19
Aspen Council, 164
assembly line, 156
The Atlantic, 174
attitudes: education system shift of, 176–77; toward error analysis, 101; nongraded system shift in, 190–91

babies, 39, 40
bait, 100–101
Baltimore grade level proficiencies, 19, 48
Baltimore Sun, 19
Beech, Marty, 82
Benedikt, Allison, 112
Bennett, William, 73
Berezin, Robert, 41
Berliner, David, 3
Billet, Leonard, 161
Black, Paul, 109
Black families: on in-person learning, 114; technology access regarding, 115
blended classroom, 200–205

Bokas, Arina, 38
Boles, Katherine, 169–70
Booth, William, 171
Bosher, Bill, 56–57
Boundless.com, 54
boys: in Chicago third grade, 55–56; observation of, 126–27
Bradshaw, Wendy, 31–32
brains: of babies, 40; child development influenced by, 40, 41; of children, 41; speech center in, 42
Brizard, Jean-Claude, 5
Bush, George W., administration, 4

calendar-driven curriculum, 177–78
California, 53
Canning, Kristen, 137
Cardona, Miguel, 1
Carver, George Washington, 3
Casserly, Michael, 86
CBAs. *See* curriculum-based assessments
charter school, 19, 159
Chetty, Raj, 6
Chicago, 55–56
child, "typical," 73, 129
child development: brain influencing, 40, 41; child activeness influencing, 40–41; cognitive development, 127; differences of, 189; disadvantages for, 39; peer utility for, 54
children: brains of, 41; differences in, 39–40, 41; standardized tests stress for, 69
Christakis, Erika, 174
class, CRTs beginning, 93
classmates, 56, 90
classroom: blended, 200–205; hypothetical, 67–68, 69; mixed-ability, 138
Clogau, Lillian, 202
clusters, 201; differentiated instruction, 138–39, 140, 141; entering skills regarding, 141–42; personalization with, 141

Coghlan, Erin, 119
cognitive development, 127
Cole, Kristen, 137–38
college, teacher-prep, 49, 212
Collis, Victoria, 115–16
Colorado, 200
commission error, 99
Common Core standards, 69, 104–5, 183
competency-based education, 53
conception, 39
conceptual errors, 102–3
Connecticut, Hartford, 5
constructs, 103
Consults, Welda, 137
"conveyor belt," 134–35
Cook, Steve, 119
Copperman, Paul, 1
Cottle, Thomas J., 18
Cotton, Kathleen, 200–201
COVID-19. *See* pandemic
Cox, Abigail, 60–61
Cox, Janelle, 139, 140
Cox, June, 52
Crew, Rudy, 23
crisis, education, 23
criterion-referenced tests (CRTs), 96; class beginning with, 93; for diverse students, 83–84; for entering skills, 89, 92; examples of, 92; information provided by, 85–86; for math skills, 88–91; in nongraded system, 203, 204; parents performing, 87; reading levels, 85; school day ended with, 91; standardized tests compared to, 86–87; teachers administering, 93; for vocabulary, 100–101
Cromer (Lord), 103–4
CRTs. *See* criterion-referenced tests
Cuban, Larry, 184
curriculum: accommodation, 48; by age, 49, 166–67, 171; calendar-driven, 177–78; child-centered approach for, 160; personalization of, 10, 38, 43; "playlist," 135

curriculum-based assessments (CBAs), 91; for diverse students, 83–84; teachers informed by, 82–83
Curriculum Development Institute, 38
curriculum mismatches, 11, 12, 47; calendar-driven curriculum causing, 177–78; formative assessment identifying, 107–8

Dallas, Plano, 197–98
Danielson, Charlotte, 111, 199
Darling-Hammond, Linda, 4, 70
data-driven instructional planning, 198, 199
Delgado-Marcano study (1965), 206–7
Delisle, James: on differentiated instruction, 146–47; "Differentiation Doesn't Work" by, 146; on lumping, 59, 134
Department of Education, U.S. (ED), 81, 126
Detroit, 7–8
Dewey, John, 168
diagnostic assessment, x, 191
Dictionary.com, 55
differences: of child development, 189; in children, 39–40, 41; of peers, 49–50, 56–57. *See also* student differences
differentiated instruction: challenges of, 142–43; clusters, 138–39, 140, 141; Delisle on, 146–47; elements of, 133–34; flexible grouping for, 138–40; heterogeneous groups, 138–39, 141, 142; homogeneous groups, 138, 142; lumping regarding, 145, 146, 147; Mann, Larry, on, 132, 134; methodology of, 132–33; in nongraded system, 203; principal regarding, 144; purpose of, 134; Schmoker on, 145; student differences regarding, 133; teachers on, 143–44; time constraints on, 143; Tomlinson on, 133–34, 136, 137, 140–41; Willis on, 132, 134

"Differentiation Doesn't Work" (Delisle), 146
Dintersmith, Ted, 74–75
discrepancy model, 27–28
distance learning, 113–14
Dodge, Judith, 109–10
Doyle, William, 70
dyslexia, 28

Eberly Center, 111
ED. *See* Department of Education, US
Edmonds, Ronald R., 4
educational disability, 28–29; labels regarding, 95–96; parents on, 95
education opportunities: inequality, 18, 161, 162, 164; nongraded system maximizing, 191
education system, 51, 91, 105, 126; alternatives regarding, 153; attitude shift for, 176–77; change to, 183, 202; in Finland, 70, 95; growth-mindset shift in, 38; limitations of, 32, 44, 129, 211; lumping in, 61; mass-production compared to, 156, 166; no-fault system for, 92; pandemic standardized test decision of, 81–82; teachers impacted by, 161; time constraints imposed by, 48, 51, 108
Education Week, 60, 141
Education Week Commentary, 146
effective teacher, 31–32
egg crates, 47–48
elementary schools. *See specific topics*
English language learners, 71, 103, 172
entering skills: clusters regarding, 141–42; CRT for, 89, 92; student differences of, 136
error analysis, 89–90; attitudes toward, 101; for math skills, 99; for vocabulary, 100–101
error types: commission error, 99; conceptual errors, 102–3; mechanical error, 102; motivational error, 102; omission error, 99

Evans, Celia, 23
Exit Card: as formative assessment, 110; prompts for, 117

Facebook, 31–32
"false positives," for student underachievement, 25
Fatherly, 22
Fessel, Murray, 202
Finland, 70, 95
Finn, Chester, 20
"Flat Earth," 144
Fleming, Nora, 117
flexible grouping: for differentiated instruction, 138–40; in nongraded system, 187, 192, 203, 207
food scarcity, 115
Ford, Henry, 156
Fordham Institute, 143
Ford Motor Company, 156
formative assessments, 145, 204; achievement gains from, 113; curriculum mismatches identified by, 107–8; Exit Card as, 110; learning improvement from, 109; on math skills, 111; for personalization, 111; for remote learning, 116–17; time constraints regarding, 109; in Wilson Reading System, 110
Forstein, Char, 129
Fountas, Irene C., 85
fourth grade, 111
Francis, Lizzy, 22
freedom, education unlocking, 3
free time, earned, 205
Friedman, Milton, 161
funding: challenges besides, 84–85; inequality, 4–6; for nongraded system materials, 195; for special education, 94–95

Galston, William, 23
Ganem, Joseph, 75–76
Gaustad, Joan, 189, 197
genes, 40

Gentry, J. Richard, 26–27
Gerber, Howard, 61
girls: in Chicago third grade, 55–56; error analysis for, 100–101; IEP meeting for, 88–89
Godsey, Michael, 112
Goodlad, John: on ability differences, 128; on diverse students, 9, 185; on graded system, 52, 177–78, 189; on Greek mythology, 188; on nongraded system, 207; on Public Law 94–142, 196
Gopnik, Alison, 40–41
Gorelick, Jacque, 173–74
government representatives, 94
governor, 75
graded system, 158; abolition of, 52–53, 194–95; administration of, 167; advantages of, 164; age-based curriculum of, 49, 166–67, 171; calendar-driven curriculum of, 177–78; cognitive development regarding, 127; fourth grade, 111; Goodlad on, 52, 177–78, 189; limitations of, 160, 166, 168, 190; nongraded system regarding, 189–92, *193–94*, *195*, *197–98*, 206, 211–13; origins of, 165, 184; retention, 157, 175, 187, 188, 204; student progress in, 187. *See also* kindergarten; third grade
grade level proficiencies: in Baltimore, 19, 48; at charter school, 19; information missing from, 85–86; math, 19, 48; parent's misperceptions of, 24; reading, 19, 29; state, 21, 29–30; teachers influence on, 29–30; from "Worst Elementary Schools," 20–21
grade levels, student differences within, 50, 51–52
grades: pandemic impacting, 22; on standardized tests, 71
Grant, Jim, 129
Greek mythology, 188
Greene, Peter, 29, 125

groups, heterogeneous, 138–39, 141, 142. *See also* flexible grouping
groups, homogeneous, 138, 142. *See also* flexible grouping
groups, multiage, 192
growth-mindset system, 38
Grundy, Paul, 42
Guardian, 155

Haley, Alex, 18
Hargrave, Kathy, 198
Hartford, Connecticut, 5
Harvey, James, 3
Hatfield, Raymond L.: on differentiated instruction, 132–33; on flexible groupings, 139–40
Hattie, John, 155
Haycock, Kati, 25–26
Hedge, Tricia, 60
heterogeneous groups, 138–39, 141, 142
Hollas, Betty, 129
homework, 90
homogeneous groups, 138, 142
horizontal nongraded education, 199–200
Hubbard, Bibb, 24

IEP. *See* Individual Educational Program
illiteracy, 20
immigrants, 165
Individual Educational Program (IEP), 67, 88–89
ineffective teachers, 29–30
inequality: of education opportunities, 18, 161, 162, 164; funding, 4–6; pandemic revealing, 164; of student advancement, ix, 23
in-person learning, 113–14
interview, 154–55
intra-pupil student differences, 130–31
inventors, 6
IQ tests, 27–28
iZone, 135

Jefferson, Israel Gillette, 3

Jefferson, Thomas, 3
job description, teacher, 198–99

Kamenetz, Anya, 24
Kaplan, Avi, 115
Kappan, 109
Katz, Lilian, 128
Kauffman, James, 13, 68
Kendi, Ibram X., 81
kindergarten: academic acceleration of, 173–74, 176; competency test for, 175
Kinlan, Carol A., 95
KM (pseudonym), 75
Koretz, D., 76
Kozol, Jonathan, 17–18

Lake, Robin, 114
Lake Wobegon, 24
Lancaster, Joseph, 131–32
language skills, 163
Latinx families, 114
Lattier, Daniel, 48–49, 188
Lawler, John M., 24
LD. *See* "learning disability"
learning: formative assessment improving, 109; nongraded products of, 205; pace differences, 47, 50, 62, 189; pandemic, 114–17
learning, in-person: pandemic regarding, 113–14; parents on, 114
learning, remote: formative assessments for, 116–17; pandemic regarding, 114–17; technology access regarding, 114–16
"learning disability" (LD), 27, 88. *See also* education disability
Leslie, Ian, 156
lesson plans, 43
Lewis, James: on nongraded system, 188–89, 199; on student differences, 93
Lindquist, Everett Franklin, 76
Lindsay Unified School District, 53
literacy, 7–8, 20

Lockhart, Shane, 133
Los Angeles, 115
low-income areas, 23
lumping: administrators regarding, 59, 60; as "conveyor belt," 134–35; Delisle on, 59, 134; differentiated instruction regarding, 145, 146, 147; downsides to, 60–61; in education system, 61; outrage against, 59–60; teachers impacted by, 61–62
Ly, Phu N., 189
Lynch, Matthew, 26; on lumping, 61–62; on teachers, 29

Magna Carta, 54
Mandela, Nelson, 1
Mann, Horace, 171, 172
Mann, Larry, 132, 134
Martinez, Clarissa, 61
mass-production, 156, 166
Math Academy, 11
Mathews, Jay, 11, 12
math grade level proficiencies, 19, 48. *See also* grade level proficiencies
math skills, 127; CRTs for, 88–91; error analysis for, 99; formative assessment on, 111; School to One program increasing, 135
McGuffey readers, 167–68
MEA. *See* Michigan Education Association
Meador, Derrick, 172–73
mechanical error, 102
medical model, 89
Merrow, John, 4
methodology: of differentiated instruction, 132–33; performance-based assessments measuring, 71; for teaching, 60, 71
Michigan Education Association (MEA), 119
middle student distribution, 48, 129–30, 172, 183
Miles, Karen Hawley, 22–23
Miller, Andre, 116–17

Miller, Richard I., 183–84
Miller, Ryan, 139
Milwaukee, 53
Minneapolis, 175
Mintrop, Rick, 119
mixed-ability classroom, 138
Montessori schools, 156
mother, 51, 88–89
motivational error, 102
Muir, Tim, 170
multiage groups, 192
multiage system alternative, 198
Mundahl, Hans, 108

National Assessment of Educational Progress (NAEP), 10; direction of, 73; homogenization of, 74
National Commission on Excellence in Education: perspective failure of, 2–3; on students, 3
National Education Association (NEA), 81, 206
National Education Association Instruction, 207
National Public Radio (NPR), 24
A Nation at Risk report, 2, 3
NEA. *See* National Education Association
neaToday, 81
New York City, 135
19th-century format, 120, 165, 207; administration of, 167; graded system age organization of, 170–71; modification of, x, 147–48, 184, 189
nobility, 54
"No Child Left Behind," 21
no-fault system, 92
Noguera, Pedro, 25
nongraded system, 157, 178; administrators regarding, 205–6; advantages of, 201–2; attitude shift in, 190–91; components of, 202–6; in countries abroad, 194; CRTs in, 203, 204; Delgado-Marcano study on, 206–7; differentiated instruction

in, 203; education opportunities maximized in, 191; entering skill differences in, 190; flexible grouping in, 187, 192, 203, 207; funding for, 195; graded system regarding, 189–92, *193–94*, *195*, *197–98*, 206, 211–13; horizontal aspects of, 199–200; learning products of, 205; Lewis on, 188, 199; NEA on, 206; one-room schoolhouse, 184; personalization of, 184, 185, 202, 203; personalized learning for, 196–97; principal adapting, 212; readiness skills in, 203; student progress continuum in, 158–59, 186, 187, 191, 197–98, 200–201, 203–4; teachers regarding, 185–86, 194, 201, 212–13; team teaching in, 200; time constraints regarding, 159–60, 205; U.S. absence of, 194–95; vertical aspects of, 200, 207
North Dakota, 53
Northern Cass School District, 53
NPR. *See* National Public Radio

Obama, Barack, 30
Obama, Michelle, 74
Obama administration, 4, 20
omission error, 99
one-room schoolhouse, nongraded, 184
opportunity gap, 6–7
Osewalt, Ginny, 136–37

pandemic, 5, 161–62; grades impacted by, 22; inequality revealed by, 164; in-person learning regarding, 113–14; remote learning regarding, 114–17; standardized test decision regarding, 81–82; students impacted by, 22–23
parents, 11, 91; CRTs performed by, 87; on education disability, 95; grade level proficiencies misperceptions of, 24; on in-person learning, 114; learning products for, 205; nongraded components regarding, 205, 212; on school closures, 119; on standardized tests, 69; student underachievement influenced by, 26–27
Parmenter, Justin, 22
Pasadena, California, 11, 92
Pavan, Barbara Nelson, 191
Pearson Publishers, 69
peers, 47, 48, 90; in Chicago third grade, 55–56; child development utilizing, 54; classmates term replacing, 56; definition of, 54, 55; differences of, 49–50, 56–57
performance-based assessments: standardized tests replaced by, 70; of students, 51, 65; teacher goals for, 72; teaching methodology measured by, 71
Perry, David M., 161
Perry, Kris, 176
personalization, 19, 51; with clusters, 141; cognitive development regarding, 127; of curriculum, 10, 38, 43; formative assessments for, 111; Lancaster system for, 131–32; Meador on, 173; NAEP against, 74; of nongraded system, 184, 185, 202, 203. *See also* differentiated instruction
personalized learning, 196–97
Petrilli, Michael J., 9–10
Pinnell, Gay Su, 85
Plano, Dallas, 197–98
Plomin, Robert, 39–40
Popham, W. James: on standardized tests, 69–70, 75, 76; on student differences, 37. *See also* curriculum-based assessments
Porter, Andy, 7
poverty: child development impacted by, 39; student underachievement influenced by, 25–26
The Power of Teacher Teams (Boles and Troen), 169–70
practice, spaced, 102
preassessment, 141, 191

preschool, academic acceleration of, 174, 176
principal, 43, 48; differentiated instruction regarding, 144; nongraded adaptation from, 212; teacher interview by, 154–55; team teaching encouraged by, 170
private school, 12, 112
Procrustes, 188
prompts, Exit Card, 117
Psychology Today, 26–27
public education: Black students failed by, 161; private schools compared to, 12, 112
Public Law 94–142, 196
publishing industry, 49, 167–68

Rapaport, Amie, 114
Ravitch, Diane, 17
readiness skills: in nongraded system, 203; student differences of, 190
reading grade level proficiencies, 19, 29. *See also* grade level proficiencies
reading levels, 85
Reagan, Ronald, 1–2, 73
"redshirting," 204
Reis, Sally, 144
RELAY Graduate School of Education, 141
retention, graded system, 157, 175, 187, 188, 204
Ritzenhein, B. A., 207
Robinson, Kimberly J., 7–8
Rock, Rod, 38
Rogers, Lois Adams, 51–52
Roosevelt, Franklin Delano, 175
Rosales, John, 81–82
Rosenberg, Alan, 156
Routzahn, Amy, 139
"Rumpelstiltskin fixation," 96

Saavedra, Anna, 114
Sahlberg, Pasi, 70
Sanders, Tony, 5
Sarason, Seymour, 8–9

SAT. *See* Scholastic Aptitude Test
Savage Inequalities (Kozol), 17–18
Schatmeyer, Kenneth, 192
Schmoker, Mike, 144–45
Schneider, Jack, 88; on education inequality, 18, 162; on standardized tests, 70–71, 74, 77, 84
Scholastic Aptitude Test (SAT), 48
school, private, 12, 112
school board, 212
schoolchildren. *See* students
school closures: for health reasons, 120; parents on, 119; student underachievement influencing, 118–20
school day: CRT ending, 91; diagnostics during, x
School Improvement Grant study, 20
schools: Montessori, 156; one-room, 184; underserved students regarding, 163–64. *See also* public education
School to One program, 135
Schweitzer, Katherine: on education system structural change, 183; on nongraded groups, 192
"seat time," 53
Shaywitz, J., 28
Shaywitz, S., 28
Shiller, Andrew, 20
Siegel, Ethan, 160–61
Silver, Dan, 114
Slate, 112
special education, 20; funding for, 94–95; personalized learning for, 197; policies on, 95; Public Law 94–142 on, 196
special needs, 67, 69
The Spectator, 103–4
speech center, in brains, 42
standardized tests: advantages and shortcomings of, 69–70, 74–75; alternative to, 76–77; children stress of, 69; CRTs compared to, 86–87; English language learners regarding, 71; grades on, 71; norm-reference

of, 73; pandemic decision regarding, 81–82; parents on, 69; performance-based assessments replacing, 70; Popham on, 69–70, 75, 76; Schneider on, 70–71, 74, 77, 84; teacher goals for, 72
Stanley, Julian, 148
State English Language Arts exam, 69
Stein, Sol, 17
Steiner, Cory, 53
Stone, Sandra, 160
Strauss, Valerie: on academic acceleration, 176; on pandemic, 22
Struntz, Amy, 137
student differences, 42, 43, 129, 159–60, 172; of ability, 37–38, 67–68, 126, 128, 131, 138, 153; differentiated instruction regarding, 133; of entering skills, 136; within grade levels, 50, 51–52; intra-pupil, 130–31; irrelevancies of, 68; Kauffman on, 13, 68; learning pace, 47, 50, 62, 189; Lewis on, 93; of readiness skills, 190; teachers regarding, 130–31; teaching regarding, 13; Tomlinson and Allan on, 125–26. *See also* differences
students: advancement inequality of, ix, 23; CBAs for, 82–83; CRTs for, 83; curriculum personalization for, 10, 38, 43; graded system progress of, 187; middle distribution, 48, 129–30, 172, 183; National Commission on Excellence in Education on, 3; nongraded system progress continuum of, 158–59, 186, 187, 191, 197–98, 200–201, 203–4; observation of, 126–27; pandemic impacting, 22–23; performance-based assessments of, 51, 65; teacher assessment decision for, 72. *See also* formative assessments; standardized tests; underachievement, student
students, advanced, 162–63
students, atypical, 11

students, Black: families, 114, 115; funding inequality impacting, 5, 6; grade level proficiencies of, 19; opportunity gap impacting, 6–7; public education failure toward, 161
students, diverse, 8, 165–66; CBAs for, 83–84; CRTs for, 83–84; Goodlad on, 9, 185
students, Latinx: families, 114; funding inequality impacting, 5, 6; opportunity gap impacting, 6–7
students, minority, 21, 118–19, 162
students, underserved, 12; grade level proficiencies of, 19; Kozol on, 17–18; labeling, 184; language skills of, 163; schools regarding, 163–64; Stein on, 17
summative assessments, 113
Sunderman, Gail L., 119
superintendent, 53, 56–57, 71; Meador as, 172–73; Minneapolis, 175
surgeon, 42
survival mode, teachers, 168–69
synapses, 41

teachers, 7, 127; benefits from, 30, 31, 155; CBAs informing, 82–83; challenges facing, ix–x, 9–10, 12, 31, 50–51, 62, 160; college, 49, 212; CRTs administered by, 93; on differentiated instruction, 143–44; education system impacting, 161; effective, 31–32; grade level proficiencies influenced by, 29–30; hypothetical classroom for, 67–68, 69; ineffectiveness of, 29–30; interview of, 154–55; job description for, 198–99; lumping impacting, 61–62; material covered by, 51; nongraded system regarding, 185–86, 194, 201, 212–13; Obama, Barack, on, 30; performance-based assessment goals for, 72; resilience of, 125; special needs regarding, 69; standardized tests goals of, 72;

student differences regarding, 130–31; survival mode of, 168–69. *See also* time constraints

teaching: methodology for, 60, 71; to middle, 48, 129–30, 172, 183; student differences regarding, 13

Teaching and learning in the language classroom (Hedge), 60

team teaching, 213; in nongraded system, 200; *The Power of Teacher Teams* on, 169–70; principal encouraging, 170

technology access: Black families regarding, 115; remote learning regarding, 114–16

textbooks, age-based, 49

third grade: Chicago peers in, 55–56; reading grade level proficiencies in, 29

Thomas, Jan, 82

Thoner, Sharon, 20

Thoreau, Henry David, 17

Thurlow, Martha L., 94

time constraints, 118; of calendar-driven curriculum, 177–78; on differentiated instruction, 143; education system imposing, 48, 51, 108; formative assessments regarding, 109; nongraded system regarding, 159–60, 205

Tomlinson, Carol Ann: on clusters, 140–41; on differentiated instruction, 133–34, 136, 137, 140–41; on student differences, 125–26

Troen, Vivian, 169–70

Tucker, Geri Coleman, 136

Tucker, Marc S., 47–48

tumor, brain, 42

21st-century symposium, 18

underachievement, student, 24; parents influencing, 26–27; poverty influencing, 25–26; school closures regarding, 118–20

ungraded system. *See* nongraded system

United States (U.S.): Department of Education, 81, 126; nongraded system absence in, 194–95; special education policies in, 95

Vegas, Emiliana, 115–16

vertical nongraded education, 200, 207

Virginia, 56

vocabulary, 100–101

voting, 156

Wagner, Tony, 118

"Wait to Fail" approach, 187

Walden (Thoreau), 17

Walker, Tim, 81–82

Wall Street Journal, 52

Washington Post, 6, 171, 176; on pandemic learning, 22; "Why are so many 8th-graders taking AP [advanced placement] calculus at this school district?" by, 11, 12

Waukesha STEM Academy, 53

Weir, Kirsten, 115

What Schools Could Be (Dintersmith), 74–75

"Why are so many 8th-graders taking AP [advanced placement] calculus at this school district?" (Mathews), 11, 12

Wiliam, Dylan, 109

Williams, Joe, 25

Willis, Scott, 132, 134

Wilson, Robert, 18

Wilson Reading System, 110

"Worst Elementary Schools," 20–21

Wright, Pam, 187

www.kidzone.ws/dolch, 87

Yale, 40

Yates, Mike, 6–7

Ysseldyke, James, 94

zebra, 100–101

zip code, 4–5

Zirpoli, Susan Bishop, 85–86

About the Author

Joel Macht served as a consultant practitioner for forty years, providing direct services to a wide variety of children, their parents, their teachers, and their administrators. Macht earned a PhD in educational psychology, a master's degree in clinical counseling psychology, and an undergraduate degree in psychology. He provided direct services to failure-to-thrive children at Children's Hospital in Denver, held a four-year consulting psychologist position at a county cooperative special school for low-incident handicapped children, served as a behavior specialist for a large urban school district, has been invited to a number of state-run institutions to provide in-services to staff and direct services to the residential children, and was a behavior consultant to a national organization that provided services to developmentally delayed adults.

As a college professor, Macht has been affiliated with graduate programs in educational psychology, school psychology, psychology, and special education, with positions at Denver University, Arizona University, McDaniel College in Maryland, and Davidson College in North Carolina, where he served as a practicum supervisor to undergraduate psychology majors with an interest in special children.

He has published seven nonfiction titles (and multiple book chapters) dealing with children, their education, and their home and school behavior (Prentice-Hall, Greenwood Press, Plenum, Longman Publishing, National Advocate for Deaf/Blind Children, John Wiley, Palgrave Macmillan, Rowman & Littlefield). One book, targeting failure-to-thrive children (Plenum, Da Capo Press, Perseus), resulted in a national CNN interview. Macht has been an invited speaker hundreds of time; he has been interviewed frequently on radio and television.

www.ingramcontent.com/pod-product-compliance
Lightning Source LLC
Chambersburg PA
CBHW030135240426
43672CB00005B/139